John Robert Seeley

**Lectures and Essays**

John Robert Seeley

**Lectures and Essays**

ISBN/EAN: 9783742826602

Manufactured in Europe, USA, Canada, Australia, Japa

Cover: Foto ©Andreas Hilbeck / pixelio.de

Manufactured and distributed by brebook publishing software (www.brebook.com)

John Robert Seeley

**Lectures and Essays**

# LECTURES AND ESSAYS.

BY

J. R. SEELEY, M.A.
PROFESSOR OF MODERN HISTORY IN THE UNIVERSITY OF CAMBRIDGE.

London:
MACMILLAN AND CO.
1870.

# CONTENTS.

## 1.

### ROMAN IMPERIALISM. I.

|  | PAGE |
|---|---|
| THE GREAT ROMAN REVOLUTION | 1 |

## 2.

### ROMAN IMPERIALISM. II.

THE PROXIMATE CAUSE OF THE FALL OF THE ROMAN EMPIRE . . 32

## 3.

### ROMAN IMPERIALISM. III.

THE LATER EMPIRE . . . . . . . . . . . . 59

## 4.

MILTON'S POLITICAL OPINIONS . . . . . . . . . 80

## 5.

MILTON'S POETRY . . . . . . . . . . . . 120

## 6.

ELEMENTARY PRINCIPLES IN ART . . . . . . 155

## 7.

LIBERAL EDUCATION IN UNIVERSITIES . . . . 182

## 8.

ENGLISH IN SCHOOLS . . . . . . . . . . 217

## 9.

THE CHURCH AS A TEACHER OF MORALITY . . . . 245

## 10.

THE TEACHING OF POLITICS:—AN INAUGURAL LECTURE DELIVERED AT CAMBRIDGE . . . . . . . 290

# LECTURES AND ESSAYS.

## I.

## ROMAN IMPERIALISM.[1]

### THE GREAT ROMAN REVOLUTION.

In the famous controversy between Julius Cæsar and Brutus the present age takes a different side from the last. Brutus used to be considered in the right, but public opinion now declares for Cæsar. Cæsar's partisans, however, may state their case in two ways. They may represent him as having simply achieved a great administrative reform, and made government more efficient at the expense of republican liberties. This they may consider to have been on the whole a necessary and useful work, and they may respect Cæsar as a practical statesman, who had the wise hardihood to abolish venerated institutions when they had become, in the lapse of time, mischievous. But it is also possible to represent him as a great popular hero, the hope of all the subject nationalities of Rome, carried to power in their arms, and executing justice in their behalf upon the tyrant aristocracy

[1] These Lectures were delivered at the Royal Institution, 1869.

that had oppressed them. If we take this view, no admiration or enthusiasm for him can be too ardent; and the judgment of our fathers upon Brutus and Cæsar is not only modified, but actually reversed: Cæsar becomes Brutus, and Brutus Cæsar. Brutus is now the tyrant, for he represents the oppressive aristocracy, and Cæsar is the tyrannicide, who armed himself in the cause of the nations, and stabbed the oppressor, once at Pharsalus, again at Thapsus, and again at Munda.

This latter view might be supported if we could assume that all the consequences of the revolution which Cæsar conducted were intended by him and by his party. By that revolution in the end the exclusive domination of the Roman aristocracy and of the city was destroyed; the provincials, who before had been insolently oppressed, now began to be more considered and more mercifully treated. If this could not have happened without the deliberate intention of those who achieved it, then the Cæsarians become at once enlightened Liberals, and Cæsar the greatest Liberal leader that ever lived. We are obliged then to suppose a vast tide of enthusiastic sentiment pervading the better part of the citizens and the provincials moved by an ecstatic hope, as the champion of mankind advances towards his final triumph, striking down one after another the enemies of the good cause. The Roman revolution is thus made to resemble the French, and Cæsar becomes a hero, a paragon, in whom appear the popular talents of Mirabeau, without his betrayal of the popular cause; the high aims of the Girondins, without their practical weakness; and the genius of Napoleon for war and administration, without his egotism and brutality.

But the truth is that what Cæsar and his party intended is to be carefully distinguished from what they actually accomplished. The revolution had many beneficial results, which were indirect and little contemplated by its principal authors. If we study the movement itself, rather than its consequences, we shall find that Cæsar was no champion of the provincials, that his party had no notion of redressing the wrongs of the provincials, that they were actuated by no desire to establish any general principle whatever, and by no devotion except a military devotion to their leader. The true nature of the revolution will very clearly appear, and its resemblance to the French Revolution will be shown to be merely superficial.

It is certain, in the first place, that Cæsar did not in any degree owe his victory to the favour of the provincials. He owed his victory to the admirable efficiency of his army, and to his admirable use of it. This army contained no doubt Gallic auxiliaries, but the great muster of provincials was on the side of the Senate. Cæsar's provincial auxiliaries were better drilled, and, like his Roman legionaries, they were no doubt personally attached to him; but that he was the champion of their interests against the Senate never occurred to them. No indication is to be found that the provinces conceived themselves to have any special interest in the quarrel. According to their personal connections with the two leaders they ranged themselves on one side or the other —the East for the most part with Pompeius, while Gaul was at the service of Cæsar. Their hearts, apparently, were not in the contest at all; but if we ask on which side were their hands, we shall be obliged to reply that so little did they understand Cæsar to be their champion that the majority of them were ranged against him on the side of their oppressors.

But let us go on to ask, Why *should* they have regarded Cæsar as their champion? What was there in his career which might lead them to suppose him more kindly disposed to them than any other proconsul of his time? His most conspicuous act was the conquest of Gaul. Let it be granted that the greatest service he could do to Gaul was to conquer it. Let us even grant, for the sake of argument, that he was himself aware of this, that he acted from purely philanthropical motives, and distinctly understood the conquest of Gaul to be a necessary stage of the evolution of humanity. Still his conduct was surely of a nature to be misunderstood by Gaul itself and by the provincials generally. His goodwill towards the non-Roman populations was not so apparent that it could not be mistaken. He stood before them covered with the blood of slaughtered Gauls, an object certainly more pleasing to Rome than to the dependents of Rome. He might not be detested so much as the plundering, peculating proconsuls, but he must have been more feared; and so far from appearing to the provincials a deliverer from the tyranny of Rome, he must have seemed to represent and embody that tyranny in its most irresistible and inexorable form.

But perhaps Cæsar had, at some earlier time, identified himself with the provincials; perhaps he had introduced measures calculated to better their condition and enlarge their franchises; perhaps he had expressed disgust at the treatment they met with, and sympathy with their suffering. The answer is, that he had not distinguished himself in any such way. One or two prosecutions of extortionate provincial governors which he had undertaken could not give him any such distinction. Such prosecutions were recognized as the established way by which young men brought themselves into notice, and also as an established way of annoying the Senate. Yet these prosecutions were the only service he had ever rendered the provinces. In his consulship, at the time when he was the recognized leader of popular legislation, he had not appeared as the champion of the provincials, but of quite a different class, whose interests were, if anything, somewhat antagonistic to the interests of the provincials—the populace of Rome.

Again, if Cæsar was no champion of the provincials, neither was his party, nor those earlier leaders of the party to whose position he had succeeded. Their constituency from the beginning had been a different one. When the great controversy was opened by Tiberius Gracchus, there were in the Roman world, not to count the slaves, three aggrieved classes: first, the populace of Rome; secondly, the Italian allies, who had not yet been admitted to the Roman citizenship; thirdly, the provincials. Now if the party which the movement of Gracchus called into existence, and which went on increasing its influence until, in the person of Julius Cæsar, it triumphed over itself and its enemies together, had really been the party of the provincials,—if the Gracchi, and Marius, and Saturninus had been representatives of the interests of the Empire as against the interests of the ruling city, they would have taken up the cause of all these aggrieved classes. The Italian allies, and still more the provincials, as the most numerous and the most oppressed class, would have claimed a larger share of their sympathy than the Roman populace. Yet, in fact, none of these leaders had ever said a word about the provincials, except, indeed, to propose that lands taken from them should be granted to Roman colonists. On the Italian allies they had not been altogether silent. Caius Gracchus had even undertaken their cause, but it then appeared clear not only that the party he represented was a different one, but that it was a party decidedly hostile to the Italians. The inclusion of the Italians in the colonization scheme of Marius also, according to Appian, "gave offence to the democracy."[1] The truth is that there had been men in Rome whose liberality was real and comprehensive, but they were not among the democratic leaders, the predecessors of Cæsar. Two men in particular had disregarded party watchwords, and had indulged sympathies not purely Roman. Both of them were aristocrats, and inclined rather to the senatorian than to the popular party. These were Scipio Æmilianus and the great Roman Whig Drusus. The former died, probably by the hand of an assassin, when he was on the point of bringing forward the cause of the Italians. The other succeeded for a moment in effecting a coalition between a section of the *noblesse*, a section of the people, and the Italians, and was prevented by an accursed dagger from earning a place among the most beneficent statesmen of all history.

The Italians were admitted within the pale of citizenship after a war in which the Senate and the democracy were allied in deadly hostility to them. Marius, the uncle and immediate predecessor of Cæsar, fought against them in this war, no less than Sulla, the champion

---

[1] " Πλεονεκτούντων δ' ἐν τῷ νόμῳ τῶν Ἰταλιωτῶν ὁ δῆ, ος ἐδυσχέραινε." App. *De Bell. Civ.* i. 29.

of the aristocracy. When Cæsar appeared upon the scene, therefore, the cause of the Italians was already won, and there remained only two aggrieved classes—the Roman populace, crushed for the time by Sulla, and the provincials. Now it was the former, not the latter, of these classes of which Cæsar made himself the champion. The provincials, as such, found no champion. Particular misgoverned provinces were from time to time patronised by rhetoricians who were equally ready, as Cicero showed himself, to take a brief from accused and evidently guilty governors; but neither Cæsar, nor any one else, ever raised the cry of justice to the provincials. Except in the case of the Transpadane province—a province only in name, being within the limits of Italy and already in possession of the inferior or Latin franchise—Cæsar connected himself before the civil war with no measure of enfranchisement, and had given no pledge to the world that any oppressed class except the Roman populace would be the better, or have any reason to be thankful, for his success. No writer of the time regards Cæsar in the light of an emancipator. Cicero gives no hint that Cæsar's partisans defended his conduct on those grounds. That somewhat vacillating politician repeatedly in his letters balances the two parties against each other. He explains why, on the whole, he prefers Pompeius, but he has much to say against Pompeius also. In these letters we might expect to find Cæsar's championship of the provincials, if he had ever undertaken or was supposed to have undertaken any such championship, discussed, and either allowed or rejected. Cicero, as a student of philosophy, was quite alive to enlarged and philanthropic considerations; if any such considerations made for

Cæsar, we should surely have heard of it. But there is nothing in his letters to show that in the hot discussions which must have been everywhere going on any general principles were appealed to by the Cæsarians; that it had occurred to any Cæsarian to suggest, what occurs so naturally to us who know the sequel, that it was a monstrous injustice that the world should be governed in the interest of a single city; that the Senate were the authors and supporters of this system; that Cæsar was the man to put it down, and had undertaken to do so. The Cæsarians were a party without ideas.

It is most easy to delude ourselves into the belief that what actually happened was intended to happen; and since in this revolution the provinces made some progress towards throwing off the yoke of Rome, to describe the revolution as a convulsive effort on the part of the provinces to throw off the yoke of Rome. But the facts are before us, the process by which the revolution was accomplished can be clearly traced, and we can see that provincial interests were not considered at all in the revolution which ultimately affected them so much; that it was a purely Roman movement; that the evil—for there was such an evil—which the revolutionaries struggled against was of quite a different nature, and that the relief which the imperial system actually brought to the provincials was an indirect and secondary consequence of a general improvement in the machinery of government.

How, then, did the revolution really come about? Undeniably the immediate cause of it was the practice, which had gradually sprung up, of conferring upon eminent generals for special purposes powers so extravagant as to enable the holders of them to rise above the laws. Where such a dangerous practice prevails revolution is at once accounted for. Such an experiment may be tried, and no revolution follow; but at Rome it was tried often, once too often. How, then, came the Romans to adopt such a practice? What, on the one hand, was the occasion which led them to appoint these dangerous dictators? On the other hand, how came they to overlook the danger? To both these questions it is possible to give a satisfactory answer, and to answer these questions is to explain the revolution.

Republicanism at Rome, though successful and glorious for so long a time, had perhaps always been, as a creed, confined to a class. Long after the expulsion of the kings, it had been necessary to watch with extreme jealousy every individual who drew public attention too exclusively to himself. Cassius, Manlius, Mœlius, perished for their eminence, and this shows how large a proportion of the citizens were felt still to retain monarchical predilections. But the republic succeeded so well that such jealousy at length became unnecessary; the glory and the regal disposition of Africanus brought no danger to liberty, though they clouded the last years of the hero himself with moody discontent. The disease, however, was only kept under, it was not cured. Personal government was the instinctive preference of the lower orders, though the great families were able, as it were, to divide their allegiance among themselves. Anything which should weaken or disorganize this firm union of ruling houses, anything which should sever the lower orders from them, would in a moment bring the monarch upon the stage again. For more than half a century after the mortal struggle with Hannibal the ascendancy of the nobles over the lower orders continued unbroken, and then, through the mere growth of the population and change of circumstances, it began to decay. It was simply a moral ascendancy; by the constitution, the rabble of Rome could at any time take into their own hands legislation and government. The first Gracchus, with perfectly pure intentions, showed them the way to do this. The second Gracchus, influenced perhaps by revenge and party-hatred, took this city rabble in hand, organized it, and formed it into a standing army of revolution. Spurius Mælius, in an earlier age, had been suspected of aiming at the tyranny when he sold corn at a low price to the poor during a famine. Caius Gracchus adopted the same plan. By his *lex frumentaria* he at once demoralized, and attached to the cause of revolution, a vast class which had before been in the tutelage of the aristocracy. The bond was now broken that attached the people to its hereditary rulers. And how little this people cared for republican liberty became apparent the moment it began to think and act for itself. It did not at once destroy the existing government. The habit of deference and obedience long remained in a people naturally as deferential and fond of aristocracy as the English themselves. But as soon as any cause of discontent arose, or public needs became pressing, they took refuge at once in a monarch, whom they created indeed only for a limited period, but from whom they neither took nor cared to take guarantees that he would ever give back into their hands the power which they had entrusted to him. Thus Caius Gracchus was supreme until his liberality began to include the Italians. Marius was supreme for five years,—had, in fact, a longer reign than Julius Cæsar. Pompey in his turn received as much power as he cared to use; and, finally, by the Vatinian law, the people plainly told Cæsar that they were his subjects as soon as he chose to be their king. At this point the people disappear; in all subsequent contentions the two parties are the Senate and the army.

Still the people showed no eagerness for Revolution. As I said, it was only in cases of need that they created a monarch. And it was only because these cases of need occurred frequently that monarchs were frequently created. And here arises the second question, What were these needs for which no other expedient could be devised? Perhaps it was the oppression practised by the senatorial governors upon the provincials. If so, then it would be true that the imperial system was introduced in the interest of the subject nationalities. But nothing of the kind appears. In the quarrels between the Senate and the moneyed class (called knights), the wrongs of the provincials are often paraded, for both the Senate and the moneyed class had a strong interest in the provincials, the former as governors, the latter as tax-farmers. But the democracy never concerned themselves in any way with the treatment of the provincials, for it was a question which did not at all affect their interests. Quite different were the reasons which led them to call in dictators, and, if we examine the different cases, we shall find that the real motive was always the same. There was one evil to which the Empire was constantly exposed; one evil to cure which, and to cure which alone, the imperial system was introduced.

What made the people give supreme power to Marius,

and continue it to him for five years? First, the
failure of the aristocratic government in the war with
Jugurtha; afterwards, the imminent danger of the
Empire from the Cimbri and Teutones. What made them
give extraordinary powers to Pompey, and afterwards
extend and increase them? First, the alarming spread of
piracy in the Mediterranean, stopping trade and threaten-
ing the capital with famine; next the necessity of exerting unusual power to crush Mithridates. What made
them give extraordinary powers to Cæsar? Rumours
of an intended emigration of the Helvetii, raising appre-
hensions of a danger similar to that which Italy had experienced from the Cimbric invasion. Nothing can be more
certain than the connection of cause and effect in these
cases. The history of the introduction of imperialism is
briefly this: government at Rome was so little centralized
that the Empire was unable to grapple with any really
formidable enemy that assailed it either from without or
within. To save themselves from destruction the Romans
were compelled, or thought themselves compelled, to resort
frequently to the obvious expedient of a dictator. The
more frequently they did this, the more did the republican government fall into disuse and contempt, the more
did men's minds and habits adapt themselves to a military *régime*. The new scheme of government, whenever
it was tried, succeeded. It accomplished that for which
it was created. It gave the Empire inward security and
good order; it crushed foreign enemies, and extended the
boundaries of dominion from the Rhone to the Straits of
Dover, and from the Mediterranean to the Euphrates.
What wonder that in the end it supplanted the older constitution, when its advantages were so unmistakeable,

and the one thing it took away, Liberty, was that which the populace of Rome and of Italy had never either understood or valued?

The Jacobins used to think of Cæsar as a great aristocrat, patriotically assassinated by the noble *sans-culotte*, Brutus. I confess it seems to me not much less untrue to describe him as a champion of nationalities, and a destroyer of aristocratic privilege and exclusiveness. It was the war-power, not the people, that triumphed in him. The people, indeed—that is, the people of Italy,—were, in the first instance, the authors of his elevation, but it was not enfranchisement that they wanted, it was simply military protection. The enemies they feared were not a Catulus or a Cato, but Helvetian or German hordes. It was not aristocratic privilege they rebelled against, but aristocratic feebleness, the feebleness which had led to the shameful treaty with Jugurtha and the bloody defeat of Arausio.

That the revolution was a triumph, not of liberalism, but of military organization, will become still clearer if we now proceed to examine the new institutions which it introduced. Had Cæsar lived longer, he would no doubt have stamped a liberal character upon his work. Though he was no champion of the provinces, and though he owed his elevation immediately to the army, and only remotely to the democracy, yet his disposition was liberal, and his statesmanship bold, original, and magnanimous. He might therefore have developed at once and forced into ripeness those germs of good in the new system which, as it was, ripened but slowly. He might have taken away from Italy that unjust precedence in the Empire which she retained for three more centuries, and raised the provinces to citizenship and participation in the honours of the state. This he might have done, but had he done it he would have accomplished another revolution. That the Empire at that time did not require such changes, even if it would have borne them, is plain from the fact that his successor Augustus was able to found a secure and durable imperial system,—was able, in fact, to conduct the movement which his uncle had begun to its natural goal, without appealing to any liberal tendencies. Augustus was in all things aristocratically disposed; his institutions bear the stamp of a conservative, exclusive, Old-Roman spirit. This did not prevent him from proving a most efficient successor to the liberal-minded Cæsar. It did not prevent him from being more completely successful than almost any statesman in history. The explanation of this is, that Liberalism was not of the essence of Cæsar's work. It adorned his character, and helped him in his early struggles, but the revolution he accomplished was independent of it, and when divorced from it could go on just as prosperously as before.

After the new system had been permanently settled in the tranquillity of the Augustan age, the great change which had passed over the Empire was found to be this : A standing army had been created and thoroughly organized, a uniform taxation had been established throughout the Empire, and a new set of officials had been created, all of a military character, all wielding greater power than the republic had been accustomed to entrust to its officials, but, on the other hand, all subject to the effective and rigorous control of the emperor. In other words, in the place of anarchy there had come centralization and responsibility.

We have heard much lately of the power which all organisms possess of differentiating special organs to meet special needs. The operation of this law is very visible in human society. In fact, it might be maintained that the whole history of a state is the record of a series of such differentiations. To take a simple example from Roman history:—At an early time the kings, and afterwards the consuls, were at the same time generals in war and judges in peace. Life had not yet become complex. But, as population and activity increased, these functions showed a tendency to separate. At first all that the citizens were conscious of was, that it was necessary to have three men instead of two to do the work. So they created a prætor, with precisely the same functions as the consuls. But Nature knew better, and by the gradual operation of a silent decree took away from the consuls their judicial functions, and from the prætor his military functions. Thus a differentiation was accomplished: and whereas there had been before but one organ of government, there were now two unlike each other; and whereas before all authority was conceived as of one kind, it was now regarded as two-fold, administrative and judicial. Now we may apply this principle to the great Roman revolution, and describe it as a differentiation. War had originally been conceived as a function devolving equally upon all the citizens. When the military season came on, the farmer or shopkeeper left his peaceful occupations, donned his armour, and presented himself before the consul in the Campus Martius. When the campaign was over, he went back to his work. But the larger the territory of the state became, the heavier the task that devolved upon its armies, the more numerous its dangers, the more extensive its vulnerable frontier, the more imperiously did Nature call for a military differentiation. The special need must be met by a special organ. A special class of men must be set apart for special military functions. I have shown that it was the necessity of defending the State against its foreign enemies that caused the revolution. In the throes of this revolution the new organ made its appearance. On the restoration of tranquillity, the Roman Empire is seen to be guarded by an institution which had been unknown to the republic, by a standing army of twenty-five legions.

This change constitutes by itself a vast social revolution in comparison with which any changes in the form of political government are insignificant. The rise of standing armies in modern Europe is well known to mark a great epoch. But it was a much less sudden and radical change than the corresponding change in the Roman Empire. For when the citizen resigned his arms to the professional soldier, he did not merely, as might at first sight appear, relieve himself of a disagreeable duty, disencumber himself of a burden which hampered his industry. He did much more than this; he placed himself under entirely new conditions of life. He parted with all his traditions, and blindly undertook to explore a new world. In the first place he resigned his liberty. We in England, who have witnessed the reconciliation of standing armies with liberty, may have some difficulty in understanding how impossible was any such reconciliation in the Roman Empire. But it is undeniable that under the imperial system the Roman did lose his liberty. With an equivalent, or without an equivalent, he parted with it, and no one who examines the history can doubt what cause principally contributed to deprive him of it. The emperor possessed in the army an overwhelming force, over which the citizens had no influence, which was totally deaf to reason or eloquence, which had no patriotism because it had no country, which had no humanity because it had no domestic ties. To this huge engine of despotism it was vain to oppose any resistance. Human free-will perished in its presence as in the presence of necessity. Not in institutions only, but in the hearts of men, liberty withered away, and its place was taken by servility, and stoicism, and Byzantine Christianity. It may occur to us that checks to the emperor's authority over the army might have been devised. But these are modern notions. The army was called into existence not by enactments, but by revolution, and there was no collective wisdom anywhere, no parliament which could call attention to the danger, or discuss it, or provide safeguards against it.

But, at the introduction of standing armies, the Roman citizen parted with something else, something which lies not less near than liberty to the springs of human character. He parted with the conception of war as the business of life. The great military nation of the world —the nation which had bred up its successive generations to the task of subduing mankind, which by unrivalled firmness of cohesion, by enduring tenacity of purpose, by methodic study and science of destruction, had crushed all the surrounding nationalities, not with a temporary prostration merely, but with utter and irretrievable dissolution—now found its work done and its occupation gone. The destructive theory of life had worked itself out. The army itself henceforth existed mainly for defence, and the ordinary citizen was no longer concerned with hostilities of any kind, whether offensive or defensive. Human life was forced to find for itself a new object. The feelings, the aspirations, the tastes, the habits, that had hitherto filled it and given it dignity, became suddenly out of date. It was as if a change had passed over the atmosphere in which men lived, as if the temperature had suddenly fallen many degrees, making all customs obsolete at once, giving an antiquated and inappropriate look to the whole framework of life. It was a revolution which struck with incongruousness and abortiveness the very instinctive impulses of men, placed an irreconcilable difference between habit and reason, preconception and fact, education and experience, temperament and reality, the world within and the world without. This might have a bright side. Poets sang of a golden age returned, and they hymned industrialism in exquisite language:—

"Agricola incurvo terram molitur aratro."

But the real enjoyment of the new state of things was still remote, and required to be nursed by habit. It was an uncomfortable transition when the old instincts and ardours were superannuated, and no new animating principle yet discovered. The new bottles had come before the new wine: the loss was felt far more keenly than the gain; the parting guest was shaken by the hand more warmly than the comer. A sullen torpor reigned in the first years of the millennium of peace; listlessness fell upon the dwellers in that uncongenial Paradise; Mars and Quirinus were dead, and He who was to consecrate peace was scarcely born. Men were conscious of a rapid cooling of the air, of a chill gathering round them—the numbness that follows a great loss, the vacancy that succeeds a great departure :

> "In urns and altars round,
> A drear and dying sound
> Affrights the flamens at their service quaint."

I hope to return to this subject. Meanwhile, let me point out how the other institutions of the imperial system were determined by the presence of the standing army. Such a great force could not be kept up, particularly as Augustus renounced the profitable course of conquest, without a rigorous system of taxation. Augustus organized a land-tax for the whole Empire, and laid the foundation of that fiscal system which in the end crushed the very life out of the people. Further, a great military system requires that great power shall be entrusted to individuals. Personal authority is the characteristic military principle. When, therefore, the standing army was organized, this principle received a great development. From the beginning the Empire had many more great posts than the republic. It created the *legatus legionis* or commander of a legion (the legion had before been commanded in a very ineffective way by the tribunes in succession). This new officer, commanding more than six thousand men, held prætorian rank, and there were not less than twenty-five such officers at once. Besides this, three new prefectures were created—the prefecture of the prætorian guard, the prefecture of the city, and the prefecture of the watch. If we compare these new city offices with the city magistracies of the republic, we find that they confer a greater amount of power because their term is not limited to a year, and also that they all bear a military character, since an armed guard is attached to each. Another office, still more characteristic of the Empire, was that of the *legatus Augusti*;[1] this was the title given to the governor of one of the great frontier provinces. He united the functions of civil governor with the command sometimes of two or three legions and as many allied troops—that is, an army of twenty or thirty thousand men. He was appointed by the emperor, and, like every one else, responsible to him. It is true that the proconsuls and proprætors of the republic had often held power as great, and with less responsibility; but when the standing army was fully organized and the frontier of the empire finally determined, these great commands became permanent, and not merely occasional. The great legates of the Rhine were regularly appointed, always with much the same range of power; and as they were not chosen by the haphazard system of popular election out of a few privileged families, but selected with tolerable impartiality, for the most part, out of those who had approved their powers of government in inferior positions, they appeared much more considerable personages than the provincial governors of the republic. This seems to me the fairest side of the imperial system. Essentially military, it was an incomparable school of great military officers. It produced in singular abundance men capable of great commands, and conducting themselves in such posts not merely with ability, but with justice and moderation, though generally also with the hardness of the military profession. Such men as Plautius, Corbulo, Vespasian, Agricola, Trajan, all held the post of *legatus Augusti*, and they are the glory of the Empire.

[1] In the most important provinces this officer was of consular rank, and is commonly called *legatus consularis*, or *consularis* simply.

Surrounded by this splendid staff of military officers, prefects, legates, and commanders of legions, appeared the Imperator. In modern history, only Napoleon or a Russian Czar has occupied a position at all similar,—absolute disposer of an army of 300,000 men, and keeping his eye at the same time on military operations as distant from each other as the Thames from the Euphrates. His power was from the beginning so great, and became so speedily unlimited, that we are apt to lose ourselves in generalities in describing it. But if we examine the process by which this power grew up, if we watch the genesis of Leviathan, we shall clearly see the special need which he was differentiated to meet—we shall plainly discover that he sprang, not out of democracy, not out of any struggle for equality between rich and poor, or between citizen and provincial, but out of the demand for administrative, and especially military, centralization. That Julius Cæsar began life as a demagogue is a fact which tends to confuse our notions of the system which he introduced. Let us rather fix our attention on Augustus, who founded and organized the Empire as it actually was and as it lasted till the time of Diocletian. He began as a professed Senatorian; he acquired the support of the army, he became ultimately emperor; but with the democracy he never had any connection. It was the object of his life to justify his own power by showing the necessity of it, and by not taking more power than he could show to be necessary. The profound tranquillity of his later years proved that he had satisfied the Empire. The uneasiness and unrest which had filled the whole century that preceded the battle of Actium had shown that the Empire wanted something which it could not find. The peace that filled the century which followed it, the general contentment which reigned, except among the representatives of the fallen republic, showed that the Empire had found that of which it was in search. Yet assuredly no comprehensive enfranchisement, no democratic levelling of classes, had taken place. If the ancient boundaries had been overleaped in the times of disturbance, Augustus devoted himself as soon as peace was restored to punishing such transgressions, and preventing the recurrence of them. His legislation is a system of exclusions, a code of privilege and class jealousy. It consists of enactments to make the enfranchisement of slaves difficult, enactments to prevent freedmen from assuming the privileges of the freeborn. He endeavoured to revive the decaying order of the patriciate, the oligarchy of the oligarchy itself—a clique which excluded Cato, and into which Augustus himself had gained admission only by adoption. He took pains to raise the character of the Senate, which was the representative of the aristocratic party, and to depress the Comitia, which represented the democracy. He bore, indeed, to his uncle a relation not unlike that which Sulla bore to Marius. Assuredly, any one who should study the Augustan age alone would conclude that, in the long contest between aristocracy and democracy, aristocracy had come out victorious. Both parties, indeed, had sacrificed much, but in the Augustan age democracy was nowhere; aristocracy was on the lips of the prince and in his legislation; it was unfashionable to mention the name of Julius; the great historian of the age spoke with admiration, and "nowhere with reproach," of his assassins, and earned from his master the epithet of the "Pompeian."[1] Yet we are told this did not interrupt their friendship. The truth is, Augustus was very much a Pompeian himself: an aristocrat to the core, and sympathising with the old republic in all things, he was yet the worthy and legitimate heir of his uncle, because he laboured successfully to complete what his uncle had begun; and this an aristocrat could do as well as a democrat, namely, to give the Roman world centralization.

Monarchy has often been used in the interest of the people as a means of coercing an insolent aristocracy. The Greek τύραννοι of the sixth century before Christ were popular sovereigns of this kind. But monarchy can also be used in the interest of aristocracy itself. Thus the monarchy of Louis XIV. was oppressive to the people, and supported itself upon the loyalty and sympathy of the *noblesse*. Now the Roman world wanted monarchy for its own sake, that is, it wanted a strong and centralized government; whether the monarchy favoured the democracy or the aristocracy was a matter comparatively of indifference. The first monarch was democratic, the second aristocratic, but both were equally successful, both equally satisfied the wants of the time. For, unlike in most respects as Augustus showed himself to Julius, he followed him closely in the one essential point. Though without much talent or taste for war, he jealously kept in his own hands the whole military administration of the Empire. Here alone he showed no reserve and wore no disguise, though in assuming civil powers no monarch was ever more cautious, or showed more anxiety not to go further than public necessity forced him. He became

[1] Tac. Ann. iv. 34.

permanent commander-in-chief; and—what shows clearly the conception which was formed of his special function—all provinces which were in the neighbourhood of an enemy, and in which a large military establishment was to be kept up, were committed to his care, and governed by his commissioners. He assumed, besides, the power of a proconsul in every province, by which means he became a kind of Governor-General of all the conquests of Rome. If we examine the powers which were given to Pompey in the war with the pirates, we shall see that they were very similar to these, and that in fact the imperial system may be considered as a kind of permanent Gabinian Law, an arrangement by which a general was empowered to wield at his discretion all the military force of the Empire, and to interfere in civil government so far as he might consider the military exigencies of the State demanded. It confirms this view to find that the most serious embarrassment which Augustus met with, particularly in his later years, was the evident superiority in military ability of Agrippa to himself, for this superiority carried with it a sort of natural title to supersede Augustus as emperor,[1] and the difficulty was only surmounted by a kind of tacit compact by which Augustus bound himself to deny Agrippa nothing, and Agrippa not to claim all, while in the meanwhile they placed themselves as much as possible in distant parts of the Empire, and so avoided the danger of a collision. This view at the same time explains the infinite alarm with which

---

[1] So Tacitus of Domitian: Id sibi maxime formidolosum, privati hominis nomen supra principis attolli; frustra studia fori et civilium artium decus in silentium acta, si militarem gloriam alius occuparet; cetera utcunque facilius dissimulari; ducis boni imperatoriam virtutem esse." *Agr.* 39.

Augustus received the news of the defeat of Varus in Germany, and the loss of three legions. Rome had weathered much worse storms than this. But what struck Augustus was that his system could not stand for a moment if it did not secure that for which it existed, the safety of the frontiers; that liberty and republican pride would be felt to have been sacrificed in vain, that Cato, and Pompey, and Cicero, and Brutus would seem to have been martyrs, if the Empire was still liable to barbaric invasion.

Considered in this light, the imperial system will appear to have had for a long time a splendid success. Though the imperial period is inferior as a period of foreign conquest to the period of Marius, Sulla, Pompey, and Cæsar, this is not owing to any military superiority of republicanism, but to the fact that the imperial system had been practically introduced long before it was legally recognized. It was not by republicanism, but by a temporary suspension of republican principles that the great generals I have just mentioned achieved their conquests. Pompey in the East and Cæsar in Gaul were as absolute as Trajan, and it was because they were so that they had so much success. Their conquests, therefore, may be claimed for the imperial system, though not for the imperial period; and to estimate the military effectiveness of the republican system, we must look back to the disastrous years when general after general succumbed to Jugurtha's gold, and army after army to Cimbric hordes. It is true that the imperial system did not in the long run succeed, that the very evil which it was created to avert fell in the end upon the Empire, that the frontier was passed at all points, and that the barbaric world overbore the Roman. But two centuries passed before the system showed any signs of inadequacy.

Such, then, in its design and in its direct working was the imperial system, simply a concentration of military force. But since it affected such a vast area, its indirect consequences are not less important than its direct ones. Of these the principal were two, the extinction of liberty, and the increase of material happiness. Of the first I have already spoken; it is displayed in a striking light throughout the history of the Senate in its relation to the emperors. The Senate had always been the vital institution of republican Rome. In it was embodied the force which had resisted Hannibal, which had made Italy into a single state, which had subjugated Sicily, Spain, Macedonia, Greece, and Carthage. Without this institution, this body of life-peers freely chosen by a people who liked neither self-government nor slavery,[1] but liberty to choose their governors—without the freedom of each senator with respect to the rest, and the freedom of the people in the election of the Senate,[2] Rome could never have become great. The popular assemblies had always been insignificant by the side of the Senate, and Augustus was right to elevate the Senate rather than the popular assemblies when he wished to persuade the people that their venerated republic still existed. Henceforward the Senate and the emperor confronted each other like the past and the present. The

---

[1] "Imperaturus es hominibus qui nec totam servitutem pati possunt nec totam libertatem." Tac. *Hist.* l. 16.

[2] The Senate consisted of those who had held or were holding magistracies, and the magistracies were filled by popular election.

Senate was respected; it was replenished with the leading men of the time; trouble was even taken by the emperors to maintain its character; it was eloquent; its debates and the lives of its members preserved the tradition of old Roman virtues; it was allowed to talk republicanism, and to canonize the "Pharsalica turba," the martyrs who had fallen in resisting Cæsar; it was highly cultivated and fond of writing history, a dignified literary club. But it had not power, in truth it had not reality. It is a painful or a majestic phenomenon, according as it acts or refrains from action. When it acts, it is like Lear with his hundred knights brawling in his daughter's palace. In a moment the wicked look comes upon Regan's face; the feeling of his helplessness returns upon the old man, and the *hysterica passio* shakes him. But so long as it remains passive it is an impressive symbol, and there is something touching in the respect with which the emperors treated it. Seldom has any State shown such a filial feeling towards its own past as the Romans showed in the tenderness with which they preserved through centuries a futile and impotent institution, because it represented the institutions of their ancestors. Like a portrait of the founder of the family in some nobleman's house, such was the Senate in the city of the Cæsars. It was not expected to move or act; nay, its moving seemed prodigious and ominous; it was expected "picture-like to hang by the wall;" and so long as it did this it was in no danger of being despised or thought superfluous, but, on the contrary, was held precious and dear.

Meanwhile liberty was actually dead, and several centuries passed in which Europe resembled Asia. That effeminacy fell upon men which always infects them when they live for a long time under the rule of an all-powerful soldiery. But with effeminacy there came in process of time a development of the feminine virtues. Men ceased to be adventurous, patriotic, just, magnanimous; but, in exchange, they became chaste, tender-hearted, loyal, religious, and capable of infinite endurance in a good cause.

The second indirect consequence was an increase of material happiness.

The want of system, which had exposed the Empire to foreign enemies, had created at the same time much internal misery. Imperialism, introducing system and unity, gave the Roman world in the first place internal tranquillity. The ferocious civil conflicts of Marius and Sulla had sprung out of republican passions, which were now for good as well as for evil stilled. The piracy which had reigned in the Mediterranean was no longer possible with a permanent Gabinian Law, with a Pompey always at the head of affairs. One new danger, indeed, was introduced—the danger of military revolutions; but, formidable as the power of the army was, it was found possible to restrain it from the worst extremities for two centuries. The dreadful year 69, which recalled the days of Cinna, was the only serious interruption to the tranquil course of government between the accession of Augustus and the death of Aurelius. Whatever Cæsar took from his country, he gave it two centuries of peaceful government.

Once more : he gave to the government of the Empire a somewhat more equitable spirit. It was not for this purpose that his army raised him to power, but centrali-

zation carried with it of necessity this result. The
cruelty with which the provinces were governed was of
the kind that is always produced in government by want
of system. There was no one upon whom it was incumbent to consider the interests of the provinces. The
Senate, to which all such affairs were left, consisted of
the very men who had the strongest interest in plunder
and extortion. The provincial governments were divided
among the aristocracy as so much preferment; the whole
order lived upon the plunder of the world, and nothing
is more manifest than that such a system could never be
reformed from within. The difficulty of getting the
House of Commons to put down bribery at elections
can but very faintly suggest to us the difficulty of
inducing the Roman Senate to reform the government of
the provinces. The new power which was now created
proved very serviceable for this end. The emperor had
no interest in any misgovernment; he was in a position
to judge it coldly, and he had power to punish it. At
the same time, in the general revision of the whole administration which now took place, the establishments
of the provincial governors were put upon a better
footing, and, in particular, stated salaries were assigned
to them. A better system undoubtedly was introduced,
and we may believe that the monstrous misgovernment
of the republic passed away. From this time it may
probably be said of the countries conquered by Rome
that they were better governed than they had been in
their times of independence. But it does not appear
that they were governed positively well. Oppression and
extortion, though on a reduced scale, seem still to be the
order of the day.

In conclusion, then, that great controversy between Cæsar and Brutus, that question whether Cæsar was a benefactor or a scourge to his kind, seems to me too vast to be answered with any confidence. The change he accomplished had remote consequences not less momentous than the immediate ones. If the nations owed to him two centuries of tranquillity, it is not less true that the supremacy which he gave to military force in the moment when he ordered the passage of the Rubicon led to the frightful military anarchy of the third century, and ultimately to the establishment of Oriental sultanism in Europe. If he relieved considerably the oppression of the provinces, he also destroyed the spirit of freedom in the Romans, and I do not feel able to calculate exactly how much is lost when freedom is lost. But what it is hard for us to compute, I am persuaded that Cæsar himself could calculate far less. Like other great conquerors, he had "the hook in his nose," and accomplished changes far more and greater and other than he knew. He had energy, versatility, and unconquerable resolution, but he was no philosopher; and yet to measure in any degree the consequences of such actions would have taxed an Aristotle. I believe that he looked very little before him, that he began life an angry demagogue, with views scarcely extended beyond the city; that in the anarchy of the time he saw his chance of rising to power by grasping the skirts of Pompey; that in Gaul he had no views that any other proconsul might not have had, only greater ability to realize them; that at the head of his army and his province he felt to the full a great man's delight in ruling strongly and well; that during this period the corruption of the Senate and the anarchy of the city became more and more contemptible to him, but that in the civil war his objects were still mainly personal; and that it was not till he found himself master of the Roman world that his ideas became as vast as his mission, and that he became in any way capable of understanding the purport of his own career.

## II.

## ROMAN IMPERIALISM.

#### THE PROXIMATE CAUSE OF THE FALL OF THE ROMAN EMPIRE.

WHAT was the cause of the fall of the Roman Empire?

That after a few centuries a fabric so artificial should fall to pieces is not in itself surprising. Great empires seldom last long; they are by their very nature liable to special evils to which in time they succumb, and so the process of their downfall is commonly the same. Rome was by no means exempt from these special causes of weakness, but we shall find that Rome did not, like other empires, succumb to them. We shall find that she weathered these most obvious dangers, and that the history of her fall is as unique as that of her greatness.

The difficulty which has been found insurmountable in most great empires is their unwieldy size, and the obstinate antipathy of the conquered nationalities to their conquerors. Government must necessarily become difficult in proportion to the extent of the territory governed and the disaffection of the inhabitants. It follows that in a great empire founded upon conquest the difficulties of government are the greatest possible. To cope with them it is found necessary to create pashas or viceroys of particular provinces, with full monarchical power. Sooner or later government breaks down, overborne partly by its insurgent subjects, partly by these viceroys shaking off its authority.

This, then, is the regular process of dissolution in empires. Subject nationalities succeed at last in recovering their independence, and subordinate governors throw off their allegiance and become kings. Sometimes the two solvents help each other, as Ali Pasha of Janina helped the early attempts of the Greek patriots. Let us take some of the more conspicuous examples which history affords. Alexander's empire was dissolved by his officers making themselves kings, and the kingdom of Pontus was formed out of it by the effort of one of the conquered nationalities. The Saracen Empire split into three independent chalifates. The Seljukian Empire of Malek Shah was divided in a few generations among independent sultans of Persia, Syria, Roum, &c. The Great Mogul lost his dominion partly to the insurgent Mahrattas, partly to his own viceroys of the Deccan and of Bengal. The German Empire became a nullity when the electors began to raise themselves to the rank of kings. In the Ottoman Empire the process of dissolution shows itself in Greece and Servia recovering their independence, and the Egyptian viceroy making himself a sovereign.

If we look for similar symptoms in the dissolution of the Roman Empire we are disappointed. The subject nationalities do not recover their independence. It is true that they make their separate influence felt long after they have been politically merged. The Greeks, for example, maintained, not only the independence, but

the superiority of their language and their culture.
Although the greatest writers of this period are Roman,
yet, within half a century after the death of Tacitus and
Juvenal, Greek not only prevailed in the eastern half of
the Empire, but had so far superseded Latin in Rome
itself, that the Emperor Aurelius uses it in meditations
intended for his own private use. The Asiatic part of
the Empire preserved its peculiar ways of thinking. Its
religions entered into a competition both with the
religions of the West and with Greek philosophy, the
religion of the cultivated classes among the Romans. In
this contest between the Western conquerors and the
Eastern subjects the conquered races had at last the
better, and imposed a religion upon their masters. Nor
were the African nationalities without their influence.
They gave to the Empire, in Severus, the master who
first gave unlimited power to the army; and they
contributed to the religious reformation its greatest
rhetorician, Tertullian; its most influential politician,
Cyprian; and, later, its greatest theologian, Augustine.

But though the nationalities retained so much intellectual independence, they never became dangerous to
the Empire. There were indeed, in the first century,
four considerable wars of independence—The rising of
the Germans under Arminius, that of the Britons under
Boadicea, that of the Germans and Gauls under Civilis,
and that of the Jews. But the first two were not rebellions of nations already conquered, but of nations in
the process of being conquered. In the case of the
Germans it was the effort by which they saved their
independence; in the case of the Britons it was the last
convulsion of despair. The other two revolts were, no

doubt, precisely of the kind which occur so frequently in great empires, and are so frequently fatal to them. But to the Roman Empire they were not fatal, and can hardly be said to have seriously endangered it. It was owing to the confusion of a revolutionary time that Civilis was able for a moment to sever the Rhenish provinces from Rome, but his success only made it more evident that his appeal to national feeling came too late, and was addressed to that which had no existence. As soon as the vigour of the central government revived, a single army, not very well commanded, extinguished the feeble spark. Far different, certainly, was the vigour and enthusiasm with which the Jews took arms. But the result was not different. The rebellious nationality only earned by the fierceness of its rising a more overwhelming ruin.

If we reckon the Jewish war of the reign of Vespasian and that of the reign of Hadrian as constituting together one great national rebellion, then the history of the Empire affords no other considerable example besides those I have mentioned of the rising of a conquered nationality. There appear, indeed, in the third and fourth centuries, some phenomena not altogether different. The third century was an age of revolution. I have spoken already of the great Roman Revolution which began with the tribunate of Gracchus and ended with the battle of Actium. It would be a convenient thing if we could accustom ourselves to the notion of a second Roman Revolution, beginning with the death of Marcus Aurelius, in A.D. 180, and ending with the accession of Diocletian, in A.D. 285. During this period the Imperial system struggled for its life, and suffered a transformation of character which enabled it to support itself over the whole extent of the empire for more than another century, and in the eastern half for many centuries. In the fearful convulsions of this revolutionary period we are able to discern the difficulties with which the Imperial system had to cope. And among these difficulties is certainly to be reckoned the unlikeness of the nations composing the Empire. The Empire shows a constant tendency to break into large fragments, each held together internally by national sympathies, and separated from the others by national differences. The Greek-speaking world tends to separate itself from the Latin-speaking world. Gaul, Britain, and Spain tend to separate themselves from Italy and Africa. These tendencies were recognized when the revolutionary period closed in Diocletian's partition of the Empire between two Augusti and two Cæsars, and, afterwards, in the four great præfectures of Constantine. The division between East and West, after being several times drawn and again effaced, was permanently recognized in the time of the sons of Theodosius, and is written in large characters on the history of the modern world.

The tendency then to division certainly existed, and might at times be dangerous. But it is not to be confounded with that working of the spirit of nationality which I have spoken of as the commonest cause of the ruin of great empires. In most great empires the subject nations have not only a want of sympathy, or it may be a positive antipathy, towards each other; they are influenced still more by an undying hostility towards their conquerors, and an undying recollection of the independence they have lost. Out of these feelings springs a fixed determination, handed down through successive generations, and shared by every individual member of the conquered race, to throw off the yoke at the first opportunity. Where this fixed determination exists, the conquerors have in the long run but a poor chance of retaining their conquest; for their energy is more likely to be corrupted by success than their victims' fixed hatred to be extinguished by delay. And this was the difficulty which, almost alone among conquering nations, the Romans were not called upon to meet. By some means or other they succeeded in destroying in the mind of Gaul, African, and Greek the remembrance of their past independence and the remembrance of the relentless cruelty with which they had been enslaved. Rome destroyed patriotism in its subject races, though it left in them a certain blind instinct of kindred. When the Empire grew weak, the atoms showed a tendency to crystallize again in the old forms, but while it continued vigorous it satisfied the nationalities that it had absorbed. Whether by its imposing grandeur, or the material happiness it bestowed, or the free career it offered, particularly to military merit, or the hopelessness of resistance, or—more particularly in the West—by the civilization it brought with it; by some of these means, or by some combination of them, the Roman Empire succeeded in giving an equivalent to those who had been deprived of everything by its unrelenting sword. As Tecmessa to Ajax, the world said to Rome—

"Σὺ γάρ μοι πατρίδ' ἥστωσας δόρει
καὶ μητέρ' ἀλλὴ μοῖρα τὸν φύσαντά τε
καθεῖλεν Ἅιδου θανασίμους οἰκήτορας.
τίς δῆτ' ἐμοὶ γένοιτ' ἂν ἀντὶ σοῦ πατρίς;
τίς πλοῦτος; ἐν σοὶ πᾶσ' ἔγωγε σώζομαι."

("Thou didst destroy my country with thy spear;
My mother and begetter a blind chance
Took to be tenants of the house of death.
Now then what country can I find but thee?
What household? on thee all my fortune hangs.")

Of all the conquered nations, that which had the noblest past was Greece. It is a striking fact—for which we have the authority of Mr. Finlay—that even a hundred years ago there existed among the Greeks no proud remembrance of their heroic ancestors. Leonidas and Miltiades were names which had no magic sound to them. But they were proud of two things,—of their religious orthodoxy and of their being the legitimate representatives of the Roman Empire.

The Roman Empire, then, did not fall as, for example, the Parthian Empire fell, by the rebellion of the conquered nationalities. But neither again did it fall by the rebellion of its great officers and viceroys, as the empire of Alexander. It was, indeed, constantly exposed to this danger. It felt, as other empires have felt, the necessity of creating these great officers. The Legati of the Rhine, the Legatus of Syria, possessed the power of independent sovereigns. They often seemed likely to use, and sometimes did use, this power against the government. In the first two centuries, Galba, Vitellius, Vespasian, Severus, were successful usurpers; Vindex, Avidius Cassius, Pescennius Niger were unsuccessful ones; Corbulo, and perhaps Agricola, paid with their lives for the greatness which made them capable of becoming usurpers. But these men usurped, or endeavoured to usurp, or were thought likely to usurp, the whole Empire, not parts of it. The danger of the Empire being divided among its great generals, did not appear till near the end of that revolutionary period of which I have spoken. Then, however, it seemed for a time very imminent. We might rather say that for some years the Empire was actually divided in this way. In what is commonly called the time of the Thirty Tyrants, Gaul and Spain were governed for some years by independent emperors, while Syria and part of Asia Minor formed the kingdom of Odenathus. In other parts of the Empire, at the same time, the authority of Rome was thrown off by several less conspicuous adventurers. At this moment, then, the Roman Empire presented the same spectacle of dissolution which other great empires have sooner or later almost always presented. It seemed likely to run the usual course, and to illustrate the insurmountable difficulty in an empire of at once concentrating great power at a number of different points, and preserving the supremacy of the central government. But the Roman Empire rallied, and by an extraordinary display of energy proved the difficulty not to be insurmountable. It escaped this danger also, and that not only for a time, but permanently. The disease of which it died at last was not this, but another.

Of the first Roman Revolution, Marius, Cæsar, and Augustus are the heroes. The first of these organized the military system, the second gave the military power predominance over the civil, the third arranged the relations of the military to the civil power, so as to make them as little oppressive and as durable as possible. The second Roman Revolution, that of the third century after Christ, had for its heroes Diocletian and Constantine. The problem for them was to give to the military power, now absolutely predominant, unity within itself. Before, the question had been of the relations between the Imperator and the Senate; now it was of the relations between the Imperator and his Legati and his army. But now, as then, the only hope of the Empire was in despotism; the one study of all statesmen was how to diminish liberty still further, and concentrate power still more absolutely in a single hand. As Rome had been saved from barbaric invasion by Cæsar, so it was saved by Diocletian from partition among viceroys. But as it was saved the first time at the expense of its republican liberties, it was saved the second time by the sacrifice of those vestiges of freedom which Cæsar had left it. The military dictator now became a sultan. The little finger of Constantine was thicker than the loins of Augustus; and if Tiberius had chastised his subjects with whips, Valentinian chastised them with scorpions.

The Revolution now effected had two stages. First came the temporary arrangement of Diocletian, who, in order to strengthen the Imperial power against the unwieldy army, created, as it were, a cabinet of emperors. He shared his power with three other generals, whom he succeeded in attaching firmly to himself. Such an arrangement could not last, for only a superior genius could suspend the operation of the law, *Nulla fides regni sociis*; but so long as it lasted the Imperial power was quadrupled, and the Empire was firmly ruled, not from one centre, but from four: from Nicomedia, Sirmium, Milan, and Trêves. This plan had all the advantages of partition, while in the undisputed ascendancy of Diocletian it retained all the advantages of unity. But it was a temporary arrangement, and gave place in due time to the permanent institution of Constantine, who broke the strength of the Legati by dividing the military power from the civil. Up to that time, the Legatus of a province had been an emperor in miniature—at the same time governor of a nation and commander of an army. Now, the two offices were divided, and there remained to the emperor an immense superiority over every subject,—the prerogative that in him alone civil and military power met. And at the same time that by disarming all inferior greatness he made himself master of the bodies, the lives, and fortunes of his subjects, he subdued their imaginations and hearts by his assumption of Asiatic state and by his alliance with the Christian Church.

Thus was the second danger successfully encountered. Rome disarmed her formidable viceroys, as she had subdued and pacified her subject nationalities. Yet in a century and a half from the time of Constantine, the Western Empire fell, and the Eastern Empire in the course of three centuries lost many of its richest provinces, and saw its capital besieged by foreign invaders. Having escaped the two principal maladies incident to great empires, she succumbed to some other, the nature of which we have now to consider.

The simple facts of the fall of the Empire are these. The Imperial system had been established, as I have shown, to protect the frontier. This it did for two centuries with eminent success. But in the reign of Marcus Aurelius, whose reign I have noted as marking the commencement of the second revolutionary period, there occurred an invasion of the Marcomanni, which was not repulsed without great difficulty, and which excited a deep alarm and foreboding throughout the Empire. In the third century the hostile powers on every frontier begin to appear more formidable. The German tribes, in whose discord Tacitus saw the safety of the Empire, present themselves now no longer in separate feebleness, but in powerful confederations. We hear no more the insignificant names of Chatti and Chauci; the history of the third century is full of Alemanni, Franks, and Goths. On the eastern frontier, the long decayed power of the Parthians now gives place to a revived and vigorous Persian Empire. The forces of the Empire are more and more taxed to defend it from these powerful enemies. One emperor is killed in battle with the Goths, another is taken prisoner by the Persians. But strengthened by internal reforms, the Empire is found still capable of making head against its assailants. In the middle of the fourth century it is visibly stronger and safer than it had been in the middle of the third. Then follows the greatest convulsion to which human society is liable, that which is to the world of man what an earthquake is to nature,—I mean an invasion of Tartars. The Huns emerge from Asia, and drive before them the populations of Central Europe. The fugitive Goths crave admission into the Empire. Admitted, they engage in war with their entertainers. They defeat and kill an emperor at Adrianople. But again the Empire is avenged by Theodosius. In the age of his degenerate sons the barbaric world decisively encroaches on the Roman. There is a constant influx of Goths. Goths fill the Roman armies, and plunder the Empire under cover of a commission from the emperor himself. Rome is sacked by Alaric. Then most of Gaul, Spain, and afterwards Africa are torn from the empire by an invasion half-Teutonic, half-Sclavonic. Barbaric chieftains make and unmake the emperors of the West. At last they assume sovereignty in Italy to themselves, and shortly afterwards the Ostrogothic kingdom is founded. The East, too, suffers gradually a great change of population. Greece is almost repeopled with Slaves and Wallachians. New kingdoms are founded on the Lower Danube. In the seventh century, Egypt and Syria are wrested from the Empire by the Saracens.

This is what we commonly understand by the fall of the Empire. It was matched in war with the barbaric world beyond the frontier, and the barbaric world was victorious. But it would be very thoughtless to suppose that this is a sufficient account of the matter, and that the fortune of war will explain such a vast phenomenon. What we call fortune may decide a battle, not so easily the shortest war; and it is evident that the Roman world would not have steadily receded through centuries before the barbaric had it not been decidedly inferior in force. To explain, then, the fall of the Empire, it is necessary to explain the inferiority in force of the Romans to the barbarians.

This inferiority of the Romans, it is to be remembered, was a new thing. At an earlier time they had been manifestly superior. When the region of barbarism was much larger; when it included warlike and aggressive nations now lost to it, such as the Gauls; and when, on the other hand, the Romans drew their armies from a much smaller area, and organized them much less elaborately, the balance had inclined decidedly the other way. In those times the Roman world, in spite of occasional reverses, had on the whole steadily encroached on the barbaric. The Gauls were such good soldiers, that the

Romans themselves acknowledged their superiority in valour: yet the Romans not only held their own against them, but conquered them, and annexed Gaul to the Empire. If we use the word "force" in its most comprehensive sense, as including all the different forces, material, intellectual, and moral, which can contribute to the military success of a nation, it is evident that the Roman world in the time of Pompey and Cæsar was as much superior in force to the barbaric world as it was inferior to it in the time of Arcadius and Honorius. Either, therefore, a vast increase of power must have taken place in the barbaric world, or a vast internal decay in the Roman.

Now the barbaric world had actually received two considerable accessions of force. It had gained considerably, through what influences we can only conjecture, in the power and habit of co-operation. As I have said before, in the third century we meet with large confederations of Germans, whereas before we read only of isolated tribes. Together with this capacity of confederation we can easily believe that the Germans had acquired new intelligence, civilization, and military skill. Moreover, it is practically to be considered as a great increase of aggressive force, that in the middle of the fourth century they were threatened in their original settlements by the Huns. The impulse of desperation which drove them against the Roman frontier was felt by the Romans as a new force acquired by the enemy. But we shall soon see that other and more considerable momenta must have been required to turn the scale. For in the first place, if in three centuries the barbaric world made a considerable advance in power, how was it that the Roman world did not make an immensely greater advance in the same time? A barbaric society is commonly almost stationary; a civilized society is indefinitely progressive. How many advantages had a vast and well-ordered empire like the Roman over barbarism! What a step towards material wealth and increase of population would seem to be necessarily made when the bars to intercourse are removed between a number of countries, and when war between those countries is abolished! If in the first two centuries of the Empire there were bloody wars within the Empire, yet they were both short and very infrequent; the permanent condition of international hostility between the nations surrounding the Mediterranean Sea, which had preceded the Roman conquests, was a tradition of the past. Never since has there been over the same area so long a period of internal peace. If we were guided by modern analogies, we should certainly expect that, while barbarism made its first tottering steps in the path of improvement, the Empire would have made gigantic strides; that its population and wealth would have increased enormously; that instead of failing to defend the frontier it would have overflowed it at all points; and that it would have annexed and romanized Germany with far greater ease than in Cæsar's time it had absorbed Gaul.

In the second place, the balance had already begun to turn before any new weights were put into the scale of barbarism. A long period intervened between the time when Rome was a conquering state and the time when she began to be conquered. During this interval barbarism had acquired no new strength, and yet the Romans had ceased to conquer. And this must have been owing, not

to any want of will, but to a consciousness of the want of
power. For when Rome ceased to conquer, she was far
more completely organized for military purposes and
governed more exclusively by military men than in her
period of conquest. With a citizen soldiery, summoned
from farms and commanded often by civilians, Rome
extended her boundaries widely; but with a magnificent
standing army, with a crowd of experienced officers, and
with an Imperator at the head of affairs, Rome ceased,
except at long intervals, to conquer. The opinion of
Augustus, that a limit ought to be set to the Empire, can
only mean that the limit of its resources had been reached,[1]
and that those resources, for some reason or other, did
not grow. And that the maxim was sound, and continued to be sound, is shown by Hadrian's re-assertion of
it when he gave up the Parthian conquests of Trajan, and
later by Aurelian's evacuation of Dacia. Aurelian was a
great general; Hadrian was an active and enterprising
man. Both of them must have known that the easiest
way to obtain popularity was to carry on wars of conquest. Both must have known that to give up conquests
was the readiest way to offend the pride of the Romans,
and to excite disaffection towards the government. We
may therefore feel sure that it was neither love of ease
nor a mere blind respect for a traditionary maxim that
induced these two emperors deliberately to narrow the
boundaries of the Empire. They must have had a knowledge of the weakness and exhaustion of the State, and
of its inadequacy to new conquests, so certain and clear
as to silence all the suggestions of ambition and interest.

[1] Observe that Augustus put this piece of advice at the end of a statement
of the resources of the Empire. (Tac. Ann. i. 11.)

We are forced, then, to the conclusion that the Roman Empire, in the midst of its greatness and civilization, must have been in a stationary and unprogressive, if not a decaying condition. Now what can have been the cause of this unproductiveness or decay? It has been common to suppose a moral degeneration in the Romans, caused by luxury and excessive good fortune. To support this it is easy to quote the satirists and cynics of the Imperial time, and to refer to such accounts as Ammianus gives of the mingled effeminacy and brutality of the aristocracy of the capital in the fourth century. But the history of the wars between Rome and the barbaric world does not show us the proofs we might expect of this decay of spirit. We do not find the Romans ceasing to be victorious in the field, and beginning to show themselves inferior in valour to their enemies. The luxury of the capital could not affect the army, which had no connection with the capital, but was levied from the peasantry of the whole Empire, a class into which luxury can never penetrate. Nor can it be said that luxury corrupted the generals, and through them the army. On the contrary, the Empire produced a remarkable series of capable generals. From Claudius Gothicus to the patrician Aetius, a period of two centuries, the series is scarcely interrupted, and for the greater part of that time the government of the Empire itself was in the hands of men bred to war and accustomed to great commands. And as in better times, the Roman arms were still commonly victorious. Julian, fighting at great odds, defeated the Alemanni; Theodosius quelled the intruding Goths; Stilicho checked Alaric and crushed Rhadagaisus; the great Tartar himself, the genius of destruction, Attila, met his match in Aetius, and retreated before the arms of Rome.

Whatever the remote and ultimate cause may have been, the immediate cause to which the fall of the Empire can be traced is a physical, not a moral, decay. In valour, discipline, and science, the Roman armies remained what they had always been, and the peasant emperors of Illyricum were worthy successors of Cincinnatus and Caius Marius. But the problem was, how to replenish those armies. Men were wanting; the Empire perished for want of men.

The proof of this is in the fact that the contest with barbarism was carried on by the help of barbarian soldiers. The Emperor Probus began this system, and under his successors it came more and more into use. As the danger of it could not be overlooked, we must suppose that the necessity of it was still more unmistakeable. It must have been because the Empire could not furnish soldiers for its own defence, that it was driven to the strange expedient of turning its enemies and plunderers into its defenders. Yet on these scarcely disguised enemies it came to depend so exclusively that in the end the Western Empire was destroyed, not by the hostile army, but by its own. The Roman army had become a barbarian horde, and for some years the Roman commander-in-chief was a barbarian prince, Ricimer, who created and deposed emperors at his pleasure. Soon after his fall, another barbarian, occupying the same position, Odoacer, terminated the line of emperors, and assumed the government into his own hands.

Nor was it only in the army that the Empire was compelled to borrow men from barbarism. To cultivate the fields whole tribes were borrowed. From the time of Marcus Aurelius, it was a practice to grant lands within the Empire sometimes to prisoners of war, sometimes to tribes applying for admission. Thus the Vandals received settlements in Pannonia, the Goths of Ulfilas in Mœsia, the Salian Franks along the Rhine. In these cases the Romans were not forced to admit the barbarians. If they were partly influenced by the wish to pacify them, it is certain also that there must have been a vast extent of unoccupied land which the Empire was glad to people in this way. However much disposed we may be to disregard rhetorical descriptions of utter devastation along the frontier, it seems at least to be clear that, however many barbaric tribes might knock for admission, there was room for them within the Empire. Nor did these large loans of men suffice the Empire. It was perpetually borrowing smaller amounts. Under the name of Læti and Coloni, there seems reason to believe that the Empire was already full of Germans before the great immigrations began.[1] Facts of this order stand in a much closer relation to the fall of the Empire than many which are habitually adduced to account for it. The drain of wealth to the East, fiscal oppression, the rapacity of officials, the tyranny by which the curiales, or respectable middle class of provincial towns, were crushed, the growth of servility and effeminacy, all these are causes which might, and probably did, bring on the ruin of the Empire. But they were causes operating indirectly and indefinitely, and they ought not to divert our attention from the immediate and adequate

[1] See "Das weströmische Reich," by Dr. Heinrich Richter; Berlin, 1865.

cause,—that want of population which made it impossible to keep a native army on foot, and which caused a perpetual and irrepressible stream of barbaric immigration. The barbarian occupied the Roman Empire almost as the Anglo-Saxon is occupying North America: he settled and peopled rather than conquered it.

The want of any principle of increase in the Roman population is attested at a much earlier time. In the second century before Christ, Polybius[1] bears witness to it, and the returns of the census from the Second Punic War to the time of Augustus show no steady increase in the number of citizens that cannot be accounted for by the extension of citizenship to new classes. A stationary population suffers from war or any other destructive plague far more, and more permanently, than a progressive one. Accordingly we are told that Julius Cæsar, when he attained to supreme power, found an alarming thinness of population ($\delta\epsilon\iota\nu\dot{\eta}\nu$ $\dot{\delta}\lambda\iota\gamma\alpha\nu\theta\rho\omega\pi\dot{\iota}\alpha\nu$).[2] Both he and his successor struggled earnestly against this evil. The grave maxim of Metellus Macedonicus, that marriage was a duty which, however painful, every citizen ought manfully to discharge, acquired great importance in the eyes of Augustus. He caused the speech in which it was contained to be read in the Senate: had he lived in our days, he would have reprinted it with a preface. To admonition he added legislation. The Lex Julia is the irrefragable proof of the existence at the beginning of the Imperial time of that very disease which, four centuries after, destroyed the Empire. How alarming the symp-

[1] Polyb. l. 64.   [2] Dion Cass. xliii. 25.

toms already were may be measured by the determined resolution with which Augustus forced his enactment upon the people, in spite of the most strenuous resistance. The enactment consisted of a number of privileges and precedences given to marriage. It was in fact a handsome bribe offered by the State to induce the citizens to marry. How strange, according to our notions, the condition of society must have been; how directly opposite from the present one the view taken by statesmen of the question of population; and how unlike the present one the view taken by people in general of marriage, may be judged from this law. Precisely as we think of marriage, the Roman of Imperial times thought of celibacy—that is, as the most comfortable but the most expensive condition of life. Marriage with us is a pleasure for which a man must be content to pay; with the Romans it was an excellent pecuniary investment,[1] but an intolerably disagreeable one.

Here lay, at least in the judgment of Augustus, the root of the evil. To inquire into the causes of this aversion to marriage in this place would lead me too far. We must be content to assume that, owing partly to this cause and partly to the prudential check of infanticide, the Roman population seems to have been in ordinary times almost stationary. The same phenomenon had shown itself in Greece before its conquest by the Romans. There the population had even greatly declined, and the shrewd observer Polybius explains that it was not owing to war or plague,[2] but mainly to a general repugnance to

[1] Plutarch, Περὶ φιλοστοργίας, c. 2.
[2] He even asserts, ii. 62, 4, that the very period in which this decline of population took place was one of very great prosperity. That matters were not much mended in the time of Trajan appears from Plutarch, who says (De Def. Or. 8), in the universal decay of population Greece had the largest share.

marriage, and reluctance to rear large families, caused by an extravagantly high standard of comfort.[1] If we can suppose a similar temper to have become common among the Roman citizens, it may still seem at first sight unlikely that the newly conquered barbarians of Gaul or Britain would fall into an effeminacy incident rather to excessive civilization. But there is reason to think, on the contrary, that the newly conquered barbarians were especially liable to it. We know how dangerous is the sudden introduction of civilized habits and manners among barbarians. We know how fatally the contact of Anglo-Saxons has worked upon Indians, Australians, and New Zealanders. The effect of Roman civilization upon Gauls and Britons was similar, if we may take the evidence of Tacitus. They exchanged too suddenly a life of rude and violent adventure for the Roman baths and schools of rhetoric. The effect upon these races was an unnatural lethargy, and apparently also a tendency to decline in numbers. The Helvetians are spoken of by Tacitus as already almost extinct;[2] and the Batavians who distinguish themselves by their high spirit in the wars of Vitellius and Vespasian,[3] have entirely disappeared when their territory is occupied in the fourth century by the Franks.

It remains to point out that the circumstances of the

---

[1] This most important passage, which was first published by Angelo Mai in 1827, and was therefore unknown to many of our writers on the population of the ancient nations, while it seems to have been overlooked by Dureau de la Malle, is to be found quoted and translated in the last chapter of Thirlwall's History of Greece. For the strange words ἀλιξαντεμίων καὶ φιλατρημοσύνην we should perhaps read with Bekker ἀλαζονείαν καὶ φιλοχρηματοσύνην.

[2] *Hist.* i. 67.  [3] Ibid. i. 59, ii. 28.

Empire between the times of Cæsar and Constantine were such as rather to aggravate than mitigate the disease. One main reason why civilization in modern times is favourable to the growth of population is that it is industrial. The Anglo-Saxon subdues physical nature to his interest and convenience. Wherever he comes, he introduces new industries. He contrives first to prosper, and next he increases. By his side the barbarian, skilled only in destruction, and without the inclination or talent to create anything, feels himself growing weaker and weaker, despairs, and then disappears. But Roman civilization was not of this creative kind. It was military, that is, destructive. The enormous wealth of the Romans had not been created by them, but simply appropriated. It had been gained not by manufacture or commerce, but by war. And it had been gained by the concentrated effort of many successive generations. Probably such a great national effort cannot be maintained for so long a time without giving to the national character a fixed warp or bias. The military inclination would remain to the Romans even when they had lost the power to gratify it. The aversion to all the arts of creation would remain even when nothing but those arts could save them. In the most successful conquering race that has appeared since the Romans,—in the Turks,—the same phenomenon appears. They have lost the power to conquer, but they cannot acquire habits of industry and accumulation. Their nature has no versatility; it enjoys nothing between fighting and torpid inaction. They could win an empire, but having won it, they allow it to fall into ruin. In a less degree the Romans seem to have had the same defect. There runs through their literature the brigand's and barbarian's contempt for honest industry, — at least when that industry is not agricultural.[1] To make wealth appears to them sordid; to take it admirable. And accordingly, when the limit of conquest and spoliation had been reached, a torpor, a Turkish helplessness, fell on them. They lived on what should have been their capital. Their wealth went to Asia in exchange for perishable luxuries,[2] a general poverty spread through the Empire, and the unwillingness to multiply must have become stronger and stronger.

Perhaps enough has now been said to explain that great enigma, which so much bewilders the reader of Gibbon; namely, the sharp contrast between the age of the Antonines and the age which followed it. A century of unparalleled tranquillity and virtuous government is followed immediately by a period of hopeless ruin and dissolution. A century of rest is followed not by renewed vigour, but by incurable exhaustion. Some principle of decay must clearly have been at work, but what principle? We answer: it was a period of sterility or barrenness in human beings; the human harvest was bad. And among the causes of this barrenness we find, in the more barbarous nations, the enfeeblement produced by the too-abrupt introduction of civilization, and universally the absence of industrial habits, and the disposition to listlessness which belongs to the military character.

---

[1] St. Just, that fanatical worshipper of antiquity, apprehended correctly in this respect the nature of the scheme of society he wished to revive. He says, "Il ne peut exister de peuple vertueux et libre qu'un peuple agriculteur. Un métier s'accorde mal avec le véritable citoyen: la main de l'homme n'est faite que pour la terre ou pour les armes." See Von Sybel's French Revolution, Eng. Trans., vol. iv. p. 48.

[2] Plin. *Hist. Nat.* vi. 23, xii. 18.

A society in such a critical position as this can ill bear a sudden shock. The sudden shock came; "a swift destruction winged from God!" Aurelius, whose reign I have marked as the end of an age, saw the flash. We might say that Heaven, pitying the long death-struggle of the Roman world, sent down the Angel Azrael to cut matters short. In A.D. 166 broke out the plague. It spread from Persia to Gaul, and, according to the historians, carried off "a majority of the population."[1] It was the first of a long series of similar visitations. Niebuhr has said that the ancient world never recovered from the blow inflicted upon it by the plague which visited it in the reign of Aurelius. We are in danger of attaching too little importance to occurrences of this kind. The historian devotes but a few lines to them because they do not often admit of being related in detail. The battle of Cressy occupies the historian more than the Black Death, yet we now know that the Black Death is a turning-point in mediæval English history. Our knowledge of the series of plagues which fell on the Roman world during the Revolutionary period from Aurelius to Diocletian, is extremely fragmentary. But the vastness of the calamity seems not doubtful, and it seems also clear that the condition of the Empire was just such as to make the blow mortal. It is also plain that the reconstructed Empire over which, when the Revolutionary period was past, Diocletian and Constantine reigned, was different in its whole character from the Empire of the Antonines, and that a new age began

---

[1] See Hecker's "Commentatio de Peste Antoniniana," where, among other things, the passages in Galen which refer to this plague are collected.

then which resembled the Middle Ages as much as it resembled Antiquity.

As the population dwindled, a new evil made its appearance. The expenses of government had always been great: when complete Oriental sultanism was introduced by Diocletian, they became enormous. And the demands of government reached their highest point when the population had been decimated (the word is probably much too weak) by the plague. The *fiscus*, which had always been burdensome, became now a millstone round the neck of the sinking Empire. The demand for money became as urgent as the demand for men. A leading characteristic of the later Empire is grinding taxation. The government being overwhelmingly powerful, there was no limit to its power of extortion, and the army of officials which had now been created plundered for themselves as well as for the government. What the plague had been to the population, that the *fiscus* was to industry. It broke the bruised reed; it converted feebleness into utter and incurable debility. Roman finance had no conception of the impolicy of laying taxation so as to depress enterprise and trade. The *fiscus* destroyed capital in the Roman Empire. The desire of accumulation languished where government lay in wait for all savings—*locupletissimus quisque in prædam correptus*. All the intricate combinations by which man is connected to man in a progressive society disappeared. The diminished population lived once more as αὐτουργοί, procuring from the soil as much as their own individual needs required, each man alone, and all alike in bondage to an omnipotent, all-grasping government. For safety they had given omnipotence to their government, but they could not give it the knowledge of political economy, nor the power to cure subtle moral evils. Accordingly all the omnipotence of government was turned to increasing the poverty, and consequently the sterility, of the population.[1]

I have not left myself space to describe in detail the pressure of the *fiscus* and the conscription upon the different classes of the people. It is related in many books with what malignant ingenuity the men of property everywhere were, so to speak, chained to the spot where they lived, that the vulture of taxation might prey upon their vitals; and how the peasantry were in like manner appropriated and enslaved to military service. But this oppression, to which government in its helplessness was driven, filled the cup. I conceive that the downfall of the Empire is thus accounted for. Barbarians might enter freely and take possession. Vandal corsairs from Carthage might outdo the work of Hannibal, and Germany avenge at her leisure the invasions of Cæsar and Drusus, for the invincible power had been tamed by a slow disease. Rome had stopped, from a misgiving she could not explain to herself, in the career of victory. A century of repose had only left her weaker than before. She was able to conquer her nationalities. She centralized herself successfully, and created a government of mighty efficiency and stability. But against this disease she was powerless; and the disease was sterility. Already enfeebled by it, she passed through a century of plague, and when the plague handed her over to the *fiscus* there remained nothing for the sufferer but gradually to sink.

[1] See Mr. Finlay's "Greece under the Romans," *passim*.

But the causes from which the disease itself had sprung were such as we can but imperfectly ascertain,—causes deeply involved in the constitution of society itself, and such as no statesmanship or philosophy then in the world could hope to contend with.[1]

[1] See Dureau de la Malle; the last chapter of Thirlwall's History of Greece; and C. G. Zumpt, "Ueber den Stand der Bevölkerung und die Volksmehrung im Alterthum." The last of these writers especially treats at length what is here dealt with but summarily. See also, for the matters discussed both in this and the following lecture, Mr. Finlay's most valuable books on the later history of Greece.

# III.

# ROMAN IMPERIALISM.

### THE LATER EMPIRE.

I HAVE already said that there are two very distinct periods in the imperial history, and that these are divided by a long revolutionary period of transition. The end of the first period I placed at Marcus Aurelius; we may be more precise if we choose and place it at the breaking out of the Marcomannic War. The beginning of the other period may be placed at the accession of Diocletian, when the unity and tranquillity of the Empire were restored and the outlines of the new system of government were sketched. The transition period which intervened is, perhaps, the most melancholy in European history. It presents some of the worst tyrannies, some of the bloodiest revolutions, and some of the most enormous calamities in history. It presents Europe suffering from two plagues at once; the one the plague properly so called; the other, a mutinous, omnipotent, and half-barbaric soldiery.

To this middle period I shall not again call your attention. I propose now to place the first and third periods before you in contrast, in order to make more clear the radical and universal change which had taken place in the interval. In other words, I propose to institute a detailed comparison between the Empire under Hadrian or the Antonines, and the Empire under Constantine or Theodosius.

First, then, in the earlier period the Roman world was clearly and broadly separated from the barbaric, but in the later period the separation has disappeared. In the earlier period certain nations belonged to the one and certain other nations to the other; the nations beyond the frontier were of a different stock from the nations within it. There was a distinction of blood, as well as of place and of institutions. In the later period the geographical boundary remains, and also the distinction of institutions; but the German blood is to be found in the Roman population as much as out of it. Germans are within the Empire, and not only so, but more diffused through the Empire than any other nationality. The Empire had before been a specific substance with a distinct form. It is still a distinct form, but the substance or stuff is no longer distinguishable from that of barbarism. The word Roman has ceased to be a national designation, and has become a legal or technical term. There are Roman citizens still in the eyes of the law, but they are as likely to have the features and habits of barbarians as those who are not Roman citizens. There is still a Roman army; there are still legions though much changed in character; but the soldiers are now very commonly Goths, Vandals, and Sarmatians. There are still famous Roman generals, as in the days of Scipio and Marius; and famous victories are won, as in old days, over barbarous hordes; but Stilicho was a Vandal and Aëtius a Sarmatian, and their victories were won perhaps with Roman science, but certainly by barbarian hands. Even the forms are in some cases barbarous. Roman soldiers now rushed to the charge with the old German war-cry, called the *barritus;* when Julian became Emperor, he was lifted on a shield like a Frankish chief.

Even in the earlier period the word Roman had been stretched considerably beyond its original meaning. There were already multitudes of Roman citizens who had never set foot in Rome. But it was still a name denoting certain nations and excluding others, and it was still justified by the fact that Rome remained the seat of government and the centre of the Empire. It was considered the strangest instance of eccentricity in Tiberius that he retired without necessity from Rome, and deliberately preferred to live elsewhere;[1] a hundred years later the first Antonine lived exclusively, and the second usually, at Rome. But now, not only had the word Roman ceased to be exclusive of any nationality, but it was used to describe an empire of which Rome was not the centre. Diocletian took the government away from Rome, and Constantine provided a worthy seat for it on the Bosphorus. Nor by this change did Rome merely cease to be the sole seat of government; it lost its metropolitan character altogether. The Emperors of the West abandoned it as well as those of the East. They preferred to it first Milan and then Ravenna. There are still other claims to the title of Roman, which the earlier Empire

[1] Tac. Ann. iv. 58.

had possessed and which the later Empire wanted. In the time of the Antonines the fact that the Empire had been founded by a conquering nation issuing from Rome, was still conspicuously seen in the distinction between those subjects of the Empire who had the Roman citizenship and those who had not. The distinction was becoming faint, but so long as it was recognized by the law, so long as in the army the legions consisting of Roman citizens were distinct from the allied cohorts and squadrons consisting of those who wanted the citizenship, so long the Empire might still be said, in a sense, to be Roman. But during the transition period this distinction also was effaced. When all the freemen of the Empire were placed on an equal footing, and the distinction between legions and allies disappeared in the army, there remained no visible record of Rome's conquest except the use of Latin as the official language.

We are accustomed to think of that Holy Roman Empire which disappeared from the world within living memory, as having been Roman only in name. The misnomer in that case was certainly more glaring, but it was hardly more real than in the case of the Empire of Constantine. It is true that the Empire of Constantine had arisen out of that of the Antonines without breach of continuity, and that the change had been gradual. Still it had been a very complete change; one by one most of the Roman characteristics had disappeared. The appropriateness of the title could only be discovered from history. The Empire might be called Roman, as Constantine might be called Cæsar. But Constantine was as much connected by blood with the old Julian gens of Alba Longa as the vast political system, half Oriental, half barbaric, in which so many nations were united, was connected with the drowsy old provincial town on the banks of the Tiber, which Ammianus has described for us.

If the Empire was no longer Roman either by nationality or in the sense of being connected as an appurtenance or dependency with the city of Rome, neither was it Roman in the sense of possessing the political institutions which had originally belonged to Rome. Here the contrast between the age of Constantine and that of the Antonines is particularly marked. Under the Antonines the Empire retained much of the political character of the old Republic. It was in fact nearer to the Republic than it had been under the first Cæsars. Just at that exceptional period the State was guided by a President for life, nominated by his predecessor from among the most promising men of the age, possessing indeed power limited by nothing but his will, but choosing for the most part to regard his Senate with deference. This Senate was a chosen body of distinguished men selected by the Emperor from the whole Empire, and required to take up their residence in Italy. They formed a dignified club at Rome, and gave a powerful expression to the feelings of the upper classes. The old Republic had often witnessed a similar government, when a Dictator had managed the State with the confidence of the aristocratic Senate. The monarchical element was there, but in the form least repugnant to Republicanism, for the monarch was not hereditary nor separated by any clear demarcation from his subjects.

In the time of Constantine the government is essentially different, for the Senate as an organ of general aristocratic opinion has practically disappeared, and the Life-President has become a Sultan. Both these changes were natural, and omens of them had appeared even before the Antonines. The Senate of Nero was almost as insignificant as that of Constantine, and no Sultan could trample on human beings more contemptuously than Caligula. When the earlier Emperors were restrained, it was by their own good sense or virtue; the system was entirely without checks. But what before only the bad Emperors had been, every Emperor was now, and the Senate was now habitually as insignificant as before a bad Emperor had occasionally made it. An Augustus, a Trajan, an Antoninus, had found it politic, and perhaps judged it right, to treat the Senate with great respect, and to secure its co-operation in government. But the Emperors of the later series who answer best to these, and who were the wisest rulers—Diocletian, Constantine, Valentinian, Theodosius—steadily disregarded and trampled on the Senate; only a weak Gratian flatters it. Nor has it only lost favour with the Emperors; it has suffered a great change of character.[1] In the first place there is now no longer a single Senate, but two, one at Rome and another at Constantinople; and next there are now a multitude of senators scattered through the provinces who do not practically attend the meetings of the body at either of the two capitals. These changes were calculated to destroy the influence of the Senate as an organ of public opinion. Its judgment was no longer the solemn decision of a picked body of distinguished men assembled at the centre of government. It was assembled partly at

[1] See Dr. Emil Kuhn's "Die städtische und bürgerliche Verfassung des römischen Reichs," p. 174.

Rome, which was not the seat of government, but a venerated ancient city, possessing a circle of very distinguished and extremely indolent noble families; and partly at Constantinople, which was sometimes nominally the seat of empire, but often only the seat of the Eastern Government. The decisions of these two bodies might be contradictory, nor did they necessarily represent the opinion of the senatorian order which was scattered through the Empire. Thus changed in character, and steadily discouraged by the Emperor, the Senate loses almost all its influence. It is preserved as a convenient nucleus of wealth for the operations of the tax-gatherer. As a political organ it becomes only once again conspicuous, and that is when the Roman Senate makes its fruitless protest in favour of the ancient gods, and once more sits, as in the old Gallic invasion, to represent a lost cause and to be bearded by victorious invaders.

When I say that the Emperor has become a Sultan, I mean, not only that he has assumed Oriental state, and a kind of sacred character as head of the Christian Church, but also that his immeasurable superiority to his subjects is admitted by them in their hearts, that the very conception of liberty has disappeared, and that that period has already begun which only ended with the French Revolution, the period during which government had a supernatural character and exercised a dazzling or enchanting power over the minds of men. This spell, which the whole seventeenth and eighteenth centuries were uneasily labouring to shake off, was first thrown "into the spongy air" by Diocletian and Constantine. By these men the deep distinction that had so long existed between the Greeks and Romans on the one hand, and the Orientals on the other, was effaced. They destroyed what we may call the classical view of life, which asserts human free will, and regards government merely as a useful and respectable machinery for economizing power, and introducing order, beauty, and virtue into human affairs. In place of it they introduced the Asiatic view, which rests upon unalterable necessity, and elevates government into a divinity, teaching the subject to endure whatever it may inflict, not only without resistance, but without even an inward murmur; and, in short, to say to government what religion commands us to say to Providence, "Thy will be done."

With the Oriental theory of government was introduced Oriental cruelty and wastefulness of human life. In the earlier Empire there had been seen cruel Emperors, but now cruelty has become part of the system. The history of this time might be written in letters of blood. Executions, tortures, massacres, make the staple of the narrative even in the reigns of good Emperors. The great Theodosius massacres thousands of innocent people in a transient fit of passion. Constantine puts to death his wife and son. Valentinian, a brave and able Emperor, sheds as much blood as Caracalla, apparently from no bad motive, but only from a kind of mania for severity which has infected government. When the Emperor is of weak character, this uniform cruelty is intensified by his fears. Constantius does not appear to have been a monster like Caligula or Nero; he was simply a weak man; yet his tyranny, as described by Ammianus, appears far more tremendous than theirs. Theirs at the utmost is European, his is Asiatic.

It is the redeeming feature of this despotism that the

rule of hereditary succession is not habitually observed in it. The ablest generals are still frequently invested with the purple, and there appeared during this period rulers who, in their merciless energy and the vastness of their views, resembled the Czar Peter. But the hereditary principle would occasionally creep in, and when it did so it always inflicted irreparable injury. The evils of hereditary succession can be guarded against when they can be calculated upon. The real burden of government can then be devolved upon ministers. But when the law of birth intrudes itself into an elective monarchy, when a weak man or a child is placed upon a throne which is commonly filled by merit, he is expected to govern personally; no adequate ministerial organization is at hand to screen his deficiencies; and his incompetence tells to its full extent upon his empire. The hereditary principle should be excluded altogether if it is not exclusively adopted. The right of nominating his successor, which was given in the Roman Empire to the Emperor, gave him the power of ruining everything by a single act. One corrupt or partial appointment was fatal. The nepotism of Aurelius brought on the dismal revolutionary period; the nepotism of Theodosius brought in the barbarians.

The worst kind of government is that which is regarded by its subjects as divine, and at the same time is really weak. Such was the government of Constantius, of Honorius, of Valentinian III.; imbecile, and at the same time despotic, plaguing the world like an angry deity, and misgoverning it like an ignorant child. But these were exceptional cases. Government during this period was commonly at a higher level. It was Asiatic, but it was commonly able. Compared with Asiatic governments it was good. If the Emperor was regarded as a divinity, at least he earned his deification for the most part by merit. He was not such a deity as those which Egypt worshipped, a sacred ape or cat, but rather a Hercules or Quirinus, who had risen by superhuman labours to divine honours. But compared with the government of the Antonines, it was barbaric. The Empire has fallen into a lower class of states. Reason and simplicity have disappeared from it. Subjects have lost all rights, and government all responsibility. The reign of political superstition has set in. Abject fear paralyses the people, and those that rule are intoxicated with insolence and cruelty. It is an Iron Age.

Government having assumed godhead, assumes at the same time the appurtenances of it. It is surrounded with "thousands of angels." A principal feature of this age as contrasted with that of the Antonines is the enormous multiplication of offices and officials. In this respect the Empire had from the beginning advanced upon the Republic. I have already shown that the most conspicuous change introduced by the imperial system was the creation of a number of great offices principally of a military character. A kind of martial regularity and strictness of discipline had been given to the State. By the side of the old civic and free organization had been placed a military organization which was despotic. Under the Antonines the two had subsisted together in harmony, and despotism had worn an almost republican dress. But the civic organization had now disappeared entirely, and had been superseded by a bureaucracy framed after the military model. The holders of function, who were originally elected by the people to rule over the people, have now become soldiers, bearing the commission and under the orders of the commander-in-chief. All officials alike bear the name of *milites*, and their service is called *militia;* even when their functions are purely civil they bear military titles, such as *centurio, primipilaris*.[1] It seemed at the beginning of this period as if the very conception of any power not military had disappeared from the world. Where is now the toga of Cicero? The Empire has become a camp. But this state of things was not to last. It was indeed destined that all power should assume the military type; civil life was to be re-organized on the model of military life. But the distinction between the civil and the military power was brought back by Constantine soon after it had seemed to be lost. Civil life is merged for a moment in military, and is then again differentiated; but when it reappears, the military stamp is on it. The military title of prætorian prefect is given to four men whose functions are purely civil, and who exercise supreme jurisdiction each over a quarter of the Empire. Meanwhile the military functions are committed to new officers called *Duces*, the originals of our modern dukes; a war-office is created; there is a commander-in-chief of the infantry and a commander of the cavalry. The old Legatus, such as he is described in the life of Agricola,—a despotic sovereign within his own province, a general and a judge at the same time—has disappeared. The civil and military professions have been created, and each is elaborately organized; but the civil profession is an offshoot from the military. The Army, as it were,

[1] For the details see Emil Kuhn, p. 149.

destroyed the State, and then created a new State out of itself.

Upon the system of the Antonines this is, in one sense, a great improvement. Such a vast empire evidently could not be satisfactorily governed without a complicated organization, nor could it be safe from disturbances without a separation of the civil and military governments. The distribution of the Empire into præfectures, vicariates, dioceses; the creation of an army, of public servants embodied and drilled with all the formality of an army; these were administrative reforms of the first magnitude, and they make the government of Constantine seem a far more finished machine than that of the Antonines. But the well-being of a State does not always increase with the administrative efficiency of its government. An all-powerful government was created: since liberty in that age was out of the question, such a government, had it been wise, might have been the best thing for the State. But it was all-powerful for evil as well as for good, and ruined the Empire after saving it.

I showed in my last lecture that the Empire was essentially weak for want of the first conditions of vigour in a society,—population and industry. It was too weak to bear the ponderous weight of such a government. For, besides the cruelty, this government had all the wastefulness of Oriental rule. The army of officials might be necessary to carry on government, but they ruined the people. Their enormous number of itself entailed ruinous expense. Moreover, in making ostentation a principle, the government had, as it were, committed itself to extravagance. Extravagance involved oppressive taxation, and the agents of this taxation, the official class, inevitably formed the habit of rapacity. Thus for the tyranny of an Emperor, to which in earlier times the people were sometimes exposed, was now substituted the uniform, universal, crushing tyranny of an official class.

Evils seldom come in this world without their compensations. I have been enumerating the symptoms of a long decay, the decay of a world. Steadily downward to a lower level of civilization and of happiness sank the Roman Empire. Its population barbarized by immigrations from beyond the frontier; its old civic freedom disappearing even from memory; its organ of opinion, the Senate, sinking into an insignificant committee of placemen; its Emperor putting off the sense of responsibility, and along with it all restraints of human feeling; its administration assuming a military ruthlessness and peremptoriness; its government generally becoming its own triumphant and insolent enemy,—Rome, the representative of European civilization, the inventor of civilized jurisprudence, and the inheritor of Greek philosophy, descends to the level of an Asiatic State. She passes through the fire to that military Moloch whose minister she had made herself. With genius dead, and the intellect fallen into such rudeness that she can scarcely tell us articulately the story of her woes, we see her more than once prostrate before one of those monstrous human idols that are worshipped in Asia, a Sultan governed by eunuchs and concubines, cruel and irresistible, deriving all his strength from human weakness, yet exacting copious libations of human blood and the utmost farthing of treasure. But to all these losses there were compensations, and these I proceed to consider.

The Asiatic despotism had some points of advantage over the classic. Liberty, which in its old forms had disappeared, began to spring up in new ones. In the first place, at the moment when freemen sank to be slaves, slaves began to turn into freemen. We do not know distinctly the steps of the transformation, but, like all the other changes to which I have called attention, it took place between the age of the Antonines and that of Constantine. A class of agricultural serfs came into existence, attached to the soil and irremovable from the spot on which they lived. They are sometimes called slaves, but they appear to have had property, and they had rights against their masters and duties to the State. In the decay of population human beings had risen in value. The government wanted recruits for its legions, and began to lay claim to the services of those who before had been the chattels of private citizens. In the decay of industry it was necessary to provide for the cultivation of the soil. One of the peculiarities of this government, in which human free-will was almost suppressed, was its principle of assigning vocations by arbitrary compulsion to whole classes of men. Many governments have assumed the right of pressing people against their will into some vocations, particularly into military service. But in the age of Constantine a principle of forced enlistment is applied to almost all functions. Men are forced into municipal offices against their will, in some cases they are pressed into trade. It was by another application of the same principle that one class of the population is bound to agricultural labour.[1] The government, as it were, enlists an army of cultivators, whom it controls with as much rigour as its army, properly so called. These cultivators are in the strictest sense servants of the soil. They have a definite function in the community, and for the fulfilment of it they are responsible to the State.[2] The State was no merciful master, but so far as it assumed authority over the serf it rescued him from the authority of his master. As the harshest system is better than individual caprice, we may believe that the lot of the *coloni* was better than that of the agricultural slaves of the earlier time. If so, an improvement is caused by the very principle of decay and dissolution, and the very rottenness of the carcase breeds new life.

At the same time there was spread through society a new principle, which, if it cannot properly be called liberty, was a most powerful substitute for it. I have said that government had been erected into a divinity, and that the very tradition of liberty was lost. This is true, and yet a certain kind of resistance to government was carried on upon a vast scale, with unalterable resolution and with success. The edict of Diocletian commanding the Christians to sacrifice was resisted throughout the Empire; the resistance was maintained for seven years, until Diocletian's successor succumbed to it. Athanasius

---

[1] "Die Gebundenheit der Colonen an ihren Stand wie an den Boden.... entspricht lediglich der gleichen Gebundenheit des Standes der Curie, der Collegiati, der Angehörigen des Soldaten und Offizianten-Standes, der Münzknechte, Purpurfärber, Schwerdtfeger, der Kornschiffer, Viehhändler und Bäcker in den beiden Hauptstädten." Kuhn, p. 258. Cf. Finlay, "Greece under the Romans," p. 181.

[2] That their duty was to the soil and not to the master is expressed by Augustine (*De Civ. Dei*, x. 1): "Coloni qui condicionem debent genitali solo propter agriculturam sub dominio possessorum."

resisted Constantine and Constantius successfully. Ambrose not merely resisted, but rebuked and humbled Theodosius. This new spirit had indeed appeared in the Empire before the age of the Antonines. Aurelius had remarked what he called the "party-spirit"[1] of a class of his subjects, but in his time the phenomenon, though striking, was not yet formidable. It became formidable early in the revolutionary period; and at the accession of Diocletian this party-spirit had spread so widely, organized itself so well, and rehearsed its part so carefully, that it proved irresistible.

This party-spirit in the Empire achieved deeds as memorable as had been achieved by liberty in the Republic. Yet it was not liberty. Liberty is a proud spirit; it regards government as a mere instrument of human happiness, and resists it when it becomes evidently prejudicial to happiness. Liberty flashes out against the government that murders innocent men and dishonours women. Liberty is force of character roused by the sense of wrong. It is consistent, indeed, with a sense of duty and a willingness to bear just restraint; uncombined with these it achieves nothing lasting; but it is more often allied with turbulence and impatience of discipline. Such had been liberty in the old Republic, the rebellion of strong spirits against laws strained too far, self-assertion, sturdiness, combativeness. Such was not the Christian spirit. In this when it was genuine there was no rebellion, there was no assertion of right. Those who practised it were not less obedient, but more

[1] In the well-known passage, *Med.* xi. 3: "Μὴ κατὰ ψιλὴν παράταξιν, ὡς οἱ Χριστιανοί," κ.τ.λ.

obedient than others. They had no turn for liberty; they had no quarrel with the despotism of the Cæsars; this they met, not in the spirit of Brutus or Virginius, but with religious resignation. The truth was, they were under two despotisms while others were under only one. They were not satisfied with submitting to the Cæsar who assuredly did not "bear the sword in vain;" they endeavoured to obey the law of Christ also. They bore the double burden with all patience. Those were not the times for free spirits to flourish in. In the soldier-ridden Empire there was no atmosphere of hope in which a spark of independence could live or a breath of free heroism be drawn. The Christian resistance to authority was indeed more than heroic, but it was not heroic. It arose from no impatience of restraint, but from a conflict of laws. The law of Christ carried it over the law of Cæsar. The spiritual sovereign prevailed over the temporal. Obedience was driven out by obedience and loyalty by loyalty. Therefore, saving the law of Christ, the Christians were the most loyal of the Emperor's subjects, and Christianity confirmed as much as it controlled despotism. It produced a complete change in the attitude of the people to the Emperor. It made their loyalty more intense, but confined it within definite limits. It strengthened in them the feeling of submissive reverence for government as such; it encouraged the disposition of the time to political passiveness. It was intensely conservative, and gave to power with one hand as much as it took away with the other. Constantine, if he was influenced by policy, was influenced by a wise policy when he extended his patronage to the Church. By doing so he may be said to have purchased an indefeasible title by a charter. He gave certain liberties, and he received in return passive obedience. He gained a sanction for the Oriental theory of government; in return he accepted the law of the Church. He became irresponsible with respect to his subjects on condition of becoming responsible to Christ.

The difference, then, between the later series of Emperors and the earlier is this. The earlier Emperors were nominally Republican magistrates, but practically their power was unlimited. The later Emperors were avowedly Oriental despots, but their power had one important and definite limitation. On the other hand, the later Emperors had not so much active resistance to fear as the earlier. The spirit of liberty which prompts to active resistance was in the earlier period not quite dead; the spirit of religion and morality which was vigorous in the later period prompted only to passive resistance. The practical result was that the earlier Emperors could not venture upon so much cruelty as the later, and the later Emperors could not indulge so much caprice as the earlier. In the first century the Romans submitted for years to all the frantic whims of the lunatic Caligula; at last they killed him for his cruelty. At the beginning of the third century the aristocracy of Rome looked on with an enormous patience while a shameless Syrian priest insulted its gods and its religion. The later Romans, however much oppression they might suffer, seldom resorted to tyrannicide; but they firmly resisted the virtuous Julian when he tried to change their institutions.

The position assumed by the Church at this time towards government has determined its attitude throughout modern history. It has often controlled and defied kings, as Ambrose did; but it has for the most part remained cold towards the spirit of liberty. Not that there is anything in a living Christianity incompatible with liberty, but a living Christianity is rarer than a Christianity that depends on traditions and documents. Christianity sprang up and shaped its institutions at a time when liberty was impossible, and when the wisest course for men in existing circumstances was to abandon the dream of it. Therefore, the earliest documents of Christianity, the biographies of its Founder, and the early history of the Church, bear the stamp of political quietism. In all disputes between authority and liberty the traditions of Christianity are on the side of authority. Passive obedience was plausibly preached by the Anglican clergy out of the New Testament; when the opposite party sought Scriptural sanction for the principles of freedom, they were swayed irresistibly back upon the Old Testament, where rebellions and tyrannicides may be found similar to those which fill classical history. The whole modern struggle for civil and national liberty has been conducted not indeed without help from Christianity, but without help from the authoritative documents of Christianity. Liberty has had to make its appeal to those classical examples and that literature which were superseded by Christianity. In the French Revolution men turned from the New Testament to Plutarch. The former they connected with tyranny; the latter was their text-book of liberty. Plutarch furnished them with the teaching they required for their special purpose, but the New Testament met all their new-born political ardour with a silence broken only here and there by exhortations to submission.

But this, which has been the weakness of Christianity in recent times, was its strength in the first ages of its existence. The spirit of Liberty and the spirit of Nationality were once for all dead; to sit weeping by their grave might for a time be a pious duty, but it could not continue always expedient or profitable. Yet this is the attitude of the age of Trajan. Tacitus makes it his object to nurse the ancient spirit as much as possible. He canonizes the martyrs of the Senate—Pœtus, Rusticus, Helvidius. He studies to feel like a senator, though conscious that the dignity of that name is only traditional. He studies to feel like a Roman, but he cannot prevent the corruption of Roman blood, nor check the inundating flood of foreign manners. Plutarch buries himself in the past, and by the power of imagination re-peoples with its ancient heroes the depopulated and demoralized Greece into which he was born. In the age of Trajan, to read of Epaminondas, Dion, Timoleon, might be entertaining and elevating, but it could not be practically useful, for it was neither possible nor desirable to imitate such examples. A literary man, like Plutarch, might not keenly feel the hopeless contrast between the reality and his ideal, but Tacitus, in the Roman senate, feels it, and hence the cynical despair that pervades his works. It was, therefore, the strength of Christianity that it renounced this unprofitable ideal. When it came forward, in the age of Constantine, to lead the thought of the Empire, it presented a programme in which Liberty and Nationality were omitted. A noble life had before been necessarily a free and public life, but the New Testament shows how virtue may live under the yoke of an absolute government, and in a complete retirement from politics. Patriotism had been the great nurse of morality; the πόλις had been the centre by which human beings had been held together. Christianity arose from the destruction of a nationality, and showed its power principally in effacing national distinctions, and in uniting first Jew and Gentile, and afterwards Roman and Barbarian. Who can wonder at its success? To a universal empire it offered a universal morality; by limiting despotism it relieved the people, and by inculcating obedience it in some degree compensated the despot.

Thus the age was made somewhat happier by receding further from liberty. Under the Antonines it was fully conscious of its loss, and looked back with regret; but now it had forgotten its loss, had found for itself new objects, and was again looking forward. Tyranny was more cruel, and misery was more wide-spread, than in the days of the Antonines; but it was less felt, because the age had occupations which absorbed it, and was possessed with thoughts which, in a measure, numbed the sense of pain. The political languor of the age of the Antonines was not compensated by any intellectual or speculative activity. The old ideas were still before men's minds, but constantly becoming more obsolete; the old creeds were still officially accepted, but with less and less belief; the old sacrifices were still performed, but with less and less devotion. Seldom, perhaps, has there been a time when ideas have had so little power over a highly civilized community. Roman literature was asleep; a movement was taking place in Greek literature, but it was of a popular and superficial kind. The itinerant Sophists, who travelled over the Greek world at this time delivering lectures or discourses, created perhaps something nearer to the popular literature of our own day than was known at any other period of antiquity. But they aim only at amusement, or very moderate edification; and the only one of them who has attained permanent fame, Lucian, exhibits most vividly the spiritual emptiness of the time. His dialogues are a universal satire—a satire upon what men do, but still more upon what they think, upon what they profess to believe and to venerate. They give a low impression of the philosophy of the age; religious belief, except in the form of a grossly deceived credulity they represent as absolutely dead. Lucian writes for and of the people; a very different writer, a writer much too noble to be a fair representative of his age, the Emperor Aurelius, still shows us what was going on at the same time in the minds of the most cultivated. The ancient gods have disappeared from his creed, and no new objects of worship have taken their place. Piety remains, and serves to him as a kind of proof of the existence of its objects, but sometimes he feels the proof insufficient. If there are no gods, he says, why should I care to live in a world void of gods and void of a Providence?[1]

Pass over the revolutionary period, and what a contrast? We find ourselves in an age when ideas, good and bad, have an overmastering influence, and when, in particular, the sense of religion is more universal and more profound than it had ever been in the world before.

---

"Εἰ δὲ μὴ εἰσί, τί μοι ζῆν ἐν κόσμῳ κενῷ θεῶν καὶ προνοίας κενῷ".— *Med.* ii. 11.

Thoughts, reasonings, controversies, which in the age of the Antonines had been but languid in the schools, had now made their way into the world, and lived with an intense life. The populace, which in the age of the Antonines lies, as it were, outside the province of history, having neither opinions nor purposes, which counts in politics only as something to be fed and to be amused, as a reason for bringing corn-fleets from Egypt and Africa, and for building amphitheatres—this populace, now in still greater poverty, and falling into a misery from which no government could any longer relieve it, is filled with vehement opinions, ardent beliefs, disinterested enthusiasm. Under the iron military rule human will and character begin to live again. Violent passions surge again, party divisions reappear, acts of free choice are done, men fight once more for a cause, once more choose leaders and follow them faithfully, and reward them with immortal fame. The trance of human nature is over, men are again busy and at work, in spite of tyranny and misery. The sense of a common interest thrills again through a vast mass, as it had thrilled through the citizens of Rome in old republican days; but the mass is now composed, not of the citizens of a single city, but of the population of a world-wide empire. Representatives of many nations appear in the great parliament at Nicæa; the leaders in the party conflict which raged there had their enthusiastic followers in almost every country in which Roman camps had ever been pitched. For the first time it might be said that the Empire was alive. Up to this time the nations of which it was composed had been held together but by military force. Now for the first time they thought and felt in unison; now they had an organization not imposed from without, but developing from within; now they had a common imperial culture and system of philosophy.

Yet all this vivid activity, which contrasts so strongly with the languor of the age of the Antonines, was compatible with a despotism much more absolute than that of the Antonines. Under the paternal rule of Aurelius the people had remained inert and lifeless; under the afflicting tyranny of Valentinian they lived, willed, and acted with spirit and energy. The explanation of this is that, as I have said, the later despotism was one which secured itself by accepting limitations. Its subjects surrendered finally one half of their liberties on condition of enjoying securely the other half. For a nominal freedom, which was in fact an unlimited slavery, they accepted an undisguised but limited slavery. Human free-will made terms with the victorious power of government, and accepted a fraction, but a secure fraction, of its original possessions. The corporate life of man, which hitherto had been one and undivided, began now to be regarded as twofold. A distinction was introduced like that which we now recognize between political life and social life. In political life despotism reigned with more undisputed title than ever, and was more remorselessly cruel. But from social life despotism was almost expelled; within this not narrow domain a government was set up which, whatever its faults, had influential parliaments and popular magistrates. The distinction was drawn roughly enough, and between the two authorities there was frequent border war; but the distinction was maintained, and was no small compensation to those unfortunate generations, the hard-pressed garrison of the beleaguered citadel of civilization.

It was in this way that a considerable share of liberty was reconquered in the Roman Empire, that the distinction between political and social life was first established, and that human free-will, expelled from the channels in which it had been accustomed to flow, found for itself a new channel. But what was the force by which this change was effected? It was a force which had seemed almost dead—the force of Theology. During the revolutionary period the sceptical philosophies lost their influence, and so did that system of moral philosophy which threw man back upon himself. An age of faith set in, an age in which a large class had found a view of the universe which was satisfying and inspiring to them; and in which even those who had not, acknowledged the necessity of finding such a view, and endeavoured in various ways to do so. A theology was the necessity of this age: those who had not got one wished for one; those who rejected the most powerful and satisfying theology had recourse to less satisfying systems, and to spasmodic revivals of systems that were at the point of death Outside the Christian Church, as well as within it, Theology was everywhere. In the time of the Antonines the most conspicuous fact, as I have said, is the decline of old beliefs. Doubtless the routine of rustic superstition went on as in earlier times; nor did philosophers speak generally with Lucian's contempt of the ancient gods. Plutarch has an explanation of them which warrants a sort of belief, but this explanation is evidently a concession to conservative feeling. The Gods are venerated in the same way as the Senate, that is, for the sake of the past and on the condition of doing nothing. The exceptions to this, such as Apollonius Tyaneus, who had a more positive religious feeling, were in the earlier age only numerous enough to show the possibility of a Pagan revival. During the revolutionary period this revival took place. The philosophers passed to theology over the bridge of Platonism. Among the vulgar the expiring credit of the Greek and Roman theologies was revived by the fusion of them with the more substantial systems of the East, which were far older, yet far more vigorous. The close juxtaposition into which the different systems of religion prevailing in the different parts of the Empire had been brought, revealed certain features common to all. The revivalists fastened upon these common features, and Paganism in its last age returned to what was perhaps its earliest form, and became Sun-worship.

We are mistaken if we imagine Christianity as having made religious and believing a world which before had been irreligious and incredulous. Scepticism had died out in the age before Christianity triumphed. It was in the third century that theology won the day against philosophy. Then began a religious age. From that time, though there was little religious agreement, there was strong religious feeling. The rationalistic period had come to an end. Feelings and emotions were now again experienced among high and low, such as had been rare among the cultivated classes of Rome since the Punic wars. The later persecutors of Christianity had as much religiousness as their victims. Religiousness is a prominent trait in the character of Diocletian.[1] It is expressly in the name of religion that Julian assails the

[1] See Vogel, Der Kaiser Diocletian.

Church. His watchword is, "The worship of the gods; no worship of dead men." As in the Reformation of the sixteenth century, all parties who agreed in nothing else agreed in being religious. Epicureanism and Pyrrhonism as Julian expressly says, had passed away. Although in the age of Julian the general disposition to belief may have been partly produced even in the antagonists of Christianity by Christianity itself, it is sufficiently plain that the special influence of the Christian religion was preceded by influences inclining men to a religious view of things, and rendering them averse to rationalism and to scepticism. To enumerate these influences is not in my present plan, but two among them are directly suggested by those characteristics of Roman Imperialism which we have been considering.

First, then, the age was religious, because it was an age of servitude. Religious feeling is generally strong in proportion to the sense of weakness and helplessness. It is when man's own resources fail that he looks most anxiously to find a friend in the universe. Religion is man's consolation in the presence of a necessity which he cannot resist, his refuge when he is deserted by his own power, or energy, or ingenuity. Negroes are religious, the primitive races in the presence of natural phenomena which they could not calculate or resist were intensely religious; women, in their dependence, are more religious than men; Orientals under despotic governments are more religious than the nations of the West. On the other hand, a time of great advance in power, whether scientific power over Nature, or the power to avert evils, given by wealth and prosperity, is commonly a time of decline in religious feeling, until man's wants, ever growing with his acquisitions, strike again against the impassable boundary. The Roman Empire, like the Jewish nation, was made religious by a Babylonish captivity.

Secondly, the Empire was made religious by vast calamities and miseries. It was during the revolutionary period that it took the religious stamp, and that, as I have pointed out, was the age of the Plague and also of unparalleled political disasters. The beginning of the religious revival corresponds accurately with the beginning of those disasters, for the solemn lectisternium and lustration of the city held by Aurelius were occasioned by the breaking out of the Marcomannic War. That was the formal act of homage rendered by philosophy to theology; it marks the beginning of the ages of faith. In the presence of the evils which then began, there was no choice but between religious resignation and a stoical apathy of which few are capable. Men cried to any deity that might be able to aid, and renounced the scepticism that left them helpless in their utmost need. Common men then felt life the tragedy which in ordinary times only men of sensibility feel it. And as the weather did not clear, as plague followed plague through nearly a century, and when this evil was removed the *fiscus* and the barbarian afflicted society almost as heavily, men must have come to consider existence itself an evil, had not religion held before their eyes a future state. Those whose whole lives were spent in watching decay and dissolution, who were borne upon a steadfast backward current, who were familiar with the dwindling of population, the disappearance of wealth, the fall of noble institutions, the degradation of manners and culture, could not have been reconciled to life by any plain view of things, by any realistic calculations. They could only repair such losses and relieve such beggary out of the inexhaustible treasury of hope and faith. It was well that, in their painful search after objects of worship and after supernatural protection, men were not finally driven back upon the outworn imaginations of mythology. Those imaginations had been lovely in their spring-time, in the days of Homer or Æschylus, but it was late autumn with them now; they were wholesome no longer. There is nothing more pestilential in the social atmosphere than the exhalations of stale poetry It was also well that they found in the end something better than that Sun-worship which was gradually evolved out of the comparison of religions. This worship, indeed, was far from being utterly hollow or spasmodic, but men could no longer be content with the most dazzling material glory. "Two things fill me with wonder," said Kant, "the starry heaven without, and the moral principle within." It was these two awful things that contended for empire over the hearts of men in the fourth century. The invisible Deity vanquished the visible one. There was superstition on both sides, and a Claudian might fancy that to worship beauty in Ceres and Proserpina was as ennobling as to worship corruption in the ashes of Peter and Paul.[1] But it was not corruption that was worshipped at the shrines of the martyrs, but a higher thing than beauty—moral goodness.

It was because in that revolutionary period, that great chasm between the Old World and the New, the depth and breadth of which I hope I have now made clear to

---

[1] See the sarcastic epigram ascribed to him beginning—
"Per cineres Petri, cani per limina Pauli."

you, the Roman Empire, searching eagerly to find a religion, discovered in its bosom a worship which had the two things which the age demanded—a supernatural pretension, and an ideal of moral goodness; and it was in a secondary degree because that ideal was of a type suiting the age, presenting virtue in the social sphere which was still open to it, and not in the political from which it was now excluded: it was for these reasons that when in the later period all the liberty which had still lingered in the age of the Antonines disappeared, when Asiatic sultanism was set up and all public functions fell into the hands of military officials, when tyranny was most oppressive and searching, when human life was cramped and stunted to the utmost, the spirit of freedom was able to assert itself in a form hitherto undreamed of, and when expelled from the State to reappear in the Church.

## IV.

## MILTON'S POLITICAL OPINIONS.

Such times as the Commonwealth, and such political writers as Milton, are separated from us by a gulf. They do not immediately concern the England of the present. Politicians have little occasion to study them; they are seldom referred to in the House of Commons. Political precedents taken from the reign of Charles I. are not now held to be applicable; the opinions of the writers of that time are not now authoritative. It is understood that we stand upon a basis which was laid later, that a radically different conception of the state and of government separates us from the politics of that age. Through this very fact, therefore, that age becomes more interesting than it was for the historical student. Now that it is dead, it becomes ready for the dissecting knife. Because it no longer excites our passions, or appeals to our party prejudices, because in fact our sympathies have cooled towards it, for that very reason it appeals to our reason more strongly, and excites a keener philosophical curiosity.

This is the feeling which pervades all the recent literature of this subject, beginning with Carlyle's "Cromwell."

That book may be regarded as the transfiguration or apotheosis of the whole subject. It was the removal of it from the warm but cloudy atmosphere of party passions and quarrels into a cold but clear sky of philosophical inquiry. Not that the writer himself can be called cold or impartially philosophical; far from it. But with respect to the old party divisions he is impartial. To the old Cavalier and Roundhead, Tory and Whig, controversy, which resounds like an interminable parliamentary debate through previous histories ending with Macaulay, he is absolutely indifferent. He is obliged to translate it into quite a new dialect before he can attach any meaning to it. And if he imports new party feelings almost equally vehement into the subject, yet these do not so readily infect the reader as his coldness to the old. His hero-worship, his thorough-going idolatry of Cromwell, is taken up only by a reader here or there; but almost all his readers feel that he has lifted Cromwell out of the region of political controversy, and has taken the first step towards a philosophical estimate of him by doing so.

The view which the present generation takes of Cromwell himself is no longer a party view. He now takes his rank among the great men of history. His figure stands in the Pantheon beside William the Liberator of Holland, Gustavus Adolphus, and William the Liberator of England, in the corner where the heroes of Protestantism are placed together. We lift our hats to him; for his deeds, we neither blame them altogether nor praise them altogether; but alike in praising and blaming, we totally disregard the old Royalist invectives. But it seems to me that Cromwell is still the only man of the period who has fairly emerged from the mist of advocacy and abuse. He has taken his permanent place in the national imagination; but his contemporaries, it seems to me, have not yet done so. We do not yet quite know what to make of them; when we hear the names of Pym, Hampden, Falkland, Marten, Sidney, and others, we feel a vague sentiment of respect and pride. We feel that they were a powerful generation of men, that they combated in a great cause with an elevation of earnestness and an exaltation of valour that makes the civil wars almost a heroic age in our history. But our conceptions of them are indistinct and doubtful, our judgment about them, in a manner, suspended.

One among them, intellectually the most accomplished of all, has escaped from the destiny of the others. On the ruin of his party and his political hopes, Milton betook himself to literature, and there, in spite of all the prejudices of the ruling party, conquered for himself an illustrious place; and, before the last sovereign of the House of Stuart died, was as eminent in the world of books as Cromwell had been in the political world, and made English genius to be respected in Europe almost as much as Cromwell had made English arms. About Milton's poetry there is, on the whole, but one voice. But when from his poetry we turn to the man himself, and his opinions and political career, we experience a change of feeling. We cannot help admiring. A powerful man, we say; a towering spirit. The family-likeness is visible. He has the large manner of Hampden and Sydney. But are there not great drawbacks? He defended regicide, he was a determined republican, he had dangerous opinions about Church government, about religion, about marriage. On the other hand, it is not to be denied that he was one of the most eloquent assertors of the responsibility of rulers, one of the earliest and strongest assertors of the freedom of the press. These have been the conflicting reflections which have blurred Milton's memory, and left his countrymen divided about him, as they long were about Cromwell, between admiration and disapprobation. But about him, too, we may, I think, now feel that it begins to be possible to form a more definite opinion. His dangerous opinions do not endanger us. If we are ever converted to them it will not be by *his* arguments, but by reasonings more adapted to the present age. Political philosophy has entered upon quite a new stage since his time, and adopted new methods. He is not now referred to as an authority by any school, either in politics or religion. There is no reason why our impartiality should now be disturbed in reading him; no bias need now prevent us from estimating him calmly. And because he is removed from us by such a distance, and his direct influence has ceased, our curiosity to understand his views and enter into them may well increase. He is not only the pride of our poetry, but one of the most powerful and independent characters that our nation has produced. A man who travelled so far out of the common and traditional line of thought must be worth contemplating, and his opinions worth appreciating, even in an age occupied with other problems, and following other guides.

I seldom find myself quite agreeing with the views of Milton as a politician taken by his biographers and critics. They are commonly perverted in two ways. First, by the influence of which I have spoken, party-spirit. Neither the studied attack upon him which is called Johnson's Life, nor the rhetorical panegyric of Macaulay, which Macaulay himself afterwards confessed to be overdone, can satisfy any one who does not consider the subject from the party point of view. But, in order to arrive at a true view it is not enough to put aside party-spirit and to be impartial. It is also important to understand distinctly to what class of political writers Milton belongs. For there are more ways than one of treating political subjects, and this fact his biographers overlook.

"He was an impracticable dreamer," says one; "his politics were the mere imaginations of a poet, which statesmen treated with contempt; it is a pity that he did not stick to his trade." Another is more indulgent, and thinks that Milton did quite right to interest himself in politics; not that his political speculations are of any value, but that his mind was braced by them, and so his poetry improved. It is significantly noted that he himself said that he was conscious of having only the use of his left hand when he wrote prose, and it is forgotten that the left hand of such a man might be as good as the right hand of another, that his prose might be less good than his poetry, and yet be exceedingly good. Even the most thorough-going of his admirers, Macaulay, seems to me to render his fame a doubtful service when he expresses his wonder that Milton's prose writings should be so little read, seeing that they abound in passages beside which the finest declamations in Burke sink into insignificance. This is well meant, but Burke himself is generally considered somewhat too declamatory, too easily carried away by his imagination. Burke's contemporaries used to complain that he imported poetry into politics; still, no one doubts his great practical knowledge of the subjects he discusses. It is not his occasional outbursts of rhetoric which give value to his works; we can admire these in their degree; but he is remembered as a great political philosopher. Now, when those who doubt the value of Milton's political writings are told that they surpass Burke's in declamation, their doubts can only be confirmed. The besetting sin of an amateur literary politician is declamation. The author of "Paradise Lost" was not likely to be surpassed by any one in eloquence; that we scarcely require to be told: the question is of his competence to treat political subjects, of the soundness of his judgment; and, on this head, we should feel, perhaps, more satisfaction if we learnt that he carefully abstained from rhetoric, than when we learn that he outshines the most florid of orators.

By using language like this, the critics leave on our minds the impression, that, with the exception of a brilliant period here and there, Milton's political writings are failures, and that it is only out of respect for a great poet that they are honoured with remembrance or criticism. Now this is certainly unjust, and it arises from not noting carefully to what class of political writers he belongs. We should do him some injustice if we compared him with Burke or Macaulay, on the one hand, or with such writers as Hobbes or Locke on the other. He was neither a politician by profession, familiar with all public questions through perpetual study, nor was he a philosopher by profession, who had worked out a systematic theory of politics. It is because he

falls under neither of these heads, but belongs to
another class of political writers, which in his own time
was hardly recognized, and is not altogether recognized
now, that he neither gained then, nor gains now, his
proper rank. In his own time Harrington sneered at
him for always confining himself to generalities, or, as
they were then called, universals; and this was not
untrue. Hobbes is said to have pronounced on his
"Defensio Populi" and Salmasius' "Defensio Regis"
the sentence, "Both are very good Latin, so that I know
not which is best, and both are very bad reasoning, so
that I know not which is worst," which is also a tenable
proposition. And this middle character of these books,
the fact that they neither express the popular opinion nor
yet the purely philosophical opinion, has caused them
to be somewhat disregarded, both in their author's own
age and since. They had too much thought and depth
for the purposes of party-conflict; they have too little
method for the purposes of political philosophy to most
students now. But because he cannot be referred to
either of these classes of political writers, does it follow
that he was not a practical politician at all? Granted
that as a politician he was neglected by his own age, and
has only partially been remembered by posterity. But
was this owing to deficiencies of his own? or to other
circumstances? Is there anything requiring indulgence
or excuse, as many of his critics hint, in these prose
writings of his? If so, it is important, because it will
degrade him altogether into a lower class of men. If his
political efforts are in the main a series of failures, if they
show an inability to grasp the affairs of practical life,
an unbridled imagination recklessly tampering with what

is most sacred and fundamental in the constitution of society,—if, in short, they require indulgence and allowance, then it will be necessary to place him in a much lower rank than we might otherwise think his due. It is the crowning glory of a great poet to be a sensible man. Shakespeare was a sensible man. Are we to deny this praise to Milton? Are we to class him with those crazy geniuses, those inspired idiots, that have been so common in the literary world? If so, our estimate even of his poetry will be lowered. For his poetry certainly aims at gravity and solidity; his taste in his later years became austere, his style simple and unadorned: if we disbelieve in the soundness of his judgments, if we degrade him from the rank of wise and profound poets, we shall find, except in the poems of his youth, little of that exquisite wildness and lawless profusion of fancy which the world falls in love with, even when it neither respects nor approves. And our estimate of his moral character will also inevitably suffer. For there runs through his works a certain assumption of authority, a grave self-approval and self-confidence, which, if it be not justified by the real weight of his understanding, and the real value of the sentiments he expresses, can be attributed to nothing but egotism. The splendour of his style, which is most impressive if we consider it as the appropriate dress of rare and precious thoughts, would become histrionic and contemptible if it clothed idle hallucinations. He aims so high, and claims so much, that if we cannot consider him as in some sense or other a great political writer, we must pronounce him a very hollow and shallow rhetorician.

The true view, I think, may be thus expressed,—Milton

was a pamphleteer, only a pamphleteer of original genius. Had he had less originality, with the same power of language, he would probably have figured more in the history of the time, because he would have become more distinctly the mouthpiece of a party. But because the weight of his mind always carries him below the surface of the subject, because in these pamphlets he appeals constantly to first principles, opens the largest questions, propounds the most general maxims, we are not therefore unfairly to compare them with complete treatises on politics, or to forget that they are essentially pamphlets still. We have in our own day a multitude of political writers who are neither experienced politicians nor political philosophers, yet who continually publish their opinions in reviews, magazine articles, leaders, pamphlets. Now we shall have a parallel to Milton's political character if among these various kinds of journalists there has appeared anywhere a man unable to merge himself in his party, having a strong personality, and doctrines in which at first nobody agrees with him, yet never quite rising into a systematic political philosopher, and leaving works which are impressive, but only sometimes convincing, and more suggestive than satisfactory. Such a man we have among us now in Mr. Carlyle, a writer in many respects as different as possible from Milton: a humorist, whereas Milton is habitually grave; a cynic, whereas few people have had a more generous belief in human nature than Milton; a hero-worshipper, which Milton never was, though he tolerated, as a temporary necessity, the dictatorship of Cromwell; but a writer closely resembling Milton in the position and point of view from which he regards politics. Another name of the present century may be quoted as a parallel. Coleridge, in his political essays, is exceedingly like Milton, partly, no doubt, because he imitates him. He is not, however, at bottom so close a parallel as Carlyle, because, being superior both to Carlyle and Milton in philosophic depth, he approaches more nearly to the class of systematic political thinkers. Mr. Ruskin in his recent writings affords another parallel.

The characteristic of this whole class of writers is that they apply to politics one or two intense convictions. As men of genius, some particular class of truths is exceptionally clear to them. At some point or other their nature and their sensibilities are keener than other men's. And so, without feeling it necessary to work out a complete theory of society, and without waiting to become familiar with political details, they take courage to announce their convictions with an emphasis corresponding to the firmness with which they hold them, and to apply them to any political case which may arise. It generally happens that these convictions, we may call them ideas, are few in number; a single mind may hold a vast variety of images, but not many ideas. Accordingly, though such men may write a great deal, as Mr. Carlyle has done, yet in reality they say little. It is one air with infinite variations, one principle with a multitude of applications. And the principle is not generally hard to find, for the writer's sole object is to make it as vividly clear to others as it is to himself, and this is the express purpose of the endless variety of forms in which he presents it. Hasty readers make it a reproach against such authors that they always say in reality the same thing, though they use different words, as though they were indigent people contriving to make a great show of their small property. This very monotony is in fact their glory; they perpetually reiterate the same thing, because they feel it so deeply, and are anxious that others should feel it also; and if they present it constantly in new forms, they do so not to conceal it but to make it plainer, as a teacher makes his pupil understand a principle thoroughly by putting before him the greatest possible number of examples.

Thus the one conviction which runs through Coleridge's political writings is the hollowness of all hand-to-mouth statesmanship, and the necessity of grounding politics upon universal principles of philosophy and religion. Mr. Ruskin has been led into politics from art. Deeply feeling that the happiness of man is to take delight in nature, and that this delight exhibits itself in simple, genuine, faithful, artistic imitation of nature, he is led to see that particular social conditions are indispensable to such a happy state of mind. He takes art as the index of national well-being, and denounces all institutions and usages which interfere with that condition of the mind and feelings out of which art in natures artistically gifted flows unadulterated and genuine. Mr. Carlyle is penetrated with two thoughts: first, that national well-being depends, not upon laws or institutions, or machinery of any kind, but upon an elemental human energy, of which institutions are but the manifestations; that this human energy dwells in individuals, and is virtue or wisdom or power, and in the ripest developments is all three, but is in all cases first and essentially a force. Secondly, he is penetrated with the extreme rarity of this elemental energy, the extreme difficulty of procuring enough of it for the purposes of society, and consequently the urgent importance of making the most of the amount of it which can be procured.

Now, as I have classed Milton along with these writers, whom we might call "genius politicians," let me try to draw out in like manner from Milton's works the ideas which principally animated him. Let me try to sum up his political creed. Times have changed in England since he wrote. But if the substance of that old controversy can never become obsolete, it is, as I have said, an advantage that the circumstances of it and the actors in it are removed to a certain distance. And assuredly the controversy of Milton's time is not yet obsolete in substance. Theories of a divine right and of an original compact may pass away, but the problem how to introduce new forces into society when the old ones are wearing out remains where it was. Presbyterian and Episcopalian controversies may have little interest now, but in our sense of the importance of spiritual enlightenment and guidance we are even nearer to the seventeenth century than to the eighteenth. I care indeed very little to weigh Milton's arguments against those of Hall or Salmasius. But it is instructive to compare his general views with those of Burke, or Carlyle, or Mill. It is interesting to compare his strong imaginations of what England ought to be, and his anticipations of what it would be, with its actual condition and with the ideals of its present thinkers. He was a man of genius, and if his genius produced its masterpieces in other departments, it was not working altogether against the grain when it treated politics. It seeks by a kind of instinct what is substantial and fundamental in the questions it handles.

The only treatise of Milton's which can be said to live in English literature is his "Apology for the Freedom of the Press." The service he did to liberty by this is generally acknowledged; nor are his arguments at all obsolete. His tract on education may also still be read with interest. Then there is a series of treatises, all more or less neglected, which fall into two classes—those attacking the government of the Stuarts, and vindicating the rebellion against it; and those which attack what he calls Prelaty, and urge reformation in the Church.

On all these questions, the interests of literature, education, civil reformation, ecclesiastical reformation, we find him equally interested and earnest. Now this is the first peculiarity I note in him—the comprehensive view he takes of national well-being. Of the revolution in which he took part, he was one of the few who understood the full scope. To most men of the time, and, indeed, to most historians since, it has seemed a complex movement, not a single change, but an accidental combination of two changes. We see that on the one hand it was a rebellion against arbitrary government, a violent reaction against the king-worship of the sixteenth century; and that with this was conjoined a rebellion against that Anglican Papacy, as I may call it, which had been set up in the Church when we broke with Rome without giving up at the same time the notion of an absolute authority in spiritual matters. For mutual help the arbitrary king and the arbitrary bishop had coalesced; and when the rebellion began, political reformers coalesced in the same way with ecclesiastical reformers. But few men at the time cared for more than one-half of the movement. Some were eager for the destruction of prerogative, but cared little for Church reform—they were rebels without being Puritans; others were bitter against Prelaty, but lukewarm in their opposition to arbitrary power. Pym was not, in the proper sense, a Puritan, still less was Marten; on the other hand, we know how ready the Presbyterian party showed themselves to make up their quarrel with the Crown. We find the same one-sided view in the historians of the movement. Macaulay has as little sympathy with the Puritans as Marten had; no Cavalier could betray a much greater contempt than he shows for their religious peculiarities. In his eyes, the movement is a political reform, which by great good luck was helped by an outbreak of religious fanaticism. On the other hand, Carlyle declares, with his usual emphasis, that it was not for questions of ship-money, or liberty of the people to tax themselves, that war was waged, but for fear of Popery. And a similar view is presented by the whole series of our ecclesiastical historians on both sides.

Milton is one of the few who were equally interested in both movements. He was a politician, but he had also a religion and a faith; he was a religious man, but his religion did not make him a political quietist. Nor was he only these two things, a politician and a religious man; he was besides a man of high cultivation and a man of genius. Therefore not only did he sympathize at the same time with both the political and religious impulse which stirred his age, but he discerned in the revolution other tendencies which neither politicians nor religionists discerned. To him literature was an interest, as well as the State and the Church; he anticipated from the revolution a great development of genius: and further still than this, he did not forget education, and frequently urged the national and fundamental importance of the question.

And because he took so comprehensive a view of national well-being, to him the revolution seemed a single movement, not the combination of two movements. The impatience of political tyranny seemed essentially connected with impatience of ecclesiastical tyranny. He felt the unity of national life. He saw in the nation a strong man shaking himself from sleep, and it seemed to him natural that an awakening of the mind should go along with the awakening of the body. It was a throwing off of tutelage, an assuming of the rights of manhood upon the part of the nation, and it seemed to him natural that this should involve a repudiation of authoritative teaching, as well as a resistance to material and civil restraints. The Church and the State to him appeared related as mind and body, constituting together one nation, suffering together, and needing to be healed together. The same comprehensive view led him to recognize those other interests—unorganized as yet, and almost unnamed—of literature and education, as equally essential to the national life, and as equally concerned in a revolution which threw that national life into new forms.

This comprehensiveness is a very rare quality among our political writers. It is a merit in Milton which particularly deserves to be recognized now, for it is only now that our political notions begin to be comprehensive, and to take in all the conditions of national well-being. The political writers of the eighteenth century limit their views very much to material happiness, to the preservation of life and property, and the encouragement of trade. Many of them, indeed, expressly maintain that the proper province of government is limited to this; but even if it be so, national well-being is certainly not so limited, and neither therefore should the thoughts and studies be, of those who interest themselves in the national well-being. On the Continent, at the present day, we may find examples of an opposite narrowness. We find the Papal States, where the main object of government is the spiritual welfare of the people, where, in M. About's words, "faith, hope, and charity are cultivated, but agriculture and commerce are neglected." We find, also, the Culturstaat of the Germans, where the cultivation and intellectual improvement of the people is made the principal object, and where the State tends to merge itself in a University, as at Rome it merges itself in a Church.

We are beginning in England to see the necessity of widening our contracted view of politics. Politics have been long enough among us the mere tool of wealth and trade. Macaulay's method of estimating well-being by the growth of population, and the number of new streets built in great towns, begins to seem insufficient. Even personal liberty and free speech begin to seem, not indeed less valuable, but less all-sufficient, results, than they seemed to the eighteenth century. When a man has been made as free as possible to do what he pleases, it is important also, we begin to think, that he should know what it is best to do. We begin to hanker after the Culturstaat.

Now, however much may be obsolete in the politics of Milton, this at least deserves appreciation at the present day,—that, throughout his works, he contemplates the State in this larger sense. It is never with him a mere market or trade-union. He did not so much by a prophetic spirit anticipate the larger views of the nineteenth century, as recur to the ideals of the ancient world, to which the tendency of modern thought seems also to be leading us. With him a State is a community living together in the practice of virtue, in the worship of God, in the pursuit of truth. Material happiness, prosperity, riches, and warlike glory appear to him something, but he requires also good things for the higher part of men; true religious and moral teaching appear to him much, but even this does not satisfy him, he requires also cultivation for the mind,—arts, sciences, literature. He has adopted without reserve the maxim of Aristotle, τῶν καλῶν πραξέων χάριν θετίον εἶναι τὴν πολιτικὴν κοινωνίαν ἀλλ' οὐ τοῦ συζῆν—we must hold political society to exist for the sake of honourable deeds, not for the sake of joint livelihood.

Let us now approach nearer, and ask ourselves what principles, what measures Milton held to conduce most to this comprehensive well-being at which he aimed. It lies on the surface of his works, that he was a believer in liberty. Here, again, classical ideals influenced him. He turned his back upon the mediæval world, with its ruthless despotic drill, recurred to Greece and Rome, and became the apostle of a political Renaissance. So far he resembles the eighteenth-century school. But as he takes a larger view of the State than they, so he takes a larger view of liberty. As he aims at much more than material happiness, so he resists other kinds of tyranny beside that of mere arbitrary force. The liberty which he preaches is a thing as much more developed than the classical liberty as modern civilization is more complex than ancient. It was in comparison but a rudimentary liberty of which the favourite examples of ancient patriotism—a Harmodius, a Brutus, a William Tell—were the champions. It is the mere freedom of the body from arbitrary injury, the freedom of the domestic hearth from arbitrary insult. It is the freedom which an infant State desires, and which is idolized now by those only who confine their views to the material happiness of a people, like the eighteenth-century politicians. The goddess Milton worships is to this ideal as Minerva to a wood-nymph. It is not the liberty of shepherds, or small farmers, but the liberty of scholars, thinkers, and cultivated men. It is not merely the right to be tried by jury, or to tax oneself. It comprehends in addition certain rights of the mind and of the conscience, franchises of the study, of the library, and of the pulpit. It is security, not only for person and purse, but for thought and imagination and belief, for literature, education, and the Church.

Milton tells us that he had been intended by his parents for holy orders, but that he had given up the prospect on finding that he must subscribe slave! Apparently, then, he would have the teachers of the nation left free to teach whatever their understandings, after sufficient study, may tell them to be true. He tells us that he attacked episcopacy because he saw that, under the obscure yoke of Prelaty, no free and splendid wit could flourish. And when he saw that, under the government of the Long Parliament, licensers were still appointed to control the publication of books, he addressed the Lords and Commons in that memorable discourse in which he maintains the right of error itself to be published and to have a fair fight with truth.

But what is it that Milton means by liberty, and what does he find so valuable in it? Men cry out sometimes for liberty because they are suffering intolerable oppression. What made the French break loose? Famine and misery in the lower classes, taxes falling heaviest on those who had least, wild stories about the Bastille and *lettres de cachet.* There was not much in England that corresponded to this: we hear nothing of any intolerable misery; neither the King nor the Archbishop, nor even the system they administered, were regarded as monstrously cruel. It is certainly no mere feeling of indignation at wrong that makes Milton an apostle of liberty. There is another aspect, in which liberty often charms men of genius, and sometimes through their influence captivates a whole people. Sometimes the yoke of law and authority, the fixed institutions of society, oppress ardent minds, and fatigue them with a sense of artificiality and superstitious pedantry. They long to be rid of the cumbrous shackles of political society, and to return to some simpler, more natural mode of life, in which, as they imagine, instinctive good feelings would take the place of law and the rude methods of compulsion altogether be abandoned. Was it this impatience of restraint that influenced Milton? Far from it. Or his party? Not in the least. Milton's party was a party of precisians. Their tendency was rather to strictness than to laxity, their excess was on the side of over-government. These advocates of liberty were the most strait-laced and severe of politicians. The grievances that they allege are often curiously unlike the ordinary grievances of oppressed men, and certainly such as show no excessive impatience of law. Their principal complaint against the bishops is, that they encourage the people to sports on Sunday, and discourage preaching. What cruel taskmasters! And Milton himself, though not altogether a Puritan, has assuredly no impatience of the yoke of law; it is not dissolution and destruction that he has in view; if he sets his hand to destroy the massive Gothic structure that he found, it is in order that he may raise on its ruins another building in a purer style, but not less massive.

In fact, the free commonwealth of which he published a scheme on the eve of the Restoration was far from being very free in our sense of the word. It was a tolerably close aristocracy, not unlike that government by the Senate which existed practically, though never legally, for many ages at Rome. Democracy, though he seems to favour it speculatively, he regards as dangerous until our corrupt and faulty education be mended.

It is not in fact against severity, but against inefficiency in government that Milton and his party revolt. What they want in liberty is evidently not liberty itself, not permission to do as they like. What they want is efficient government; teachers that will teach instead of shirking the work, rulers that will govern instead of throwing the rein on the beast's neck. And here, as it seems to me, we come within sight of Milton's fundamental idea, which is not liberty for itself, but liberty as increasing vigour.

A free government is not only happier than a hereditary despotic government, but it has commonly much more vigour. A revolutionary despotic government such as that of Napoleon, or the despotism of a hereditary king who happens to be a great man, such as that of Frederick, may of course be more vigorous than liberty itself. But free government is on the average far more vigorous than hereditary despotism. The reason of this is evident. It lies in the *carrière ouverte aux talents*. In the despotism the disposal of everything falls to a man who is not likely to have great ability, since he is determined by the chance of primogeniture in a single family; who is likely to have been educated exceedingly ill, because of his artificial elevation above his kind; and who is likely also to be exceedingly prejudiced, owing to his seclusion from ordinary life. On the other hand, where there is liberty, government falls into the hands of those who, in fair competition and before the eyes of the world, have surpassed their equals in some of the qualifications required in government. If liberty be imperfect, and extend only to a privileged class, it is still better than despotism, as the best man in a number of families is more likely to be a capable governor than the eldest-born of one. If liberty be complete, and the whole population may enter for the race, it is evident that, *ceteris paribus*, there is a chance of getting better governors still. Liberty, in fact, means, just so far as it is realized, the right man in the right place.

This is a common observation with the advocates of liberal institutions. But they commonly apply it to government only. Milton, as we have seen, habitually thinks of government as only one of many institutions on which national well-being depends. Extend then the notion of the vigour which a nation derives from liberty beyond the province of government, and apply it also to education, literature, moral and religious teaching,—apply it, in short, not only to the State, but also to that which I may call, in a large sense, the Church,—and you have, I believe, Milton's fundamental idea, and the key to all which is interesting in his prose works.

In Milton's time, not only was the government of the country enfeebled by the real and not merely nominal sovereignty of hereditary kings, but its intellectual life also was under tutelage. Literature was under the control of clerical licensers; education was mainly in clerical hands; and the pulpit had in that age all the influence which in these days belongs to journalism. In other words, the whole culture of the nation was in the hands of the clergy. Now, who were the clergy? If they had been simply men specially prepared for the work, men certified to have gone through the studies likely to qualify them for the position of instructors and guides to the people, Milton would have found no fault with this state of things. He would probably have preferred it to the state of things at which we have actually arrived—the absolute liberty of all persons, whether wise or foolish, enlightened or ignorant, to teach any one who will listen to them. But the clergy were not merely this. They were men bound and pledged to a definite and very minute system of doctrine. By this restraint culture in England was fettered, just as civil liberty by the prerogative of the Stuarts. And against this restraint Milton protests, not so much for its severity as for its enfeebling effect.

To impose a dogmatic system upon the teaching class

of a nation is inevitably to enfeeble the influence of culture upon that nation; and that equally whether the system imposed be absolutely true, absolutely false, or partly one and partly the other. It enfeebles precisely in the same way in which the hereditary principle enfeebles government. It closes the *carrière ouverte aux talents*. If the system imposed is at all minute, it must shut out from the teaching class a large number of the men who ought to be in it. There is one class which it must almost infallibly shut out, men of genius, for these will generally have something too peculiar and special in their thoughts to square with any dogmatic system, and, even if they have not, they will be offended, as Milton seems to have been, by the attempt to rob them of their intellectual liberty.

If it is bad when the government of a nation is enfeebled, it is a still greater calamity when its culture is emasculated. This is a slavery of the mind against which the patriots of antiquity were never called to contend, and it saps the national energy more fatally than the most despotic Court. When the boy grows up amid teachers whose lessons have been prescribed to them by authority, and the youth studies in an intimidated and bribed University, and men can get no instruction except from preachers whose mouths have been bridled by subscriptions, or from books all the pith of which has been extracted by the licenser; when the awakening utterances of honest conviction and the inspiring music of genius are silenced; when decorum and demure conventionalism and sentimentalism are in the ascendant; when the best influence which is allowed to operate is a feminine, panic-struck pietism, and the faint sweet odour of this is used to conceal the rottenness of corruption; when all the intellectual vigour of the country is driven to revolt; and, worse still, when all great interests are entrusted to narrow and common minds, and timid respectability is set to do the tasks of magnanimity;—this is enslaved culture, and this is the feebleness of it. In his strong perception of this, Milton is very like our own Carlyle, and I know no writer between the two who exhibits it. But there is this great difference between Milton and Carlyle, that Milton sees the possible good much more strongly, and Carlyle the actual evil. Carlyle, as we know, is a cynic, and despairs of the republic. He hardly believes that any better state of things will come, and therefore reserves all his vigour and humour for his delineations of the bad. But Milton is of a sanguine temperament. He has a trait in common with that Cromwell by whose side he will for ever stand in history, and of whom it was said, that hope shone like a fiery pillar in him when it had gone out in all others. His mind is firmly fixed upon the future; his face is radiant with the sunrise he intently watches. Therefore in his best works, in his "Areopagitica," his "Tract on Education," and parts of his "Reason of Church Government," you see the reverse of that picture which Carlyle presents to us. Carlyle has described to us an Age of Shams,—that is, the result of enslaved and enfeebled culture. He shows how, when strong convictions and originality are discouraged, and timid mediocrity applauded and advanced, there begins a universal reign of insincerity; that men's language becomes official and conventional, their thoughts indistinct, their actions irresolute; that education loses itself in verbal prettiness,

Universities languish in sloth and obscurantism, literature becomes affected or spasmodic, the Church loses sight of the facts of life, and quarrels about words. He explains how from this enfeeblement of institutions, from the short supply everywhere of genius and original energy, the whole surface of society becomes gradually obscured with a misty atmosphere of insincerity, superficiality, scepticism, cant, and how the whole fabric of the State, which stands upon convictions, grows more and more insecure as these languish or die, until at last nothing keeps it standing but inertia and the agonized solicitude of its rulers to shield it from any external impact. He has written in fact a most striking chapter of the pathology of States, and has described the course of an atrophy which sets in through an insufficient. supply of the proper food of States,—human virtue and genius, and which ends in that which to States is death,—revolution. Now what Milton has done is the precise opposite. A man, in spite of his Puritanism, of a singularly happy temper, impatient of all saddening and depressing contemplations, with an imagination that might be called luxurious, only that it deals rather with images of action and movement than with images of pleasure, he turns away from the state of things around him, and taxes himself to picture what a State might become, to what a bloom of vigour and greatness it might arrive, through a comprehensive liberty both in government and culture. He is the prophet of national health, as Carlyle is the prophet of national decay.

Both believe national health to consist in the same thing,—in the promotion of virtue and genius to the highest posts, and the careful confinement of mediocrity to positions of secondary importance. But Carlyle believes it unspeakably difficult, or only possible through some lucky accident, for a State to reach this healthy condition, because he believes virtue and genius to be exceedingly rare, and the recognition or appreciation of them to be rarer still. He comes, therefore, to hero-worship; which means that a State must always groan under the management of fools or knaves, except in the rare case where virtue appears in so transcendent an incarnation as to overpower all opposition. What has led him to form this low opinion of his kind, and how he has convinced himself that there are no means of raising the average of intelligence, so that we might count always upon a supply of competent heroes, it is impossible to discover, since it is not his custom to reason, or produce in form the evidence which supports his conclusions. But one may conjecture that he has never comprehensively considered the question of cultivation. If virtue and genius are exceedingly rare, is it not also certain that vast quantities of both are lost through neglect? In the lower classes this neglect has been almost total. Whatever great capacities Nature has sown there have been almost entirely lost to the world—left to themselves, and stifled under low cares and drudgery. In the higher classes there has been cultivation, but it is equally certain that great mistakes have been committed in the method of it,—that much of it has ended in perversion or stunting, rather than the improvement of the plant. All this Carlyle certainly knows well. He has written forcibly on Education and the Church, and on the function of literature. But perhaps he has not seen how much depends upon culture, and what infinite hope lies in it. It is scarcely too much to say that culture is the larger half of politics. The first great speculator in politics, Plato, wrote a book on the ideal Republic, and what Rousseau says of it is perfectly true, that Plato's Republic is a treatise on education.

Culture, like government, requires two things, liberty and organization,—liberty to ensure a supply of power, organization to bring the power to bear. Carlyle is always complaining of the want of organization in our modern culture, of the anarchic isolation of literary men and journalists. In Milton's time organization was not wanting; as I have said, the whole machinery of culture was in the hands of the clergy. Perhaps it was this imposing system and unity of culture gathered up and embodied in the Church, that enabled Milton to see better than our later political writers how vast the results of culture might be if it could only add to its organization liberty. Milton has none of Carlyle's despair, none of his sense of the extreme rarity of virtue and genius. He believes that by the improvement of education it will be possible to obtain the necessary supply. And he hopes, by giving liberty to the Church and to literature, to subject the whole nation to such a perpetual stream of noble influence as may elevate its tone of feeling, and make it capable of vigorous self-government.

The scheme of education which Milton gives, labours, no doubt, under the defect of greatly overrating the average power of boys. "Before this time, they may easily have learnt at any odd hour the Italian tongue!" The reader of it must also bear in mind that it belongs to a time when both modern literature and modern science were in their infancy. But when these deductions are made, it will be found to be distinctly in advance of our present system in several particulars. First it includes a systematic training for the body as well as the mind. Next, by laying stress upon music, it introduces, at least in a rudimentary form, the notion of æsthetic education. Next, though the authors prescribed are mainly Greek and Latin, as was at that time inevitable, the subject-matter of them is everywhere made prominent, and education in things is put by the side of education in words.

For the next great instrument of culture, literature, he saw that the one thing needed was liberty. In this he was before his age, but more than twenty years after his death the nation entered the path he had pointed out. Of journalism, which is now perhaps the most powerful intellectual influence to which the nation is subjected, he saw only the germ. Evidently it could never have existed in any influential form without that liberty of the press of which Milton was amongst the very first advocates.

To the Church also he would give liberty—such liberty as could be conceived in his age—and at the same time he would take from it all worldly authority. With the one hand he would increase its moral influence, by reinforcing it with all that ability and genius which was excluded from it by the system of tests, and with the other hand he would confine it to this moral influence. We have adopted his views in the latter particular, but only partially in the former. We have deprived the Church of its invidious secular authority, and many of its monopolies. We have deprived it of the power which it might derive from positive institution, but we are only beginning to give it in exchange the vigour that comes from liberty. Milton's Church seems to me the Church of the future—a muster of all the piety, genius, and ability of the country, relieved from all tests, save tests of character and competence, and set in charge of the religious and moral guidance of the nation.

Such, then, was Milton's political idea. Himself the most cultivated man of his time, perhaps we might say the most cultivated man that has ever lived in England, he viewed politics from a certain elevation above the standing point of the ordinary politician. He viewed the questions of the day, not with the eyes of an English lawyer or churchman or citizen, but as a scholar, a traveller, and a thinker. He had his memory full of Greek, Roman, Byzantine, and Italian histories. He had lived in Florence, and observed Italian literati chafing at the system of tutelage and paternal government which had been established in the city of Dante. Thus his conceptions of national well-being had been enlarged. Being at the same time the son of one who had suffered for his religious belief, he had inherited a militant unbending character, and a capacity for self-sacrifice. The result was a rare union in his personal character of stern energy with fastidious refinement, and in his politics an equally striking combination of the desire for vitality with reverence for law. Once more when I think of him I am reminded of Carlyle. Elements which in Carlyle struggle were reconciled in him. How strangely in Carlyle do the two convictions battle with each other!—We must have liberty, else there can be no life; and we must have despotism, else there can be no organization. And so he has given us in his "Cromwell" and "French Revolution" two great historical dramas, both of which begin with the throwing-off of despotism in order to gain power, and end with the recurrence to despotism in order to gain organization. But Milton never ceased to believe that life and organization, liberty and order, could be reconciled; his faith does not seem to have been shaken even by the failure of the experiment in his own age. As I have said, this was owing not merely to a sanguine temperament. It was owing to a higher view of what can be done by culture. Milton held it possible to produce by training, in no short supply, the manhood and moderation which can do without heroes, because it is itself heroic. If Carlyle does not hold this possible, it is perhaps because culture itself has grown anarchic, and the perpetual warfare of sects and schools has fairly shaken the basis of virtue.

But there seems to me another reason why Milton is more sanguine than Carlyle. I have compared Milton to one watching the sunrise. It is equally true that the glow on Carlyle's face is that of sunset. In other words, Milton belongs to the beginning of an age, Carlyle to the end of an age. Carlyle's despair was produced in him by his failure to find in the society around him the forces necessary to supply the place of those that were dying. Everywhere he thought he saw institutions in decay, a languid society living upon conventionalisms, and, instead of convictions, having only opinions, which they held because they had never heard the other side. Efforts there were at reformation, considerable improvements here and there, but not the mighty and universal impulse that he believed to be needed. He saw no proportion between the work to be done and the forces that were at hand to do it. But Milton lived in a golden age of hope and energy. There was throughout the

nation a confidence of strength, a readiness for great
and stirring deeds. Behind them lay two great ages, the
age of Reformation and the Elizabethan age. Nearly a
century of spiritual freedom, many years of glory and
prosperity, and a newly-acquired treasure of literature,
had enlarged their minds and filled them with confidence.
They intended to add a third great age to the two great
ages that had passed. They pressed on, as Milton says,
to reform Reformation. And they succeeded, not indeed
in all that they attempted, but in opening a new age.
The reaction did not completely undo their work; the
impulse they had given never died out completely. They
let in a flood of new vigour, both into government and
culture; they inaugurated a time of responsible government, free literature, religious toleration.

But in time these new forces too wore out, and this
period in its turn drew to an end. Carlyle has all his
life been watching its decay. It has not fallen to his lot
to use the language of hope or exulting expectation.
The gladness of Milton's style would not suit him. The
difference is not so much in the men as in their position.
The Evening Star and the Morning Star are one; they
differ only in place. We address the one as—

> "Sad Hesper o'er the buried sun,
> And ready, thou, to die with him,
> Thou watchest all things ever dim
> And dimmer, and a glory done."

But to Milton we say—

> "Bright Phosphor, fresher for the night,
> By thee the world's great work is heard
> Beginning, and the wakeful bird;
> Behind thee comes the greater light."

## V.

## MILTON'S POETRY.

Of all arts poetry is the most various. The forms that it assumes are as much more numerous than those assumed by painting, for example, or by music, as its instrument, speech, is a more comprehensive organ than colour or sound. Poetry is rhythmical, like music, and it is also graphic and imitative like painting; but, besides this, it sometimes appears in a form resembling oratory, sometimes it passes into philosophy, at other times it becomes story-telling, at other times wit. Accordingly men of the most various characters, aims, and tastes have all alike taken up poetry, and the word "poet" has to be understood in very different senses when it is applied to different men.

But there are several leading types of poetry, and of these types one becomes fashionable in one age and another in another. How poetry was regarded in the seventeenth century may be judged by the phrase with which Bacon checks himself when he is tempted to philosophize upon it "But it is not good to stay too long in the theatre;" and still more by the following curious passage from Locke: "Poetry and gaming, which usually go together, are alike in this too, that they seldom bring any advantage but to those who have nothing else to live on. . . . If, therefore, you would not have your son the fiddle to every jovial company, without whom the sparks could not relish their wine nor know how to pass an afternoon idly . . . I do not think you will much care he should be a poet, or that his schoolmaster should enter him in versifying."[1] In the biographies of our poets, from Marlowe to Cibber, we may read the explanation of this contemptuous language. Poetry in those days, we may see, was regarded as an appendage to city-life; the poet was a town-wit. He was very merry, and generally rather needy. He amused great men and busy men in their hours of leisure, fought their battles with lampoon and satire, presided over Court merrymakings, wrote masques and songs; above all things, wrote plays. Such a life does not seem to have been a good school of manners, but it was a good school of poetry to this extent, that it brought the poet into perpetual contact with life and society, and so taught him a racy, popular, universally intelligible style. It effectually saved him from pedantry and obscurity. The most agreeable English ever written is that of the wits of the later Stuarts,—that of Dryden, Swift, Addison, Steele. On the other hand, the best thing about this school in general is their English. Their masterpieces are for the most part in inferior styles. They were not conscious of any high vocation, they seldom aimed at substantial or permanent fame. They were too much dependent on great men, and they corrupted poetry with servility and party spirit.

[1] The whole is quoted in Mr. Quick's excellent "Essays on Educational Reformers."

Milton belongs to the age of these wits. He knew Dryden personally. As a boy, he may have seen Shakespeare. But evidently he does not belong to their school. He was not only excluded from their society by his politics; it is evident that he had a totally different view of the objects of poetry and the function of a poet. The reigning sovereign of English poetry in Milton's last years was Dryden, and him Milton denied to be a poet at all. In considering Milton's poetry, the first remark that suggests itself is the total unlikeness of it to the other poetry of that time.

The school of wit-poets has passed gradually away since theatres went out of fashion, and the reading public ceased to be co-extensive with the town. There prevails now a different notion of poetry. We now think of the poet not as a wit, but as an *artist*. We connect poetry not so much with pamphleteering and politics, as with painting and the fine arts generally. In the seventeenth century there was no considerable school of painting in England, and, therefore, there was no art-world with which the poets could come into connection, and Englishmen had too little knowledge of the fine arts, and too little the habit of thinking about them, to perceive clearly the relation of poetry to them. Goethe first brought home to the minds of men the conception of art as a genus under which poetry, painting, and the rest were to be classified, and gave the conception importance by dedicating to it his long and unique life. At the same time, a large reading public has sprung up, so that the poet is no longer dependent upon patronage, and instead of flattering great men, or taking up their quarrels, he has now only to suit his productions to the taste of some considerable section of his countrymen. Hence the modern art-poetry is entirely free from the great vice of the old wit-poetry. Waller's poems are almost entirely made up of flattery, and two-thirds of Dryden consist of flattery and party satire. But the modern school almost always aims high, sometimes too high. It deals with great subjects, and often in a difficult style; so far is it from being corrupted by too much contact with or dependence on society. It has also gained greatly from having mastered the large conception of *art*. It thinks much less of mere language and more of invention and imagination. The wit-poets seem often to have considered their business to be nothing more than the production of polished couplets. The art-poet knows that he must study nature, and that it is his function to reflect nature. Hence a great improvement in power of description and abundance of imagery, and, with some loss of elegance, a great advance in word-painting and word-music.

Milton is evidently more of the modern type than of the ancient, more like the artist-poet than the wit-poet. Not one word of flattery did his pen ever let fall, not one word of insincere or interested party spirit. He fed no patron with soft dedication, nor was received in the undistinguished race of wits in the library of any Bufo. He had not even the merits of the wit-poets, none of their sprightliness or ease or point—there is not one polished couplet in his works—none of the exquisite miniature-painting of the "Rape of the Lock." He has, on the other hand, all the descriptive richness and distinctness and all the music of the modern art-poets. He gives large range to his imagination, and in fact does the very opposite of what Pope boasted to have done, when he said,

> "That not in Fancy's maze he wandered long,
> But stooped to truth, and moralized his song,"

though he would have strongly protested against the colour which Pope puts upon the matter.

But if there is a marked resemblance between Milton and the art-poets, there is also a marked difference. It is characteristic of the art-poets to be quietists. Their maxim is, Art for its own sake; and as Art is the reflection of Nature, they consider that it is the business of the poet to be as placid and tranquil as possible, in order that his mind may be the more perfect mirror. He must not, therefore, allow the tumult of human affairs to break in upon his tranquillity. He must stand aloof from whatever is exciting or disturbing. Goethe, the master of the school, understood everything in the world except politics, and found everything interesting except the fact that Napoleon was trampling upon Germany. His disciples have often imitated his indifference. They have thus placed an artificial check upon their sympathies for the sake of Art. And what they have professed to do for the sake of Art, they have at least lain under strong temptation to do for the sake of mere enjoyment. He who refuses to embark in any cause, and places himself towards human life in the attitude of a mere spectator, may perhaps improve himself as an artist, but he certainly saves himself a world of trouble. He runs a risk of being made effeminate by his neutrality; and whether he is so or not, he incurs the suspicion of being so. The maxim, "Art for its own sake," which, properly understood, is true, slides insensibly into the maxim, "Art for my own sake."

It is certainly better that the poet should not be a politician at all, than that he should be a reckless pamphleteer like Dryden or Swift. If there be no politics but party conflict, as has been too much the case in England, or if they be the monotonous and empty politics of despotism, as for a long time they were over the Continent, certainly the poet can be little interested in them. Goethe's indifference, however it shocked the patriots of 1813, is to be excused by his youth having been passed in that old despot-ridden Germany, which had entirely lost the political sense, and in which a man like Lessing could write, "Patriotism is a thing I have no conception of, and it seems to me at the very highest a heroic weakness which I am very glad to be without."[1] But the word "politics" may bear a nobler sense than either of these. If the greatest subject for the poet is human beings, and scarcely any human affairs can be so insignificant as to be below the poet's scope, it is surely strange that they should become unpoetical just when they appear on the largest scale. What are politics but the greatest and most important of human pursuits? If they are below the notice of poetry, it can only be because they have fallen into a corrupt and unnatural state. The great political movement of the present century ought, it seems to me, to have a poetical side. I do not mean that poems ought to be written on the Italian war, or the American war, or the German war —poems on contemporary events are generally failures; I mean that poets ought to feed their imagination upon

[1] In a letter to Gleim, dated 14th February, 1759.

contemporary history, draw from the new phenomena new conceptions of human character, new reflections upon human destiny; and that, as their study is Nature, one of the most important chapters in that book, and which should be studied as much as or even more than the visible appearances which the descriptive poet studies, or the individual men that are the study of the dramatist, is Man in communities, as we see him in the time, transforming institutions, dissolving and recombining States, struggling forward towards some ever-brightening ideal under a vast providential law, which slowly reveals itself, of secular progress.

The modern school are the monks of the religion of Art. Milton had as strong an objection to monachism in Art as in the Church. It was one of his cardinal doctrines that the great poet must lead a great life. He therefore plunged deliberately, and probably also doing some force to his inclinations, into the great controversy of his time. He would not pursue his own tranquil enjoyments at a time when his country was disturbed by a great contest. He recorded this resolve in a well-known and impressive passage of one of his earliest works. This was no mere flourish of rhetoric. It is not generally perceived how great the sacrifice was which Milton made to this sense of duty. When the civil troubles began, Milton was thirty-two. He had already written poems which, few as they were, would have given him a high rank among the English poets. If any man was ever conscious of his powers, it was Milton. He is far from being vain; I should not call him, in any bad sense, even egotistical. But he makes no concealment of his high estimate of himself, and with a singular self-confidence announced to the world, and that in a controversial pamphlet, his purpose to produce at some future time a work which should be immortal. Having given this bold pledge to the public, what does Milton do? He abandons poetry for twenty years. From the beginning of the disturbances, when he was thirty-two, to the Restoration, when he was fifty-two, he wrote no poetry except his few sonnets. When he returned to his favourite pursuit he was at the age when Shakespeare died—at the age when poets very frequently feel the spring of their inspiration drying up. The great work he promised he actually produced, but he was growing old before he even set about it.

It is worth while to remark the effect upon Milton's genius of this long breathing-time, or rather, I should say, this long course of discipline that he gave it. The chief characteristic of his later poetry is greatness. It is distinguished by daring, condensed force, sublimity. These qualities do not appear in his earlier poems. In these he is a disciple of Spenser, almost surpassing his master in sweetness and luxury of imagination. His college companions remarked something feminine or rather ladylike in him, and from the speeches of the Lady in "Comus" we may gather that he was conscious of it himself, and was in a manner proud of it. Nevertheless, I have no doubt the vigour, the fire, the love of action was innate in him. In his prose he soon began to show it. But probably it would not have blended with his imaginative power so as to form the Milton of the "Paradise Lost" and the "Samson" but for that hardy school of controversy and danger in which he spent twenty years. He seems to have been himself conscious that there was something in him unformed and immature, some power as yet undeveloped, at the time when he bade his first farewell to poetry. The reader does not find "Comus" or "Penseroso" crude; yet in the opening of "Lycidas," written about the same time as the latter, Milton calls himself crude, and signifies his intention of writing no more for the present.

Milton's view of poetry then differs from that of the art-poets, as we before found that it differed from that of the wit-poets. It is in fact a middle view. The art-poets regard poetry as a serious pursuit, to be pursued for its own sake and for the sake of the artist himself, as a part of his self-cultivation. It is to them a solitary pursuit, neither connected with any public feeling, nor having any public end. The wit-poets regard it as an amusement of social life. Milton takes a serious view of it like the first, but at the same time a social view of it like the second. To him too the poetic talent is no mere knack, no mere toy, but a noble gift given to noble ends, and worthy of the most assiduous and earnest cultivation. But it is not a gift which isolates him from others, or makes him indifferent to the things which interest others, or cuts him off from the general movement of his generation. Art is indeed cultivated by him for its own sake—that is, he sings because he must sing; but the impulse in him is an impulse which is at the same time in others, of whom he becomes the representative, because he feels it more strongly. And his Puritan faith gave him, if not a clue to the progress of human affairs, yet an assured belief that there was such a clue, and disposed him instead of turning aside from the movement of his age, as Goethe did when he wrote his "Westoestlicher Divan," to study it with eagerness as a vast drama, or, in Cromwell's phrase, a great "appearance of God" in the world.

Can we find a name for the poet conceived in this third way? Milton furnishes us with one. It is always to the poets of a primitive age, the *bards*, that he compares himself—to Homer, Tiresias, and the Hebrew prophets. Orpheus and Musæus are the poets he would best like to see before him in his pensive hours.[1] Now in those primitive times the poet was almost an officer of State; he was regarded with reverence, and classed with the priest or diviner. He sang in the halls of Grecian princes, and stirred up the warriors to emulate the great deeds of their fathers. In Palestine he assumed a still greater elevation, and, mixing the praises of virtue with exalted conceptions of God and of the national vocation, became what we call a prophet. This was the ideal of poetry which suited Milton. Unlike the ideal of his own age, and like the ideal of his master Spenser, it was serious and lofty; but, besides, it was public and social, unlike the ideal of the present age. We have therefore a third name for the poet. We have seen him as wit and again as artist; we now see him as bard or prophet.

Bard and prophet, however, are not quite the same, though of the same kind. Both have the same theme, and that a public one,—great events, great deeds. But the bard is exulting and triumphant: he describes a state of things in which he delights, $\dot{a}\gamma a\theta\hat{\omega}\nu$ $\kappa\lambda\dot{\epsilon}a$ $\dot{a}\nu\delta\rho\hat{\omega}\nu$, the glories of Achilles and Ulysses. He belongs to a time and state of affairs when society is on the whole happy and satisfied. The prophet is indignant and dissatisfied,

[1] See "Il Penseroso."

not a praiser, but a reprover: he belongs to a time of transition; that which kindles his imagination is not the present, but a state of things either passed away or anticipated as to come.

We may be said to have among our English poets a good example of both. Spenser is a bard, Wordsworth is a prophet. The former celebrates the chivalrous life. It is an ideal, but an ideal towards which some tolerable approximation had been made. Spenser has no quarrel with his time; he lives among men that seem to him similar to those knights of his imagination who represent the moral virtues. Accordingly we are told that Prince Arthur, who in the first instance signifies Magnanimity, means in a secondary sense Sir Philip Sidney. And throughout the "Faerie Queene," ideal as the poem is, the poet displays the same feeling of delight and satisfaction with his own age.

On the other hand, Wordsworth, still more lofty and ideal, is no bard, but a prophet. The pure and glorious life which he conceives he cannot find realized in the world around him. Therefore his poetry, instead of being narrative and sensuous, as poetry loves to be, is compelled to become abstract, didactic, oratorical, not like Homer, but like Isaiah. That high communion with Nature, that paradisiacal life which he believed to be meant for man, and which he seems himself to have lived, he could not much illustrate from general experience. In a few Westmoreland shepherds and in himself he found it, and therefore his poetry becomes a description of pastoral life and of his own feelings, and beyond this only eloquent philosophical discourse or indignant denunciation.

Milton stands with these two as the third great ideal poet of England. He assumes a public function, that of expressing, heightening, and correcting the aspirations of the community. In the manner in which he does this he stands between them. His own genius and his training inclined him to the manner of Spenser, but the circumstances of the time drove him more and more into that of Wordsworth. He begins as bard, and ends as prophet.

The civil wars produced this change. When his career began, he was happy and contented with the age, but he closed his course in disappointment and prophetic indignation. His boyish reading seems to have been much in romances. He has described in "Il Penseroso" the enchantment they exercised upon him; he reconciled this indulgence with the seriousness of his character by always discovering in the story a secret meaning, such as that which is concealed under the "Faerie Queene." His youthful imagination was full of knights and castles, giants and dwarfs, tournaments and queens of beauty. His first long poem was a masque altogether in the taste of the age, though with a moral rather above the taste at least of the poets of the age. He evidently looked forward to a career like that of Spenser. His great poem was to be on the achievements of some knight before the Conquest, in whom it might be convenient to lay the pattern of a Christian hero. In another place he tells us it was to be on King Arthur. By the side of the "Orlando," the "Jerusalem," and the "Faerie Queene," there would have been set another fantastic cloud-palace, which could hardly have been less gorgeous than any of the three.

But a difficulty arose. Besides being a poet, Milton was a perfectly sensible and serious man. He meant nothing fantastic when he planned his "King Arthur." He contemplated a work which should be true in substance, though imaginative in form. He intended to adopt the machinery of romance, machinery which had been created by the poets whom he loved best and in whose school he had formed himself. But in romance he always held that "more is meant than meets the ear," and he was capable of disowning even his favourite imaginative types if they should cease to be symbolical of his convictions. He saw that there must be some proportion between poetry and reality; and as he grew older and became acquainted with reality, the poetical machinery of Spenser began to pall upon his taste. Spenser's ideal was obsolete, the age had altered, and it was the duty of poetry to break with chivalry once for all. The feeling which had been spreading through Europe, and which found its clearest expression in "Don Quixote," the feeling that chivalry was out of date, entered Milton's mind as he was drawn into that political party which stood opposed to the representative of chivalry, the Court. He quarrelled with all that charmed his youthful imagination, began to think that he had grown up in a wrong school, and turned his back decidedly on the whole mediæval world. It is true that he never ceased to speak of Spenser with tender reverence, and once or twice in his great poem there is, as it were, a momentary revulsion of feeling, the child's heart within the man's begins to stir, Milton is a boy again, and the gay images of mediævalism once more crowd the verse. But his deliberate opinion now is that the "Vandal and barbaric stateliness" of the Middle Age is not to be approved by a true taste.

Then followed twenty years of politics, controversy, and abstinence from poetry. A new world began in England. The old mediæval monarchy and aristocracy passed away; in their place came new principles, new feelings, new forms. The chivalrous scheme of life, which was barbarism idealized—a kind of religion of birth, war, and wandering—gave way to the civic life, which was a religion of law, duty, and simplicity. To correspond with the new view of life, there had arisen new forms, which resembled those of the ancient classical world. A grave senate took the place of a magnificent Court, classic notions of liberty came instead of mediæval notions of loyalty, and religion reassumed its ancient Judaic form of austere and ardent spiritualism. During this long period of silence, Milton's genius was slowly conforming itself to the new ideal. He was passing out of the school of Spenser, and training his imagination upon the Attic tragedians, Homer, and the Old Testament. When he returned to poetry, and produced those great works which he had so long before promised, they had a character quite peculiar, and by no means such as the earlier poems had seemed to promise. "Paradise Lost" is not much like the "Orlando," or the "Jerusalem," or the "Faerie Queene;" "Paradise Regained" and "Samson Agonistes" are exceedingly unlike them.

He is still, as much as ever, an ideal poet. He presents to us, not the world as it is, but grander and more glorious; human beings in a state of perfection or angels, and if also devils, yet sublime devils. But his ideal is no longer the ideal of his own age. Nothing in habitual English life, nothing in the European life of a thousand years past, suggested the order of things presented in these poems. Yet the ideal is not original. He does not initiate us into a new mystery, as Wordsworth into the mystery of Nature, or Goethe into that of Art. In his quarrel with the age he falls back upon antiquity. He revives the ancient world. His poems are the English Renaissance.

For two centuries before his time the European Renaissance had been going on. The ancient literatures had been rediscovered, and laboriously studied. Latin style had been purified, Greek poetry and philosophy studied in the original, Christian antiquities explored. But in most countries of Europe the revival had as yet been superficial. Some superstitions had been exploded, a new refinement added to life, but men remained on the whole what the Middle Age—with its feudalism, its chivalry, its Catholicism—had made them. There was one exception. Italy, in the fifteenth century, had revived antiquity with a strange vividness. All the sensuality and moral coldness of paganism had revived along with the arts of antiquity in the very bosom of mediæval Catholicism. Never was such a strange blending. Bishops and cardinals writing poems on sacred subjects in the easy manner of Ovid; Christian creeds, mediæval institutions, philosophic scepticism, classic taste, Machiavellian politics, pagan morals! But the hollowness of the fifteenth century had given way to a somewhat more earnest spirit near its close. French invasions and the prophesyings of Savonarola had produced a sobering effect, and the Italian Renaissance found a thoroughly dignified representative in Michael Angelo.

The name of Michael Angelo brings us naturally back

to Milton. Milton lived in antiquity as much as any fifteenth century humanist, as much almost as Marsilio Ficino or Lorenzo Valla. Of his English contemporaries, though others may have read as much, I believe none had anything like so vivid a conception of the ancient world. When he was in Italy he had intended to go on to Greece, but, on hearing of the disturbances in England, had been led by a feeling of patriotism to return home. He never saw Athens with his bodily eyes. But Milton had an inner eye, of which he speaks more than once. And it may certainly be said of him, that first of all Englishmen he saw the ancient Greeks. Shakespeare had some notion of an ancient Roman, but the Greek was rediscovered for Englishmen by Milton. He is the founder of that school of classical revival which is represented in the present age by Mr. Matthew Arnold. But further, it is characteristic of Milton that he revives Greek and Jewish antiquity together. His genius, his studies, his travels, had made him a Greek, his Puritanism made him at the same time a Jew. In this renaissance there is no taint of paganism. Under the graceful classic forms there lives the sternest sense of duty, the most ardent spirit of sacrifice.

Nevertheless, all renaissance, all revival of what is long past, has in it something unnatural. The attempt to dress Jewish feelings, transplanted to an English heart, in Greek forms has something violent in it. Milton's singular power enables him to do it in such a way that neither of the foreign elements is lost in the other, but not so as to blend them harmoniously. The Greek forms do not lose their grace under his handling, the Hebrew spirit does not lose its earnestness. But it

cannot be said that the forms sit easily, or altogether
becomingly, upon the subject-matter. When we consider
it, how strange an inconsistency lies in the very construction of "Paradise Lost." A Puritan has rebelled
against sensuous worship. He has risen in indignation
against a scheme of religion which was too material, too
sensuous, which degraded invisible and awful realities
by too near an association with what was visible and
familiar. But, in the meanwhile, a poet, who is the same
person, having a mind inveterately plastic and creative,
is quite unable to think, even on religious subjects, without forms distinctly conceived. And, therefore, while
with one hand he throws down forms, with the other he
raises them up. The iconoclast is at the same time an
idolater. For one of the most striking features of
"Paradise Lost" is the daring materialism that runs
through it, the boldness with which Divine Persons are
introduced, the distinctness with which theological doctrines are pragmatized. Milton the Puritan is not much
less sensuous than Dante the Catholic. He does not,
indeed, crowd his description with insignificant details
intended simply to produce illusion, as Dante does,
almost in the manner of Defoe. But his pictures will
always be found, if examined, to be curiously distinct;
whether his scene be the abyss of hell or the heaven of
heavens, he draws always with the same hard, firm outline. Nothing daunts him, nothing overawes him; his
style never becomes tremulous, the eye of his imagination is never dazzled, he looks straight before him where
the seraphim cover their faces; "the living throne, the
sapphire blaze, where angels tremble as they gaze," he
sees and describes with unfailing distinctness. Thus the

Puritan becomes to the full as mythological in his religious conceptions as the mediæval Catholic had been. And further, it must be said that the artificial Protestant mythology is by no means so appropriate as that which it replaces. The mediæval mythology sprang up naturally. It was the instinctive, often the innocent, product of lively religious feelings working upon untrained, infantine imaginations. It gazes upwards to the spiritual world with awe and tenderness and yearning desire. With what a beautiful reverence and love does Dante introduce the angel at the beginning of the "Purgatorio," and even Spenser the angel that meets Guion when he issues from the cave of Mammon! What a glory fills the last cantos of the "Paradiso!" If this be mythology, it is thoroughly Christian mythology; it is full of heart and full of religion. Not so the mythology of Milton; it is Greek, not Christian. Milton does not seem to feel any *awe* of the spiritual world. Even in Homer, when a deity has stood by a warrior and exhorted him to be brave, the warrior is often described as receiving a kind of spiritual intoxication from the contact. Virgil, in his supernatural apparitions, has a formula, "I stood stupefied, and my hairs stood up, and my voice clung to my throat." Milton's angels are but majestic, grave, and virtuous men. Adam behaves to them as a subject to a king, or a citizen to a great nobleman—with decorous respect, but scarcely with awe; and in a curious passage Milton flouts the notion of there being anything marvellous about an angel's mode of existence, insisting that an angel eats and drinks just like a human being; ay, *and digests his food too.*

Milton's morals, as I have said, are not the least tainted

with paganism, but his imagination is somewhat paganized. The Greek mythology, so full of graceful images, is throughout irreligious; with one or two exceptions, the Greeks felt no reverence for their own theological traditions; they found nothing sacred or impressive in them, and suffered their imaginations to play upon them with little ceremony. The later Greeks regard Homer's supernatural machinery as little better than blasphemy. But, after all, Homer took the traditions that he found; whatever their merits or demerits, they lived, they were generally believed. But the modern poet who goes out of his way to revive and imitate them has not even this excuse. Milton's pictures of the spiritual world not only fail somewhat in the awe and tenderness which the Christian imagination demands, but they do not adapt themselves to any existing belief or sympathies. One feels here the cold touch of the Renaissance. These Greek angels appearing in the costume of Achilles or Æneas, or declaiming at each other, like Æschines or Demosthenes, on their infernal Pnyx, are not such as either Catholics or Protestants have ever believed in. The workmanship is magnificent. We admire them as we should admire a dress by Veronese. But the poet speaks for himself alone. He does not appear here as the exponent of the popular imagination. He is a brilliant, but often a frigid, and once or twice, I fear, even a frivolous mythologer. I confess that I can never read without a shiver that cold-blooded myth of the creation of the constellation Libra at the end of the Fourth Book of "Paradise Lost."

This, then, seems to me the great fault of the "Paradise Lost." It is, in short, a work of the Renaissance. It belongs to the age which produced St. Paul's Cathedral; and when we compare this, the great poem of Protestantism, with the great poem of Catholicism, Dante's "Divine Comedy," we find the same difference that there is between St. Paul's and Westminster Abbey. The first is more graceful in outline, but it is colder and more artificial. The "Paradise Lost" is, as it were, a Christian temple in England, in a style of architecture neither Christian nor English. The whole form of it, imposing and magnificent in the highest degree, is outlandish, and commands wonder, but not sympathy. It expresses no one's mind but the author's. The "Divine Comedy," like Westminster Abbey, is all of a piece. Form and substance suit each other. It leaves one overpowering impression. The spirit that created it is expressed in every detail. Not by learned labour amongst past ages, not by fancying into life again exploded beliefs and forgotten ways of life, was the "Divine Comedy" written, but by living more intensely than others the life of the time, feeling more keenly what others felt, hoping more ardently, imagining more distinctly, speaking more eloquently. It has therefore not merely grandeur and beauty, but warmth.

But this coldness of the "Paradise Lost" is not due entirely to its being a work of the Renaissance. It is due also in part to the subject. Milton tells us that he was long choosing, and his choice was in some respects happy. He required an exceedingly large subject. We do him indeed imperfect justice when we speak only of his greatness or sublimity. His true excellence is that of the best Greek art; that is, the combination of greatness with grace. Grace was the quality that appeared earliest in his poetry, and it characterizes his latest poetry quite as strongly. But during that middle period of silence to which I have called attention he developed a vastness of conception hardly to be found in any other poet. He acquired a facility in picturing to himself the largest phenomena, a startling talent of presenting by a few slight touches the most stupendous images. His blindness had evidently greatly increased this faculty. How much the world owes to great sorrows! Dante was driven by the loss of his home in Florence to create a new home for himself with Beatrice beyond the grave; and Milton creates a new universe to console himself for that which he had lost with his sight. The "Paradise Lost" is the record of many lonely hours spent in gazing upon vacancy. It is a fresco painted by an imprisoned artist on the wall of his cell.

The subject, I say, was well chosen, so far as it suited the poet's turn for vastness and amplitude. It allowed the blind dreamer to wander through starry deeps, to explore unfathomable abysses, to muster innumerable hosts, to rear colossal edifices, to plant gorgeous paradises. But in another respect it is unfortunately chosen. It admits too few human beings. Here again, when we compare Milton's poem with Dante's, we are reminded of the difference between St. Paul's and Westminster Abbey. Westminster Abbey is full of human interest. A line of kings and conquerors is buried there; wherever we turn, the figures of great men, sculptured in their most characteristic attitude, confront us. St. Paul's, on the contrary, is almost barren of such human interest; it is an empty building. In the same way Dante's "Hell," and "Purgatory," and "Paradise" are full of human beings. In that vast cathedral all the great men of the Middle Ages, all the personalities that make up mediæval history, lie in glory, each one in his own place. Beside the awful divine realities are enshrined solemn and tender human memories; in the bosom of the passionless eternity we see gathered the loves and hatreds and the vicissitudes of time. But of all such interest Milton's poem is barren. He contrives indeed to introduce a part of the Old Testament history, but his plan excludes absolutely everything that he knew by personal experience, and everything that his reader can possibly know by personal experience. Down this mighty Renaissance temple as we walk we admire vast spaces, arches wide and graceful, majestic aisles: but it has no monuments, no humanities; it is an empty building.

This is the more disappointing, as the fault was certainly not in the poet, but simply in his subject. The "Paradise Lost" is no small sample of what the human mind can do, but I am persuaded that it gives us no measure of Milton's powers. He had lived in a great age, and among great men. He had occupied his mind with political questions; he had an intense and enlightened political belief. Who can doubt that all this experience of men had left in his mind an imaginative wealth of which the "Paradise Lost" gives us no intimation? If his subject had included some of the events which agitate societies of men, and rouse the powers of great characters, I doubt not that he could have drawn character and described action, not indeed in the manner of Shakespeare, but in the large and simple manner of Homer. As it is, he has given himself scarcely any room to do either. The great passion of his life, the passion for political liberty in the most comprehensive sense, finds no expression in his poetry. No subject could draw out all the powers of Milton which, besides being great and sacred, did not include a republic and a struggle for liberty. Since he chose one which had only the first condition and wanted the other two, we shall perhaps never know with what force and magnificence politics can be idealized in English. The tenderness of Dante was not in him. But he had all his fire and magnanimity, a sympathy with heroism, an ardour of spirit such as has rarely dwelt in a human breast. To display this, his subject gives him no scope. Milton, be sure, is far greater than the "Paradise Lost." The epic of liberty, virtue, and religion, which he had it in him to write, remained unwritten; the God-gifted organ-voice of England never found full or sufficient utterance.

I can well understand the story that Milton himself preferred the "Paradise Regained" to the "Paradise Lost." It had been his ambition all along to paint heroism, to celebrate ideal virtue. He conceived himself as a bard, as one whose function it was to encourage his countrymen to virtue and great deeds by putting before them great examples—"Μυρία τῶν παλαιῶν ἔργα κοσμήσασα τοὺς ἐπιγιγνομένους παιδεύει." In his early description of the poem he intended to produce, the most prominent feature is the pattern of a Christian hero. Now, in the "Paradise Lost" he had missed this mark altogether. The most prominent feature here is the gigantic figure of embodied Evil. He had summoned ideal virtue to appear, and the summons had been answered by the Prince of Darkness. Aspiring to encourage and elevate men's minds, and having himself a sanguine temperament, he had produced a dismal tragedy of the weakness and failure of humanity. He must have felt that he owed some reparation to his own genius for having employed it on a subject to which it was not naturally inclined. This reparation he made in " Paradise Regained." He presented that picture of ideal virtue which he had promised long before. But it is characteristic of the advance of his genius in boldness and elevation that, whereas he had at first meditated fixing the pattern of a Christian hero in some knight before the Conquest, he is now content with nothing short of the Christ Himself.

Every one can recognize the daring originality of the " Paradise Regained." It was the first attempt that was ever made really to study the great Ideal of Christendom. In the picture of the " Raising of Lázarus," by Sebastiano del Piombo, you may see that when the miracle is wrought Martha turns her head away, unable to bear the sight, but Mary keeps her eyes wide open, and fixes them on the face of Christ. The painter evidently thought this the more pious attitude. I know not whether it is, but it is the attitude of Milton throughout his poems. He looks hard at everything, and represents everything with the firmness of sculpture. Whether or no he found this consistent with worship, it is at least clear that he meant it to be so, and that he was not conscious of finding it otherwise.

But, supposing that we ought not to be pained with the plainness and boldness of the picture, we cannot fail to be struck with the same great characteristic that we find in " Paradise Lost,"—that is, the combination of greatness, distinctness, and grace. Nowhere, except, as

I have said before, in Greek art, is there so much of what Clough calls

> "Pure form nakedly displayed
> And all things absolutely made."

But in "Paradise Regained" there is something higher yet—a homeliness of greatness, a simplicity, wanting in "Paradise Lost." There is not a hollow or a vague sentiment, not a useless word, in the whole poem, hardly a single flight of fancy; and yet nowhere is there a touch of commonness. This perfection Milton seems to have owed to the great life he had led. The habit of "plain living and high thinking" had made him all of a piece. Earnest labour had removed from his mind everything fantastical; he had lost even the richness of his style; there remain to him the qualities which were radical in his mind, and which begin now to stand out in an impressive bareness—I mean greatness and grace. In this respect the two poems of his old age, "Paradise Regained" and "Samson Agonistes," resemble each other, and differ from all the earlier poems.

But what shall we think of the ideal of perfect virtue which is presented to us in this poem? In most Christian Churches, I imagine, it is coldly regarded. It is a high ideal, no doubt, but it does not strike most people as the Christian ideal. The truth is that we feel here, as in the "Paradise Lost," the touch of the Renaissance. Milton's source of inspiration is not—it scarcely ever is—the New Testament, but Plutarch and the Old Testament together. The great men of the Greek republics and the Jewish prophets, these were the materials out of which he constructed his ideal. Now, as virtue is essentially the same thing in all ages, no high conception of it can differ radically from any other. Still, Christianity sets out from one point, and the classical nations from another and a widely distant one. The two ideals may not be very different, but if they are the same object, it is the same object presented from widely different points of view.

Classical virtue is self-dependence, love of country, contempt for pleasure in comparison with great deeds, love of fame. It is the poverty of Fabricius, the devotion of Timoleon, the continence of Scipio, the valour of Alexander. Now Milton starts from conceptions like these. He idealizes some of them; he enlarges love of country into love of kind, but still preserves the old phrases; the love of fame, which he evidently felt strongly, he very grandly elevates into an ambition for the approbation of God, and celebrity among the angels of Heaven. He adds from Jewish antiquity an earnest Theism, the conception of zeal, and that of martyrdom for the cause of justice and truth. All these qualities he assigns to one the basis of whose character is a vast and towering, but noble ambition, a mighty statesman capable of embracing in his mind the affairs of a world. In short, it may be said at once that he draws a more gifted and energetic Marcus Aurelius.

Now the Christian ideal, as generally and I believe rightly conceived, starts from quite a different point of view. Put before your mind the man whom the Middle Ages regarded as approaching nearest to Christ, and in whom Protestants may assuredly recognize the resemblance, Francis of Assisi. Love of country, self-dependence, love of fame—what have all these phrases to do with him! His scheme of virtue is altogether different. For country, he can scarcely be said to have one, so entirely is he naturalized throughout the world; nor has he any ambition, noble or ignoble, except to serve. His moral code begins with the love of all men, nay, of all living things, (in Francis himself, you know, it went further still; witness that hymn of his, "Praised be our Lord for my sister, the water, who is very serviceable to us, and humble and precious and clean:") and arising out of this love an absolute self-surrender, a merging of desires in sympathies, and of rights in duties, which make the self-regarding virtues come latest, if they come at all. Francis shows us the Christian ideal, not, it may be, in its most perfect, but in its most extreme and one-sided form—sympathy carried to the point of self-annihilation. But we may still see the difference of Milton, if we take a less extreme example; if we compare him once more with Dante. Dante recognizes some of the classic virtues; patriotism, for example, is very strong in him: but his morality is radically Christian, founded not on self-respect, but on self-sacrifice, and looking therefore for the reward, not of fame, which is self-respect gratified, but of the beatific vision, which is the final merging of self in the transcendent Object of its love.

As then we saw the Renaissance in "Paradise Lost" in the adoption of the forms of heathen mythology, so in "Paradise Regained" we find it in the adoption of the classical conception of virtue. There remains another great work in which it may also be traced, the "Samson Agonistes."

I have always thought "Samson Agonistes" the test of a man's true appreciation of Milton, and not a bad test of his appreciation of high literature. It is the

most unadorned poem that can be found. Even in
"Paradise Regained" there is little richness of style, but
the great panorama from the mount has a certain material
magnificence which every one can appreciate. There
is no splendour of this kind in the "Samson;" colour,
which in his early poems is most rich and glowing, and
in "Paradise Lost" is still rich, begins to grow faint in
"Paradise Regained," and disappears entirely in the
"Samson." But the essential individuality of the man
seems to appear only the more impressively. What you
see here is, not the dazzling talents and accomplishments
of the man, but the man himself. It is pure greatness and
grace, a white marble statue by the hand of a Phidias.

Here, too, the Renaissance works intensely. The
forms of Attic tragedy are rigorously, almost pedanti-
cally, observed. But this produces here no serious in-
congruity, for it is not a question of Christian theology.
The hero to be described is a hero of the antique world;
no Greek, to be sure, but if a Hebrew a Hebrew of a
primitive age. He reminds one of the Ajax of Sophocles, and the resemblance gives no shock to the
imagination. His religion differs, to be sure, from that
of the heroes of Attic tragedy; it is more elevated, and
much less sensuous: still it is a religion contemporary
with theirs; it belongs to the same age of the world, the
same stage in the growth of the human mind. Form
and substance here agree, on the whole, admirably well
together. It is the only one of Milton's great poems
of which the design seems to be completely happy.

But it has another very special interest, in the fact
that the poet himself is evidently put before us in the
person of Samson. In a sense this is not peculiar to the

"Samson," for Milton, who has little dramatic genius, and who holds his opinions strongly and earnestly, allows his own personality to appear more or less in all his poems. In many speeches attributed to Raphael, to Adam, to our Saviour, you may hear unmistakeably the voice of Milton himself. The views and opinions expressed are Milton's views and opinions. But what is peculiar to the "Samson" is, that it is the expression not merely of Milton's opinions, but of his feelings under a special trial, of his indignation and disappointment at the failure of his political schemes. The Restoration had taken place. As I have said elsewhere, Milton's party had not failed—after two centuries we can see this clearly; but for the time they seemed to have failed, to have failed deplorably. The nation had surrendered at discretion to the Court; the Court-party resumed the government of affairs, having lost in the interregnum all their redeeming virtues. The men against whom the nation had rebelled were men who used bad means for what they believed to be good ends; it now submitted to men whose ends were as bad and selfish as their means. Those who had pressed on with such high hope to reform reformation, found their enterprise end in the establishment of the most shameless government that England had ever seen. This was the calamity that Milton suffered in common with his party; he was likely to feel it with a keenness corresponding to the ardour of his previous hopes. But his nature was too strenuous for despair or utter prostration. The sweet Spenserian dreamer of thirty years before, he who had been called at college the "Lady," had so schooled his mind and formed it to such heroic temper that it was proof against this blow. It bore up against the combined weight of this disappointment and blindness, and the contempt and hatred of the ruling party. Fallen on evil days—on evil days though fallen and evil tongues, with darkness and with danger compassed round—he remains unbroken, confident in the ultimate triumph both of the good cause and of his own good name. "Paradise Lost" and "Paradise Regained" are not the works of a melancholy or disappointed man. But, after all, a poet's soul is like some stringed instrument; if you strike it, it will sound. "Samson Agonistes" is the thundering reverberation of a great harp struck by the plectrum of disappointment. It was one of Milton's favourite meditations to number up all the great men who have ever been blind. There was Homer; there was the old bard mentioned in Homer, Demodocus; there was the blind prophet of Thebes, Tiresias; there was Samson. Upon this last his imagination brooded. Samson had giant strength; so, in a manner, had Milton. Samson had been betrayed by his wife; Milton had received a similar domestic wound which long rankled in him. Samson was a Nazarite, forbidden the use of wine; Milton, though he was not, at least a dozen years before, a total abstainer, was essentially an abstemious man. He admired abstemiousness in the abstract; it pleased his imagination in the same way as the exactly opposite quality of joviality pleases most English poets; he is, on the whole, one of those water-drinkers of whom Horace rashly says that their poems cannot please long nor last long. And then came the great point of resemblance. Samson had fought for the living God and had been conquered by the Philistines. He had fallen from his high position in Israel into ignominy and imprisonment. Milton felt the parallel strongly in those last years which he dragged out in obscurity in the neighbourhood of a triumphant Court, which to him was Philistine, in a city which had become to him a city of the uncircumcised. If you find a passionate force in Samson's lamentations, do not quote this as a proof that Milton's genius is dramatic. They are not dramatic, those lines:—

> "Ask for this great deliverer now, and find him
> Eyeless in Gaza, at the mill with slaves,
> Himself in bonds, under Philistian yoke."

His mind does not rest upon his triumphant enemies. The Philistine lords are left in the background, very seldom and slightly mentioned. Milton's complaint is not against them, but against Providence. He utters that cry against the order of things, that demand for justice from the Power that rules the universe, which is heard in all the highest poetry of the world, and will be heard until men can satisfy themselves that the appeal is vain, at which time of necessity it will cease, and perhaps high poetry and all high feeling will cease with it. This is the note that is heard throughout the Greek drama, and throughout the Book of Job. In the Greek drama it is generally a note of despair, and sometimes of bitter rebellion; in the Book of Job it has also bitterness, but hope and faith triumph in the end. Milton has taken the form of his poem from the Greeks, but the spirit of it is that of the Book of Job.

My sole object in this rapid review has been to bring forward Milton re-asserting for the poet his old prophetic character in times when he was held in low esteem, and doing so first by the strenuous training he gave himself, and then by three works in which the seriousness, the distinctness, the grace, and occasionally the coldness of the antique world are reproduced. This was his work: let me now draw your attention to the reward which has been assigned him. It has happened to more than one European nation to bracket as equal at the head of their roll of artists two men who to foreign nations seem to be by no means equal. All the world does homage to Raffaelle, but the equal admiration of the Italians for Michael Angelo meets with a much more doubtful response, and is to many people a perplexity. The Germans cannot be persuaded to put Schiller below Goethe. And yet a foreigner, who may feel all respect for Schiller, who may admire his glowing eloquence, who may find in him a splendid lyrical gift and an imposing, though not very exquisite, dramatic talent, remains at a loss to conceive how such merits as these can be placed in comparison with the inimitable felicity, the profound originality, and the immense variety of Goethe. Very similar, I suppose, is the feeling with which Germans, who have become mere drivellers in admiration of Shakespeare, and the French, whom he has astonished into involuntary respect, hear Milton's—the almost unknown Milton's—name familiarly coupled by Englishmen with that of the prodigy of literature.

But I think it is right that a man should be judged in one way by the world and in another by his own countrymen. In both the parallel instances which I have quoted it is evident that the world has looked simply at the artist; while the nation, following, as it were, the instinct of kindred, has passed judgment upon the whole personality of the man. Raffaelle has given the Italians beautiful pictures, but Michael Angelo, by uniting to his talents a noble character and aspirations that meant more though they achieved less than was achieved by Raffaelle, has given the Italians more than any pictures— he has increased their self-respect. And because Schiller ennobled the Germans, because he gave them a moral inspiration which they sadly wanted, they have paid him a gratitude which they probably understand must seem exaggerated to a stranger, but only because he is a stranger.

Milton has never met in England with a too cordial appreciation. He had his day of excessive poetical renown, but it was the day when it was customary to speak of his character with detestation. Now that we do more justice to his virtues, we have become conscious that the world at large, though conceding to him a good poetical rank, has placed Shakespeare immeasurably higher. Nevertheless an instinct has been at work. Before the definite verdict of Europe, our fathers said Shakespeare and Milton; and since it has been pronounced, we still say, Shakespeare and Milton. Nor need we, I think, drop the fashion. I think we might, without losing sight of moderation, admire him even somewhat more than we do. We may be fully aware that at any international competition of poets England ought to be represented not by him but by Shakespeare. It is by Shakespeare that England takes rank in the world of literature; for it is in him that we have given to mankind a new type of genius—something that cannot be paralleled, something that cannot be replaced. The mighty national character which fills so vast a space in modern history, the human type which seems destined ultimately to predominate upon the globe, is made intelligible and familiar to all the other families of mankind by Shakespeare. In him we ourselves note fondly, and foreigners note respectfully, all the English traits— careless force, kindly humour, sensibility under the control of hard sense, and varied now and then by cynicism, a lucky blending of many opposites, a happy eccentricity, a disregard of all forms, both intellectual and moral, combined with a sufficient fidelity to essential taste and substantial morality. This strange and vigorous English character, most unlike the character of all the nations that had before given laws to literature, suddenly enters into literature, and competes for supremacy there in the person of Shakespeare. Compared with this imposing phenomenon, it must seem to the world comparatively little worth attention, that England has also produced a poet who, for his severe grace, may be set by the side of Sophocles, and who, in the simple and sincere elevation of his genius, resembles an ancient patriot. Yet Milton's work also required an originality for which I doubt if he gets enough credit. There is an originality of invention and creation in which Shakespeare is supreme. But there is also an originality of taste and choice. It was Milton's originality to have an ideal different from that of others, and to remain faithful to it; when the whole cry of poets hurried in one direction, to move steadily and serenely in another, and to forfeit in consequence during life the rank that was obviously his due; in an age of conceits to disdain conceits; in an age of couplets to make no couplets; to be at the same time a Puritan among poets, and a poet among Puritans; to be an Englishman, and yet to display in eminence all those intellectual and moral qualities in which the English type is most deficient. But for him, we should never have dreamed that it lay in the English race to produce a Sophocles. More even than Shakespeare, if I may dare to say so, he enlarges our conception of our national character.

If so, we do right to allow no name to be placed altogether above his, and we should study him as one possessing a secret into which we have not yet been initiated. Unlike all other men that our country has yet produced, Milton may prove a prophecy of some future age, a model to some future generation of Englishmen. Let me collect in one closing sentence the features of this great character: a high ideal purpose maintained, a function discharged through life with unwavering consistency; austerity, but the austerity not of monks but of heroes; a temperament of uniform gladness, incapable of depression, yet also, as far as appears, entirely incapable of mirth, and supplying the place of mirth principally with music; lastly—resulting from such a temperament, ripened by such a life—the only poetical genius which has yet arisen in the Anglo-Saxon family combining in Greek perfection greatness with grace.

# VI.

## ELEMENTARY PRINCIPLES IN ART.

Art is one of the natural forms which are assumed by joy; what we call the arts are merely different ways of being happy. In the lives of most of us, fortunately, there are pauses, intervals without any prescribed occupation, in which the initiative is given back to ourselves. If we cannot fill these, or at least some of these, by Art, the chances are that they will be filled, if we have energy, by avarice or ambition; if we want energy, by *ennui*. This is particularly true in great cities. Life is stifled and overtasked when it is spent in the midst of a crowd; where the animal happiness and freedom of the country is wanting, what but Art can supply its place? A city without picture-galleries, theatres, beautiful buildings, a city where no one writes verses or reads them, or cares to talk about literary subjects, must, I imagine, be far worse than a dismal place. It need not, perhaps, be an immoral place in the common sense of the word; the average number of thefts and murders committed in it need not be greater than in other places of the same size: but in a high sense of the word I think it must be immoral; the standard will be pitched low; life will be uninteresting, and virtue will become languid and, so to speak, unprogressive. The city we live in is certainly not like this; among us all arts are practised. Still, when one seeks among the great cities of history for a parallel to London, it is not Florence or Athens that occurs to us, but rather Tyre or Carthage. If it were only politics that took precedence of the arts, one could put up with it; but when they are crowded out by mere business, this city, to say the least, is not so great morally as it is physically. It does not make a due return to those whom it deprives of the freedom of the country and the beauties of nature.

Foreigners are fond of raising the question, whether the English people are capable of Art. It seems the easiest and most triumphant answer simply to name Shakespeare and Reynolds. So long as we confine ourselves to naming our great artists, we do well; and it is certainly hard to imagine that there can be any radical artistic deficiency in a nation that has produced such men even exceptionally. But there are nations whose artistic faculty shows itself, not in isolated cases, but as a universal birthright; and among these certainly no one would reckon the English. The absolute want of susceptibility to Art seems commoner in English people than in most other nations. The Frenchman's taste may be too exclusive and intolerant, but at any rate it is not wanting; the German's somewhat too tolerant, but there is no doubt that he does enjoy a piece of music at least, and often a painting; among us pure insensibility is perfectly common, and I imagine that of the people who may be found any day walking among the Elgin Marbles, or in the National Gallery, a considerable proportion would derive accurately the same amount of enjoyment from

their promenade if the statues or the pictures were away.
Of course such insensibility, when it is natural, is irremediable. Not by thinking about it will any one find out
beauty. But a sensibility that is weak may be strengthened, and one that is confused may be cleared and
purified. Now the way to make one's perceptions clear in
Art is to consider carefully what Art is in general, what is
its object, under what conditions it works, and what may
be expected from it.

Most people in England, who are not themselves
artists, both dislike and disbelieve in Art-criticism. It
seems to be nothing but a contrivance for making out
everything that is agreeable and enjoyable to be bad, and
everything that is shocking and revolting to be admirable.
Such a contrivance would be irritating enough if works
of art existed for anything else but enjoyment, but as
they have no other end it seems to add insult to injury.
A picture is painted solely to please me, and I am to be
told that it is a masterpiece, although it makes me
shudder! I go to the theatre expressly to be amused; I
am amused, delighted, and enchanted, and next morning
the critics tell me that the piece was detestable. I might
perhaps get over this difficulty by supposing, though
the supposition is not gratifying, that my taste is in a
thoroughly morbid state, like the palate of a man in
fever, or immature, like the taste of a child who delights in
pastry and sweet things. But then the critics do not in
the least agree among themselves, and if I should educate
myself according to the doctrine of one school I met with,
and succeed in liking all that I naturally disliked and in
disliking all that I liked, I should fall at once under the
condemnation of another school, which might in the

meanwhile have superseded the former, and should be told now not that my taste was childish, but that it was artificially depraved.

Still we should not allow ourselves to suppose that Art is governed by no principles at all, because the expounders of it differ so widely among themselves. Their differences, though great, are at least not so numerous as they seem, while their agreements, though less loudly proclaimed, are much more numerous. There are standing controversies in Art which are perpetually breaking out afresh; they take new forms with every new age, but they are essentially the same always. They are always conducted hotly, with sweeping denunciations and anathemas on both sides. Each combatant represents his favourite tenet as absolutely fundamental; the opponents of it are always to him the destroyers and underminers of Art. This violence has always been characteristic of Art-controversies, from the time when the young Athenian in Aristophanes assailed his father with a cudgel for preferring the poetry of Æschylus to that of Euripides, to the time when Blake wrote, at the death of the illustrious Reynolds, "This man was here for the destruction of Art." The effect of it upon the lay-world is generally scepticism; the one party is believed to be as much in the wrong as the other. These violent dogmatic decisions crush too and wither the timid likings of plain people, which might have developed into cultivated taste; they grow ashamed of their own faint impressions and modest opinions, which they are not prepared to justify by reasons; and thus discouraged, turn their backs altogether upon Art. Yet nothing is so important to Art itself, and to general cultivation, as the formation of an intelligent lay-opinion; nothing is so desirable as that there should be a large number of persons who appreciate in some degree without appreciating perfectly, to whom Art is something without being everything, and who can be happy and comfortable in their individual preferences without dignifying those preferences with the name of critical judgments. It is curious that criticism is generally understood to mean finding faults; a really good criticism would consist much more in finding merits—nor need it for that reason become tame; at least I know that the best critic that ever lived, Goethe, scarcely ever blames anybody.

But whether or no you believe in Art-criticism, be sure that I am not going to give you to-night any of those dogmatic judgments which professed artists or critics have perhaps a right to give. I am a humble inquirer in this field, wishing my own sensibilities were greater than they are. I am not going to apply critical canons, nor yet to lay down new ones; my great object is to make persons who have never thought upon the subject aware that there are laws in Art, and laws which, if they are thoughtful, they may discover for themselves. In the short time allotted to me I shall only be able to treat a few of the most elementary laws, and throughout I propose to speak of all the arts together, or, as I may say, not of the arts, but of Art.

Let us begin by considering what we understand by Art. The word is one which we use constantly in speaking of painting, sculpture, and architecture, less commonly, but still often, in speaking of poetry and music. These are the different arts. Each of them differs in some respects from every other, but in some points all of them are alike. Now that in which all the arts resemble each other, what is common to all the arts, is called Art.

What is that one thing which shows itself in all alike, whether we are dealing with stone, as in sculpture, or with words, as in poetry; with canvas, as in painting, or with sounds, as in music? To answer this question is to make a beginning in the intelligent study of Art.

With every power that we have we can do two things: we can work, and we can play. Every power that we have is at the same time useful to us and delightful to us. Even when we are applying them to the furtherance of our personal objects, the activity of them gives us pleasure; and when we have no useful end to which to apply them, it is still pleasant to us to use them; the activity of them gives us pleasure for its own sake. There is no motion of our body or mind which we use in work, which we do not also use in play or amusement. If we walk in order to arrive at the place where our interest requires us to be, we also walk about the fields for enjoyment. If we apply our combining and analysing powers to solve the problems of mathematics, we use them sometimes also in solving double acrostics.

If this is clear, let me now go a step further, and say that as all the serious activities of man fall into certain large classes, and as each class of activities has its own method and rules, so is it with what I may call his sportive activities. What these large classes are in the former case we all know. Men's serious activities are war, manufactures, trade, science. But what are the classes or kinds into which man's activities fall when he sports with them? They are manifold, but among them are painting, sculpture, poetry, music, or what we call the arts.

This fundamental doctrine, that all art is play or sport, and exists for pleasure, is easily misconceived, and therefore often denied. To see it clearly we should consider the simplest cases of Art, not the most famous or splendid examples. If I wanted to discover what is the object of dinner, it would not be wise to take the case of a great public banquet. If I did so, I should be in danger of supposing that the object of dinner was the display of plate or the making of speeches, and that eating and drinking were mere accidents of it. My best plan would be to consider why the tired pedestrian puts up at the wayside inn. In the same way, in order to discover the object of music, let us not consider Mendelssohn's "Elijah;" this might lead us to suppose that the object of music is the inculcation of religious truth; but let us consider why the labourer whistles at his work. If I took "Faust" or "Hamlet" as examples of the drama, I might suppose the drama had a philosophical object; I understand the drama better when I consider a Christmas party making up a charade. In these simple, natural actions we see the naked notion in which the arts begin. We are present at the birth of the Muses, and we see that they are not the daughters of Memory, but the daughters of Joy. Such examples show us how, with all our faculties, we naturally play as well as work. They show that the voice is not only useful to speak with, but also delightful to sing with; the foot cannot only walk, but also dance; the hand can paint, as well as work or write; and, to take more complicated instances, the gift of speech, the serious use of which is to communicate thoughts and facts, is also used for delight and satisfaction in rhythmical forms, and thus becomes poetry;

finally, the whole variety of our serious life is reproduced for delight in the drama.

Let me endeavour to meet some of the objections which are commonly brought against this view. You may notice that artists themselves sometimes reject it as degrading to their profession. As high-minded men, and by their very function men of elevated views, they cannot bear to think that the pursuit to which their lives are devoted is a mere sport or amusement. Such a view seems to degrade them below men of business who work for a serious end, and to give them the character of idlers in the community. And this seems to them as unjust as it is humiliating, for they feel themselves not only not inferior, but distinctly superior in dignity to mere business-men; not only not idlers, but the holders of a high and almost sacred function in the community, the priesthood of the Beautiful and Becoming.

In thinking so they are perfectly right, and the feeling which in all ages has attached a certain sacredness to the character of the artist is quite reasonable. But because all Art is play, it does not follow that the artist is simply one who amuses himself. It is true that he is this in the first instance, and if he were no more, he might be justly called an unprofitable idler. But he amuses others besides himself, and thus he is a benefactor. He is the general purveyor of joy to the whole community. We know that the great secret of wealth was long ago discovered in the division of labour. It was discovered that if, instead of making our coats and shoes for ourselves, we commissioned certain persons to spend their whole lives in making coats and shoes for us, the result was that we got better coats and shoes than we could have ventured to imagine before, because they were now made by persons whose genius specially inclined them to this pursuit, and by persons whose skill was perfected by perpetual practice. Well, this division of labour extends further than we sometimes remark. It includes the art of enjoyment. As we commission the merchant to supply us with merchandise, so do we commission the artist to explore the realms of joy for us, to discover and bring home, or else to contrive, new joys for us.

The artist, then, is master of the revels, director of the amusements to the community. Will this satisfy him? It evidently satisfied Shakespeare. He seems to have been contented and happy in regarding all the world as a stage, so long as his stage might be all the world. Still I think many artists would be discontented. Where is the dignity, where is the sacredness, they ask, of such a position? We shall find the answer if we consider in what way the position is gained. It is the reward of an intrinsic superiority of nature, a superiority in the power of enjoying. Does not this place the artist at once high above the tradesman and the merchant? With a few accidental opportunities or a little capital, added to common shrewdness and perseverance, any man may succeed, and deserve to succeed, in trade. But the artist's capital is in himself; it is the gift of Nature, and incommunicable. And what is this gift? It is the gift of joy. In other words, the power of remaining young longer than other people, perpetual youth. Will it not satisfy the artist that he should be regarded as one whom Nature has favoured with a more elastic spirit than others, as one who, because he retains his freshness when others have lost it in cares and details, becomes a fountain of

freshness to the community? And if there is something
sacred in the artist's intrinsic superiority, is there not
also something sacred in his function? To regulate the
pleasures of a community! It is to have a greater moral
influence upon human beings than is directly possessed
by any class of men except those who teach, and therefore no figure of speech can be more apt than that which
compares the artist's function to a priesthood.

Still, when I repeat that Art is play, I feel that the
maxim has not yet ceased to sound paradoxical, and
that another objection of a different kind may be urged
against it.

There is a stumbling-block in the trivial associations
that are connected with the word "play." Play, people
think, cannot be important or grand or solemn, and
much of Art is important, grand, solemn; again, play
can at any rate never be melancholy, yet much of Art
is melancholy, tragic, pathetic. There is a sort of Art,
they would say, which may fairly be called play, because
it is light and amusing. To this sort belong comedies,
the painting of the Dutch school, &c. But there is
another quite different sort, solemn and akin to religion,
to which belong the poetry of Milton and Dante, and the
painting of the Cartoons; this it would be most inappropriate to call play. I would ask such persons why, if
one piece of Art differs from another so completely and
essentially, we still call both Art? Evidently the lightest
comedy and the most sombre tragedy have *something*
in common, something which leads us to class them
together as works of Art. What is this common quality?
If you will not have it to be what I have maintained,
and what we express when we call them both plays, you

ought not to be content with this negation; you ought not to rest satisfied until you have found some other common characteristic. But the shortest answer is that you misunderstand the word "play." Play is not by any means necessarily connected with mirth or the relaxation of the faculties. What can be more serious than a game at cricket? While the game is going forward, wicket-keeper does not laugh or look about him; point does not chat with cover-point. What parties are more solemn than those that sit round a whist-table? The truth is that all the better sort of games, all those which really refresh and reinvigorate, are of the strenuous, intense kind; they relax some faculties, it is true, but they do so by straining others. Well! but, you will say, if play is an energetic exertion of the faculties, how does it differ from work? It differs in this, that the exertion used in play is exertion for its own sake; while that used in work is for some ulterior object.

Vigorous persons enjoy the vigorous use of their faculties, and of *all* their faculties. This is true far more universally than we are apt to suppose. The same impulse which leads us to stretch our limbs in racing and rowing, the same desire to feel and enjoy our powers, extends to the mind, and, beyond the mind, to the feelings and the moral sense. It devises for itself games or sports suited for each faculty, and for the higher faculties exercises of so exalted a kind that we scruple to call them sports. Such are the higher forms of poetry. They are the forms in which the imagination,—that is, the power of bringing before the mind forms and combinations like those which are furnished by experience,— and the sympathies,—or the power of feeling by reflection

what other people, even imaginary people, feel,—exercise
and amuse themselves. Like other sports, these amusements of the higher faculties will be with vigorous people
vigorous. The imagination will draw upon all the wealth
of earth and heaven; it will find its materials in whatever is most solemn, most venerable, most terrible; it
will play at bowls with the sun and moon. So too the
power of sympathy, when it plays, will not be contented
with pleasurable images; it will deliberately create griefs
in order that it may share them. It will not be mirthful;
for indeed sympathy, when it is strongly excited, is never
mirthful. But not the less on that account is this
activity of sympathy a sport, for it has no ulterior
object, and ends in itself. It will not indeed be a sport
to all. As in every school there are commonly weakly
or effeminate boys who do not care to mix in the more
vigorous sports of their schoolfellows, so will these larger
and intellectual exercises of manhood be too strenuous
and formidable for intellectual weaklings. Such are
pleased with a ballad, but fatigued with "Paradise Lost,"
because their imagination is not equal to a sustained
flight; or their feelings are not lively enough, or their
characters elevated enough, to enable them to enter into
great and impressive situations, so that while they may
feel a genuine interest in the "Ticket of Leave Man,"
they are entirely unmoved by "Philip Van Artevelde."
And indeed among the greater excursions of imagination
are some which, to all but the most robust mind, are
ponderous sport. When the powers of man are at the
highest, his gambols are not less mighty than his labours.
Man, working, has contrived the Atlantic cable, but I
declare that it astonishes me far more to think that for

his mere amusement, that to entertain a vacant hour, he has created Othello and Lear, and I am more than astonished, I am awe-struck, at that inexplicable elasticity of his nature which enables him, instead of turning away from calamity and grief, or instead of merely defying them, actually to make them the material of his amusement, and to draw from the wildest agonies of the human spirit a pleasure which is not only not cruel but is in the highest degree pure and ennobling.

If now I may assume this fundamental position, that Art is in all cases the same spirit of free self-delight, creating for itself various forms and modes of expression, there follows immediately from it one great law, which notwithstanding is often violated. It is that every work of Art must be in its total effect pleasurable. Not that pain is to be excluded; as I have just remarked, pain is one of the principal instruments with which the tragic poet works. But it must be used as the painter uses shadow, that is, by way of contrast to light, and in order to set off or relieve light. Every work of Art is bad, however powerful, which leaves on the mind a predominant feeling of dissatisfaction, or disgust, or horror. And yet it is very common to hear the works of Art judged simply by their power, by the amount of effect they produce, without regard to the quality of the effect. At Bologna, for example, there is a very powerful picture by Domenichino, of the Martyrdom of St. Agnes. Now to see a human being put to a violent death is a dreadful thing, and, as a general rule, I had rather not see even any representation of it. But when the death is martyrdom, when faith and hope triumph over bodily torture, then no doubt, instead of being merely painful, it becomes sublime. It then becomes a fair subject for Art, because the contemplation of it produces on the whole a predominant feeling of triumph and satisfaction. But the artist's special problem is to convey the sense of this victory of faith over pain. If he merely paints with great power the change produced in the human body by the agonies of death, he misses the mark altogether. And this was the effect produced on me by Domenichino's picture. I felt as I should feel if I saw a woman stabbed to the heart in the street. I thought I had seldom seen anything so powerful, and I wished I had never seen it at all.

Another law which follows at once from the principle that Art exists for pleasure, is that all works of Art which have a practical purpose are not properly works of Art. It was a fashion a few years ago—I think it is somewhat less fashionable now—if anybody had a view that he wished to put before the world, a new theory of politics or morals or religion, to dress it up in a novel. You remember how Young Englandism was put before the world in "Coningsby." It was thought that people who might find a series of political dissertations dull, would read with pleasure that a brilliant young man of great expectations, conversing at Cambridge with a brilliant friend, expressed certain views about the Tory party; that he then visited a duke, and in conversation with the heir to the title discussed the prospects of nobility in England; then discussed manufactures with a Manchester millionaire; then the prospects of the Jewish race with an all-accomplished Hebrew capitalist. This was the plan of the story; the reader's imagination was filled with ducal palaces, splendid London and Paris parties, and love-scenes; only now and then was he expected to imbibe a little of the new political philosophy: but gradually the whole dose was administered; and then the brilliant young man, his work being done, is translated to Parliament and a rich wife, and the story ends. Critics, who saw that the object of a novel is pleasure, and the object of a political discussion profit, justly pointed out that, considered as a work of Art, this and similar works were altogether vicious. It does not follow, however, that they are intrinsically bad, and that they ought not to be written. They are simply not works of Art. But if a man can recommend his views to the public by borrowing the machinery of Art, I know no reason why he should not do so. If people will take in a political doctrine when it is explained by a fictitious peer to a fictitious M.P., and will not take it in when the author delivers it *in propriâ personâ*, I know no reason why their peer and their M.P. should be grudged them; only I think that wrong opinions are better conveyed in this mode than right ones, and that hazy conceptions will get more advantage from it than clear ones.

It is by no means true that Art ought always in practice to be kept apart from that which is not Art. On the contrary, there are large classes of the works of men which are partly artistic and partly not. All things that make what I may call the furniture of man's life are of this kind, the articles of utility that habitually surround him, from the clothes that he wears and the chairs that he sits on, to the halls in which he meets his fellow-citizens in council and the temples in which he worships. All such things exist in the first place for use and convenience, and so far are not artistic. Use, convenience, is the paramount law to which all such things are subject. It is a breach not so much of taste as of good sense when we wear clothes that trip us up, or give us colds, because they are graceful, put up with dark rooms for the sake of tracery in the windows, build lecture-halls or churches in which no human voice can make itself heard. But in all such matters, as soon as Use is fully satisfied, Art takes her turn. Man likes to draw delight from the things that habitually surround him. Wherever his mind has freedom for enjoyment, there will he provide the materials of enjoyment, contrivances of Art which may exhilarate the sense. Hence arises the Art of Decoration, reaching its highest dignity in Architecture, which, therefore, differs from the other arts, such as Painting or Poetry, in this, that it is attached like a parasite to that which is not an Art, but a mechanical craft governed by convenience, namely, building. From this peculiarity in Architecture, there follow at once certain practical rules of criticism. For instance, a building may be as good as possible and yet not beautiful, for the conditions of utility may not allow much beauty; and, again, a building may be very beautiful and yet very bad, for the beauty may have been introduced in defiance of the conditions of utility.

Let me take another example of these mixed arts, one in which I have always noticed men's critical judgments to be especially confused on account of their overlooking its mixed character—I mean Oratory. It is evident that this, in the first instance, is not an Art. It is not to give pleasure that men make speeches, but to produce persuasion. The first and indispensable merit of a good speech, therefore, is that it produces persuasion, — that is, as much persuasion as is possible in the circumstances. If a speech does not do this, if it does not, when spoken, attract and hold the attention of the audience, it is of no sort of importance how well it reads. All its merits are out of place, and therefore out of taste. The performance is essentially a failure, and to praise it because, in a different audience, or in the minds of readers some time afterwards, it produces persuasion, is like saying of a general's tactics that they were admirable, only not adapted to overcome the particular enemy with whom he had to contend. I am thinking particularly, as you will guess, of Burke, whose speeches are so full of good thinking and fine writing, but who is said to have " thought of convincing while his hearers thought of dining," and so got the name of the Dinner Bell. If he really did think of convincing, and was so totally unable to do it, all we can say is, that he must have been a thoroughly incapable orator. But I fancy he did not really think of convincing, at least not of convincing that particular audience. I suppose he fancied himself speaking to Johnson and Reynolds, or perhaps to future times, and it may be happy for us that he did so. But, critically, a speech which is not listened to can never be anything but a bad speech, and the speaker who makes it, who, as they say, is above his audience, commits the capital fault in Art; for as the capital fault in war is cowardice, and the capital fault in common life is dishonesty, so in Art the capital fault is inappropriateness.

As in architecture, so in oratory, directly utility is satisfied, Art takes her turn. Speech, when it is already clear and strong, is all the better for being also agreeable; sentences that have been so arranged as to be perspicuous may as well be further so arranged as to be musical. But in oratory, as in architecture and everything else, all true ornament is a shy and diffident thing. It cannot bear to appear out of place; it hates to be intrusive and impertinent. When men are intensely occupied or anxious, it slips out of view; and therefore architectural ornament is displeasing in a counting-house or shop, and oratorical ornament is insufferable in a scientific demonstration, and must be introduced with caution in a budget-speech. But when men have leisure, when the work that occupies them does not absorb all their minds, or press for instant decision, when, however earnest or solemn, it allows of being considered in the way of brooding contemplation rather than of close calculation or reasoning, then, again, Art is in place; and so, for example, architectural ornament is appropriate in a church, and rhetorical ornament in a sermon. And there are cases where both architecture and oratory become almost purely artistic, and the element of utility is nearly eliminated from both. Such are, in architecture, memorial buildings and mausoleums; in oratory, panegyrical speeches.

Now all that I have said hitherto has been deduced from one simple principle. Knowing nothing more of Art than that it is enjoyment, I can deduce with confidence that what does not produce enjoyment on the whole is not truly artistic. I can deduce that what assumes the form and outward appearance of Art, but really has in view, not enjoyment, but the spreading of some doctrine, the detecting of some abuse, or the recommending of some virtue, is again not truly artistic, however useful it may sometimes be. Further, I can deduce that Art is not always independent, but, in some cases, as architecture and oratory, parasitic; and accordingly, that, in judging of particular performances in these departments, it is necessary to apply two standards in succession, the practical standard and the artistic standard, and that the great and decisive test of merit in this case is what I may call the free play of Art in subordination.

But let us now come somewhat nearer to Art, and inquire more closely into its nature. I have said that it is activity for its own sake; in short, that it is sport. It may occur to you as an objection that it would be absurd to call cricket or whist Art, or to class them with painting and poetry. Certainly: but what I said was that Art is sport, not that sport is always Art. The two propositions are perfectly different. Art, I affirm, is sport, that is, activity for its own sake; but then it is sport of a particular kind. Now how do the games that I have mentioned differ from Art? They differ in this respect, that though their object is pleasure, their laws are the same as those of men's serious activities. What makes the serious business of life serious is the cares, the dangers, the anxieties attending it. Remove these, and it becomes a game. This is the theory of games. They are, for the most part, imitations of one of the most serious activities of life—war, with the element of danger and pain removed. Cricket, chess, cards, are only different forms of mimic war; they call into play precisely the same faculties and in the same way as real war, only the object being trifling, danger removed, and the time given to them short, the play has some of the excitement and bustle of real conflict with none of its fatigues and pains. Now Art is like these games in respect of its sole object being pleasure, but it is unlike them in this respect, that it does not merely repeat the activities of serious life, but has laws and modes of activity of its own. Let us try and discover some of these laws, confining ourselves to the simplest and most elementary.

The different kinds of Art answer to different faculties; let us pass them in review and see if we cannot discover a likeness running through them. Such a likeness strikes us at once. There is an obvious correspondence between the art of music and the art of dancing; there is another correspondence equally plain between music and poetry. Dancing is the way or mode in which we express delight in bodily movement; music is the mode in which we express delight in the power of producing sound, whether by voice or instrument; poetry is the way in which we express delight in speech. But the mode of expressing delight is in all three cases the same: it is by *rhythm*. What is dancing but rhythmical movement? What is music but rhythmical sound? What is poetry but rhythmical speech? We may say then that rhythm is one of the primary modes of Art.

Rhythm is nothing but proportion, and to say that it is a primary mode of Art is merely to say that human beings delight in regularity, in pattern, in proportion. In the commonest actions, even where the question is entirely of utility and not of gratification, we use as much regularity, or what we call neatness, as we can. The commonest objects which surround us in daily life must have arrangement and pattern, or they offend our eyes. What we seek even when we are principally concerned with utility, we affect much more earnestly when pleasure is our object. Rhythm runs through our whole existence: subdued and little perceived, and of a simple kind, it is present everywhere as a kind of seasoning; without it life would be slovenly, disgusting, comfortless. But in Art, instead of an accessory, it becomes a principal thing; it is cultivated for its own sake; the more elaborate and intricate forms of it are employed, which are capable of affecting the mind with a far stronger feeling than a quiet soothing satisfaction, and which possesses the secret of rapture and of inspiration.

But am I justified in speaking of rhythm as common to all arts when I have only shown it to exist in some? I have shown it in music and poetry, but not in painting, sculpture, and architecture. No doubt in this latter kind of Art it assumes a somewhat different shape, but it is not the less present. Music and poetry are arts which deal with time; painting and sculpture deal with space. A picture is at rest, always the same, and occupying a certain portion of space; a song begins and ends, and occupies a certain portion of time. Now, if the principle of regularity or proportion enters into both these kinds of Art, it is evident that it must conform to these varying conditions. Regularity in time is what is called rhythm, and therefore rhythm appears in all the arts that deal with time. Now what is regularity in space? Regularity in space is what we call *form;* and accordingly form takes the place of rhythm in all the arts which deal with space. Form and rhythm differ from each other as the sense of sight from the sense of hearing; and the pleasure which the ear receives from a Spenserian stanza, from the regular beat of the iambic cadence, the ordered recurrence of the rhymes, and the swelling Alexandrine at the close, is precisely analogous to the pleasure which the eye receives from the spire of Salisbury or the dome of St. Paul's.

But though regularity, as rhythm or form, pervades all Art, yet it does not by itself constitute that which is highest in Art. It fills a very important place in music and in architecture; but when we examine the arts of painting and the literary arts, that is, poetry and artistic prose, we see another principle taking precedence of it. What is the chief source of the pleasure which we derive from a picture? It is not certainly regularity or beauty of form. A party of Dutch boors by Teniers do not exhibit much of this characteristic. What, then, is it which pleases in the Teniers? It is the likeness of the painted Dutchmen to real Dutchmen. And if we pass at once from a low style of Art to the highest, and consider what pleases us in a Raffaelle, we shall find that, though form is distinctly present here, and though the eye is charmed by a multitude of subtly-contrived proportions, yet still the principal charm is the resemblance of the painted figures to real human beings, the faithful imitation of reality. We have found, then, the second of what I call the primary modes of art, imitation. To recur to my former language, the human faculties, when they sport, amuse themselves, first, with introducing regularity or rhythm into their movements; secondly, with imitating all kinds of objects.

You must see plainly that, though I am near the end of my time, I am still at the beginning of my subject. But my purpose was merely to furnish a few hints; if any one of you to whom these questions are new has been interested, he will pursue for himself the analysis from the point where I leave it. I will bring this lecture to a close by a few inferences from the principles just stated.

It is this principle of imitation which gives to Art its boundless range. Without it painting would not rise beyond arabesque, and poetry beyond metrical rhetoric. With it painting acquires a field as large as the visible universe, and poetry a field even more unlimited, comprehending the world of thought and the world of sense together. And as Art extends its range, so does the character of the artist become more important and dignified. I have described the artist as being a person superior to others in freshness and joyfulness of spirit. But this freshness implies much more than could at first sight appear. It is not merely that he is still mirthful or rapturous when others become sedate, not merely that where others speak he sings, where others step he dances. It is besides that he has an imitative faculty that others want, an observant eye, a penetrating insight, a retentive memory for form and images, a power of sympathy which carries with it a power of divination. Now we can imitate only what interests us strongly; he, therefore, who can imitate many things, is he who is interested in many things; and the artist, whose mind mirrors and reflects everything, has this power simply because he lives more intensely than others. This explains to us how it is that the great artists of the world stand out so prominently. It is true that they did but undertake to find amusement, sport, recreation for their fellow-men; but because true joy is true insight, and intense life is profound knowledge, therefore we rank Shakespeare, Dante, Goethe with great philosophers, the men who have truly and clearly mirrored the universe with those who have rightly analysed it.

But among all the arts it is only poetry that can confer this supreme kind of fame, because speech is the only mirror in which the whole universe can be reflected. With colours or in marble we can express only what we see, but there is nothing that the mind can think which cannot be uttered in speech. And, therefore, in the poetry of all ages we possess, as it were, a shifting view of the universe as it has appeared to successive generations of men. According to the predominant inclination of the human mind in each age is the poetry of that age. At one time it is busy with the brave deeds of the hero, the contest and the laurel wreath; at another time with mere enjoyment, with wine and love. Then it describes the struggle of man against destiny, heroic fortitude and endurance in the midst of little hope; at another time it pictures man as in probation, purified in adversity, and having a hope beyond the grave. At one time it becomes idyllic, delights in country life, simple pleasures, simple loves, a wholesome and peaceful existence; at another time it loves cities, and deals in refinements, courtesies, gallantries, gaieties. And sometimes it takes a philosophical tone, delights in the grandeur of eternal laws, aspires to communion with the soul of the world, or endeavours to discover, in the construction of things, the traces of a beneficent plan.

So far the mind of the artist is passive. Its function so far is to receive impressions from without and to reflect them faithfully. But then comes in that other principle, which we may call the active principle of Art, the principle of regularity or rhythm. The mass of impressions received from without is reduced to shape and unity by the artist. And in this shaping, arrangement, and unification he may show as much mastery as in the correctness of his imitation of Nature. But now it is to be noticed that the taste for imitation and the taste for regularity or rhythm are very distinct things. Often no doubt the same man has both, perhaps oftener than not; but it sometimes happens that an artist has one but not the other, and very often that he has the two faculties in very unequal degrees. Hence there are in Art, and have been ever since Art began, two styles, two schools, two tendencies, which are always at war, by turns almost victorious, but never quite destroying their foe. The watchword of the one school is Nature; with them Art is nothing but careful observation and exact representation; they deify Nature, and almost think it a sin to exercise any choice among the materials she presents to them. The other school think more of what the artist gives than of what he finds; to them Nature is the quarry out of which Art draws shapeless blocks, and informs them with beauty, Nature is the chaos out of which Art makes a Cosmos. The besetting sin of the first school is ugliness; the besetting sin of the last is falseness and feebleness.

All through history these schools have contended, and indeed you have little else in the history of Art but the perpetual veering of fashion and opinion between these two extremes. There is but one other question, which has been so much debated between artists, and this is the question with which I began, whether Art exists for pleasure or for moral improvement. I said that the confusion which generally seems to the lay-world to reign in Art-criticism was not so great as it appeared, and that great judges do not differ in Art so irreconcilably as they themselves love to declare. I have now put before you the two great points of difference to which almost all disagreements in Art may be traced. It is a clue through the maze of Art-criticism to know that its intricacies are caused mainly by two fundamental disagreements. Let me repeat the two great questions of debate. The first is the question whether Art exists for pleasure, or for instruction and moral improvement. The second is the question how much Art derives from Nature, and how much Art adds to Nature.

In conclusion let me say that this latter controversy does not much affect the greatest artists. They are for the most part practically above it. It is the second class of artists who run into mere imitation, like the Dutch school of painting, or to false prettiness, like the pastoral poets. And so with critics, it is generally an immature taste that excludes and condemns either the Realist or the Idealistic school. Young readers of poetry who have a strong sense of rhythm, and a strong appreciation of what is formed, finished, and regular in conception, delight in Milton, and for a time find Shakespeare slovenly, loose, irregular. On the other hand, those who have strong feelings and a strong sense of reality delight in Shakespeare, and find Milton cold and unreal. At the present day it is the lovers of rhythm, form, and harmony that stand firm by Tennyson, the lovers of reality and variety that desert him for Browning. Of course of these two factions one or the other must be right,—Tennyson must be greater than Browning, or he must be less. But assuredly both these artists, and all really great artists, are Realists and Idealists at once. Milton did not know Nature nearly so well as Shakespeare, but assuredly he had a keen eye for reality, as well as a powerful imagination to form new combinations above Nature and greater than Nature: Shakespeare had not Milton's shapeliness nor his elaborate and complex rhythms, but assuredly he too had Art as well as Nature, form as well as matter, unity as well as variety. All the great artists both draw from Nature and add to Nature. If Tennyson is exquisite in form and composition, he is also faithful in imitation and rich in knowledge: if Browning is inexhaustible in knowledge and variety, there are rhythms in him too, if quaint ones; methods, if difficult to follow; unity, or a powerful struggle for it.

has been so much debated between artists, and this is the question with which I began, whether Art exists for pleasure or for moral improvement. I said that the confusion which generally seems to the lay-world to reign in Art-criticism was not so great as it appeared, and that great judges do not differ in Art so irreconcilably as they themselves love to declare. I have now put before you the two great points of difference to which almost all disagreements in Art may be traced. It is a clue through the maze of Art-criticism to know that its intricacies are caused mainly by two fundamental disagreements. Let me repeat the two great questions of debate. The first is the question whether Art exists for pleasure, or for instruction and moral improvement. The second is the question how much Art derives from Nature, and how much Art adds to Nature.

In conclusion let me say that this latter controversy does not much affect the greatest artists. They are for the most part practically above it. It is the second class of artists who run into mere imitation, like the Dutch school of painting, or to false prettiness, like the pastoral poets. And so with critics, it is generally an immature taste that excludes and condemns either the Realist or the Idealistic school. Young readers of poetry who have a strong sense of rhythm, and a strong appreciation of what is formed, finished, and regular in conception, delight in Milton, and for a time find Shakespeare slovenly, loose, irregular. On the other hand, those who have strong feelings and a strong sense of reality delight in Shakespeare, and find Milton cold and unreal. At the present day it is the lovers of rhythm, form, and harmony that stand firm by Tennyson, the lovers of reality and variety that desert him for Browning. Of course of these two factions one or the other must be right,—Tennyson must be greater than Browning, or he must be less. But assuredly both these artists, and all really great artists, are Realists and Idealists at once. Milton did not know Nature nearly so well as Shakespeare, but assuredly he had a keen eye for reality, as well as a powerful imagination to form new combinations above Nature and greater than Nature: Shakespeare had not Milton's shapeliness nor his elaborate and complex rhythms, but assuredly he too had Art as well as Nature, form as well as matter, unity as well as variety. All the great artists both draw from Nature and add to Nature. If Tennyson is exquisite in form and composition, he is also faithful in imitation and rich in knowledge: if Browning is inexhaustible in knowledge and variety, there are rhythms in him too, if quaint ones; methods, if difficult to follow; unity, or a powerful struggle for it.

# VII.

## LIBERAL EDUCATION IN UNIVERSITIES.[1]

"In Würtemberg wird locirt bis in's Mannes alter hinein. Ausser China wird in keinem Lande so viel examinirt und locirt, als in diesem. Die Locationen werden gedruckt; sie sind der Maasstab bei den späteren Anstellungen. Nach seinem Locus misst man den Mann."—"*Life of Hegel,*" by *Rosenkranz.*

"In Würtemberg they arrange in order of merit even grown men. In no country but China is there so much examining and *placing* as in this. The lists are printed; they regulate the subsequent appointments. A man is estimated according to his place."

THE state of the English Universities is a subject sufficiently important in itself, but it is discussed here mainly on account of its intimate connection with the state of English schools. In the leading schools it does not rest simply with the Head-master to decide what the higher

---

[1] This paper appeared first in 1867, in "Essays on a Liberal Education," edited by the Rev. F. W. Farrar. As was to be expected, it gave some offence and provoked some angry criticisms. But I have not felt called upon to alter anything except a phrase or two the meaning of which had been misunderstood. That Cambridge has of late years produced some eminent names, both in science and scholarship, I know as well as my critics; all I say is that I think, and many high authorities think, that she ought to produce a greater number. But the reader must bear in mind that the paper is now three years old. In three years, though no great change has taken place, yet the evils here complained of have steadily diminished. The College system is gradually relaxing: in some cases a particular course of

forms shall study. The College authorities at Oxford and Cambridge take this question very much out of his hands by their examinations for entrance exhibitions, and the University authorities by their degree examinations. In the second place, the Universities are practically our Normal Schools, the places where our schoolmasters are trained. It is not, to be sure, a methodical training, but it is the only training they receive. The opinions about education which they imbibe there are the opinions upon which they act, so far as they act freely, in the work of education. The subjects they will consider most important in education will be, as a rule, the subjects which were most in repute at College when they were there; and they will commonly teach by the same methods by which they themselves were taught. The experience of teaching may afterwards modify their views, but it is less likely to do so in respect of the subjects than of the methods. A schoolmaster may discover by trial a better way of teaching a subject than the way he began with, but it will not so readily occur to him to doubt the expediency of teaching a particular subject at all. A master's faith in the Eton Grammar breaks down long before his faith in Latin itself is even shaken, and this profound faith in Latin depends ultimately upon the value which is attached to it at the Universities. In the third place,

---

lectures has been thrown open to the students of more than one College; other courses have been instituted entirely independent of the Colleges. Perhaps the change which is likely to prove most beneficial is the increase in the number of married lecturers retaining their fellowships. In them the University gains a class of teachers prepared to devote to her their whole lives and their ripe experience, and at the same time not forced to give up their whole day to tuition.

it is to be noticed that the Universities have lately, with much spirit, taken upon themselves the function of directing education even in those schools which do not send their boys to them. By the Middle Class Examinations a number of schools were brought under the control of a common system, which before had had neither control nor system. This was a great step; but at the same time it greatly increased the influence of Universities over Schools, and made the nature of that influence a more serious question.

Education, in fact, in England is what the Universities choose to make it. This seems to me too great a power to be possessed by two corporations, however venerable and illustrious, especially since we know them to have grown up under very peculiar circumstances, and to be fortified by endowments against all modern influences, good or bad. I wish we had several more Universities; I mean teaching as well as examining Universities. I hope that the scheme which was announced some time ago, of creating a University for Manchester, will not be allowed to sleep. I should like to see similar schemes started in three or four more centres of population and industry. Could any investment of money in philanthropy be less questionable at this time? Is there anything more undeniable than that our material progress has outrun our intellectual,—that we want more cultivation, more of the higher education, more ideas?

But in the meanwhile, since education in England is, in the main, what Oxford and Cambridge make it, how important is it that Oxford and Cambridge should disseminate just and profound views on education!

There is no greater or deeper subject; there is no subject which demands more comprehensive knowledge or more fresh observation. There are general principles to be grasped, and there are particular circumstances of age and country to be noted, by the men who would legislate for the education of a nation. Oxford and Cambridge legislate for us, and we may be sure that if those Universities labour at present under any serious defect of system, the whole education of the country will suffer for it: our schoolmasters will want just views of their duty, and they will also be fettered in the performance of it.

The remarks which follow refer principally to Cambridge, the University I know best. They endeavour to point out a serious defect, which has the effect of lowering the whole intellectual tone of the University. If I can make my case good, I may expect to be pardoned, even though I venture to criticise an institution to which personally I owe much: if I do not succeed in convincing the reader, then he is likely to think my language ungracious, and I can only defend myself by assuring him that I echo the thoughts of very many who have had experience of the system, and also that, serious as we think the evil, we none of us doubt that both Universities are doing much faithful and valuable work.

Oxford and Cambridge, then, are just now in low repute upon the Continent, and it is common with foreigners to remark that they have made few contributions of late to science and scholarship. Whatever it may be possible to urge on the other side, it is at least undeniable that original research is not prosecuted so methodically, so habitually, nor by so many people at Oxford or Cambridge as at Berlin or Leipzig. We may have isolated celebrities equal to the greatest of Germany, but we have not anything like the number of students engaged, each in his own department, upon original and fundamental inquiry. This will hardly be disputed; and, taken by itself, it is a fact which every one would deplore. But some regard it as inevitable, and as arising from an inherent inferiority of the English character to the German in intellectual industry; while others consider that the energy withdrawn from original study at our Universities is given to the instruction of the undergraduates, and that this is a better application of it. The theory of radical inferiority will certainly not bear examination. There is plenty of industry at Cambridge; among the undergraduates a good deal of over-work, and among the graduates a considerable class whose intellectual industry is incessant and would not bear much increase. The other explanation is obviously to a certain extent true. The industry, for example, of the class just mentioned, is absorbed in tuition. They are the private tutors whose services are in so much request at Cambridge. Though they are generally the most distinguished men of their respective years, they are unable to pursue their studies further because they are engaged for eight or ten hours of every day with their pupils. The College lecturers, if they formed a distinct class, would have the necessary leisure, but they are commonly private tutors at the same time. There remain the professors. These, as they are in the position most favourable to production, do actually produce the most. But how small is their number compared with that of the men equally well circumstanced in a German University!

There are, however, other impediments besides want of leisure. As the habit and fashion of original production has long gone out, as no one beyond the handful of professors regards it as lying within his functions to extend the bounds of knowledge, all the arrangements which might facilitate production are neglected. This is seen particularly in the case of the College lecturers. Why are not these more productive? They form a considerable band. When they can resist the temptation to waste their leisure in private tuition, they have the first condition of production—leisure, and also the second condition—a prescribed task. What more do they need? In the first place they need a subject carefully limited, so that they may hope to master it thoroughly. For example, if you make a man lecturer on classics, you spoil him for the purposes of original production. The subject is too wide. If he is required to lecture one term on a Dialogue of Plato, the next on an Oration of Cicero, and the next on Theocritus, he will lecture at best in a second-rate manner upon each. And if he hold such a lectureship for ten years, he will not, at the end of it, be necessarily much more learned than when he began. On the other hand, if an able man lecture on Aristotle for ten years, his lectures will soon become first-rate instead of second-rate, and he himself will hardly fail to become an accomplished Aristotelian. Now, this condition of production is neglected at Cambridge, and the consequence is, that a College lecturer who was promising at twenty-two is often no nearer to performance at thirty.

Again, in this great band of College lecturers, there is scarcely any division of labour. As each College thinks it necessary to furnish all the needful instruction to its students, and admits to its lecture-rooms only its own students, the same subjects are lectured upon at the same time in all the Colleges. In the German Universities the whole field of knowledge is elaborately divided, and assigned in lots to different lecturers. In a prospectus of Heidelberg University I count about sixty, each lecturing on his own peculiar subject; at Cambridge scarcely anything but classics and mathematics is lectured on in the Colleges at all, and at every College the lectures are substantially the same.

In Germany, every lecture-room being open to the whole University, the size of a lecturer's class bears some proportion to its merits. At Cambridge the best lecturer is no better attended than the worst, and not only his salary, but also his reputation, is hardly at all affected by the merit of his lectures.

Again, not only do good lectures attract no more attention than bad ones, but neither good nor bad lectures attract any attention worth speaking of. The attendance in most cases is compulsory, and purely formal.

Once more, the College lecturers being commonly chosen from the Fellows, and the Fellows not from the University at large but from the students of each College, though they can never be incompetent or fall below a certain level of ability, yet they are not by any means invariably the most competent men.

In fact, if the conditions of original research are leisure and special ability, a limited field, and rewards in reputation and money proportionate to exertion, there is no class at Cambridge, except the professors, that possess them in any moderate degree. And these conditions failing, another condition, also important, fails with them—the stimulus of the success of others in such research, and of a public opinion demanding it. There is no occasion, therefore, to suppose any natural inaptitude for original study in the Englishman; the present insignificance of our Universities in the world of science and scholarship explains itself very naturally by the system pursued in them. I am not at this moment considering whether that system is good or bad; I am only remarking that it has quite a different object from the advance of knowledge, and therefore, naturally enough, does not favour the advance of knowledge.

There are persons who, acknowledging all this, maintain that it is not to be regretted. Their position is, that a University may exist for one of two objects—either for the cultivation of science, as the German Universities, or for the education of youth, as the English ones; but that it is impossible to attain both these objects at once; that a choice must be made between them; and that if we have definitely chosen the former, and therefore to a considerable extent sacrificed the latter, it is equally true that the Germans have purchased the learning of their professors at the expense of the education of their young men. This is a perfectly logical position, and if we were really driven to make such a choice, I should admit that something might be said for education as against learning. Only if Oxford and Cambridge devote themselves to education, we ought to have other Universities that will devote themselves to learning. Or is the country already so impregnated with ideas that we can afford to sacrifice, without equivalent, our two principal nurseries of thought? Perhaps philosophy will grow of itself in England; perhaps every Englishman's head is such a hotbed of generalizations that it is unnecessary here, as in every other country in Europe, to encourage thought and study by special arrangements!

But I will endeavour to show that we are not driven to make such a choice. I will maintain that the two things help each other; that where the spirit of original inquiry is most active among the teachers, there the teaching is best; and on the other hand, that where it is languid or dormant, the teaching, however assiduous or conscientious, is degraded in character, and that such a University tends to become a mere school.

It will be admitted that teaching boys is very different from teaching men. If we inquire in what the difference consists, we find that the boy requires to be constantly supplied with motives for working, while the man brings these with him. On the other hand, the man needs above all things learned and profound instruction, which is less necessary for the half-formed mind of the boy. It is by no means necessary that the masters of a school should be deeply learned. If they have tact, firmness, and a lively way of teaching, with competent knowledge, they will do all that can be done in a school. Moderate learning will be sufficient to command the respect and stimulate the minds of boys. The qualifications most important to a lecturer are quite different. The liveliness and attractiveness which interest boys are not required in teaching young men. Manner is here much less important, and matter much more. The lecturer deals with a riper stage of intellect. In order to be a useful guide to the cleverest young men at their most impressionable age, he must be before all things a man of power and learning. In short, the success of a schoolmaster depends mainly upon his force of character, the success of a college lecturer mainly upon his force and ripeness of intellect.

For this reason I maintain that in a University education and learning can only flourish together, or, in other words, that even if University teachers devote themselves absolutely to the work of education, they will find that the way to influence the students most powerfully is by becoming as learned as possible. I beg the reader to observe that this position is not the same as that which is often maintained by the same arguments. I do not assert that the professorial system ought to be revived and made to supersede the tutorial. The professorial system, as commonly understood, differs from the tutorial in two points, and it is only in one that I think it superior. Greater concentration upon his subject, and within the limits of it greater learning than the college tutor commonly has, I think all-important; but I do not advocate the rhetorical method of instruction which belongs to the professor as better than the catechetical method of the tutor.

The existing system of moderately learned College lecturers and over-worked private tutors—in short, of teachers who are not at the same time students—defends itself not so much on abstract grounds as on the ground of the present exigencies of the University. The argument runs as follows: The undergraduates are reading for triposes; upon their success in these triposes depend their chances of a fellowship, their chances of success in the scholastic profession, and to a considerable extent their chances of success in life generally. The teacher's business is to conform himself to these triposes, and to give such instruction as will give his student success in them. Now it is not practically found that this is best done by the men of great learning and original research. On the contrary, it is found that such men generally fail, and that the most successful teacher is the man who devotes himself most exclusively to his pupils, who considers most carefully their wants and what is likely to be set; in short, who trains them most diligently for the race. It follows that the interests of education and learning, whatever they may theoretically be, are not practically the same, but conflicting. To this we might reply, "But perhaps it is *not* the teacher's business to conform himself to the triposes. Perhaps the influence of the triposes is not beneficial, or only partially beneficial, or only beneficial to some students. In these cases would it not be the teacher's business to dissuade his pupils, or some of them, from reading for the triposes, or to warn them that success in a tripos is not the ultimate end of education, nor an infallible test?" What answer would be given to this? Some would answer very simply, "We do not think so. We are convinced that the best thing a student can do is to devote himself to a tripos, and to measure himself by his success in it. The simple contrivance of a tripos cures all freakishness of mind, absolutely identifies interest and duty both for teacher and taught, and renders moral considerations in education once for all superfluous." *O fortunatos nimium*, those who have found out how to do their duty by machinery! But a larger class would urge very plausibly, "Whether they will or not, the teachers *must* conform themselves to the triposes. If they do not, if they teach what they themselves hold to be important, without considering whether it will pay, their pupils will simply refuse to listen to them, and nothing will be learnt at all." There is no doubt that this is in a great degree true, and it brings to light another great impediment to learning which exists at the English Universities. We have seen that there exists no large class there which has at the same time leisure and a strong motive for profound study. We now see that the triposes act powerfully upon the teaching class, and draw them by motives of interest, and what almost seems duty, into a method of instruction which makes profound study unnecessary and scarcely possible.

The question then rises, Is the machinery of triposes actually so admirable for purposes of education? Is it the best way of educating a young man to place before him the prospect of a great race, for which he is to train himself through a series of years? If so, his teachers will do their work best by becoming trainers; for this purpose they will have to sacrifice original study, and it will be necessary to admit that the interests of education are irreconcilable in a University with the interests of learning. I fully recognize the use of a system of rigorous examination, and the advantage of sifting the men to some extent, and arranging them with some reference to merit. But I do earnestly maintain that when this examining and placing are made the principal thing, when the tripos is made the heart of the whole system, the great central pump which propels the life-blood through all the arteries of the University, the system becomes mischievous, and lowers the whole tone of education.

Let me point out the mischievous consequences of the system.

The object of a tripos is to discriminate accurately the merit of the students. Now it is found that the difficulty of doing this varies very much with the subject of the examination. There are some subjects upon which it is hardly possible to gauge a man's real knowledge by any set of questions that can be devised. There are other subjects upon which it is much more easy to do so. And unfortunately the suitableness of a subject for the purposes of examination is not at all in proportion to the importance of the subject in education. Whatever theory of University education you adopt—whether you hold that it should aim at a complete training of the faculties, or that it should prepare the student for the pursuits of later life—it is evident that the curriculum ought to be determined by other considerations than the convenience of examination. To be able accurately to measure the amount of knowledge a student has acquired may be important; but it is infinitely more important that the knowledge be valuable. Yet, when a tripos is made the principal thing, this very obvious fact is apt to be forgotten. The imparting of knowledge begins to be regarded as less important than the testing or gauging of knowledge. Then subjects in which attainments can be accurately tested come to take precedence of subjects in which they cannot. These latter, however important they may be, gradually cease to be valued or taught or learned, while the former come into repute and acquire an artificial value. This cannot take place without an extraordinary perversion of views both in the taught and the teachers. They learn to weigh the sciences in a perfectly new scale, and one which gives perfectly new results. They reject, as worthless for educational purposes, the greatest questions which can occupy the human mind, and attach unbounded importance to some of the least. Philosophy, for example, is in little repute at Cambridge. The subjects it deals with may be of vast importance; the study of them may be most improving and stimulating: but the fatal objection to philosophy is that you cannot satisfactorily examine in it; you cannot say confidently, as the result of an examination in it, A is better than B, or B is better than A. The consequence is that a student may run a most distinguished career and finish his education in utter ignorance of philosophy. Meanwhile the whole mind of a large section of the University is occupied by the grammar of the classical languages, simply because it is found possible to examine in this; and lads are taught to be ashamed of falling short of perfect knowledge in the genders of Latin nouns, which involve no principle at all, and in which a minute accuracy can hardly be attained without a certain frivolity or eccentricity of memory!

No one will deny the importance of rigorously testing knowledge. A student will often suppose himself to understand a proof or a principle; but, if he is required to write the proof out, or to do some exercise involving the principle, he shows by his failure that his knowledge was superficial, incomplete, or even imaginary. And it is true that the student who studies for a long time, without ever undergoing strict examination, fills his mind with these vague and imperfect conceptions, and, if he have at the same time a gift of ready expression, is in danger of becoming a rank impostor. It is also a useful thing that the men should be arranged in groups, so that a man may know of himself, and others may know of him, whether he is to pass in a particular department as a first-rate, or second-rate, or third-rate man. All this is very valuable; but there is much to be said on the other side. In the first place this testing is much more necessary to bad men than to good. It should, in fact, be comparatively little needed at a University. With a rigorous examination-system at schools the better men might form the habit of exact thought before going up to College, they might learn to criticize themselves, and might be fit, as indeed many are fit, to leave prizes and examinations behind them at school with the other toys and trammels of boyhood. And though it be useful to classify men, yet as soon as the classification pretends to be exact it becomes delusive. A difference of twenty places commonly has meaning; but a difference of four or five places has not necessarily any meaning. And if it had, what is gained by such accurate discrimination? Who is the better for learning that of two good men one is slightly better than the other? I can imagine no useful result that is gained by all the conscientious care that is bestowed by examiners upon these nice determinations. In this case, at least, the result seems to me none the better for being quantitative. To act upon it,—to give, for example, an appointment to the man who was fourth rather than to the man who was eighth,—is, I am sure, a folly. And to many such follies and injustices does this system of placing men practically lead.

Meanwhile the state of mind which is produced in the student by his perpetual preparation for the tripos is far from wholesome. In saying this I am confident I speak the sentiments of many who have had opportunities of observing it. I do not now speak of cramming. It is true that at Cambridge, by great care in the conduct of the examination, but still more by the summary process of eliminating out of education all subjects, important or unimportant, that can be crammed, cramming, in the ordinary sense, is rendered almost impossible. What I complain of is the vulgarizing of the student's mind. Surely nothing is more important at a University than to keep up the dignity of learning. Nothing surely is more indispensable than an intellectual tone, a sense of the value of knowledge, a respect for ideas and for culture, a scholarly and scientific enthusiasm, or what Wordsworth calls a strong book-mindedness. Now the spirit of competition, when too far indulged, is distinctly antagonistic to all this. In the case of boys I suppose it must be called in, because boys have not yet felt the higher motive to study. But it vulgarizes a mind capable of this higher motive to apply to it the lower motive in overwhelming force. Students at the University are no longer boys. They differ from boys principally in this, that they are old enough to form an opinion of the value of their studies. And that they should form such an opinion is most desirable; it is, in fact, one of the principal things they have to do. The student should be always considering what subjects it is most important for him to study, what knowledges and acquirements his after-life is likely to demand, what his own intellectual powers and defects are, and in what way he may best develop the one and correct the other. His mind should be intent upon his future life, his ambitions should anticipate his mature manhood. Now in this matter the business of the University is by a quiet guidance to give these ambitions a liberal and elevated turn. All the influences of the place and of the teachers should lead the student to form a high conception of success in life. They should accustom him to despise mere getting on and surpassing rivals in comparison with internal progress in enlightenment, and they should teach him to look further forward than he might of himself be disposed to do, and to desire slow and permanent results rather than immediate and glittering ones. Now I say that intense competition vulgarizes, because, instead of having this tendency, it has a tendency precisely contrary. Instead of enlarging the range of the student's anticipations it narrows them. It makes him careless of his future life, regardless of his higher interests, and concentrates all his thoughts upon the paltry examination upon which perhaps a fellowship depends, or success in some profession is supposed to depend. It is well understood that the examination demands this concentration. It is well known that the man who hesitates is lost; that any one who asks himself the question, "Is this course of study good for me? does it favour my real progress, my ultimate success?" is not fit for the tripos. Thinking of any kind is regarded as dangerous: it is the well-known saying of a Cambridge private tutor, "If So-and-so did not *think* so much, he might do very well." The tutor in question probably defended what sounds so startling by arguing that it is really wise not to indulge the power of discursive thinking too soon, or with too little restraint. I am not now concerned with this, and may content myself with remarking that the particular student who *did* think too much, and who, perhaps, as a consequence, was beaten in the tripos, now stands in scientific reputation above all his contemporaries. But whether or no such self-restraint be wholesome in itself, it is vulgarizing to those who practise it as a means of success in the examination. It is a violence done to all the better nature of the student. He does not inquire whether it is wholesome or not; the process of reasoning which goes on in his mind, and which you may hear avowed in his conversation, is this: "I know what I should like to be doing; I know what seems to do my mind good; I know what I shall study as soon as I am at liberty, if my taste for study lives as long: but at the same time I know what will procure me marks, what will procure me a fellowship; and it is my business now to narrow my mind, and for three years"—three of the most progressive years of a man's life—" to consider not what is true, but what will be set; not Newton or Aristotle, but papers in Newton or papers in Aristotle, and to prepare, not for life, but solely and simply for the Senate House." It is only persons ignorant of the facts who will consider this description exaggerated. And the worst is that this vulgarity in study infects not, as might be supposed, only an inferior class of men, but the men of the greatest ability and promise—so diligently have the glories of the tripos been trumpeted. I knew a man who had an almost unprecedented career of success at Cambridge, who had so completely made success of this sort his end, that when he had exhausted the prizes of the University he confessed that he did not know what next to do, or how to employ himself. Another Alexander!

Yet is even this quite the worst? I think it is worse still that the teaching should be vulgarized as well as the learning. It is bad enough that our youth should resort to the shades of Academe simply to seek marks, but it is worse still that the Platos of Academe should teach and earnestly preach that marks are the *summum bonum*. I can only wonder at the blindness of those teachers who do so under the belief that marks are the symbol of sound and accurate knowledge. Can they not see every year high places becoming the reward of schoolboy abilities and schoolboy knowledge? I can quite understand that others may be carried away by the torrent, and may think that it is useless to struggle against an influence which is overwhelming, and which at the same time is not purely bad. But, whatever may be the cause, I think it the greatest misfortune in a University that success in an examination should be held up by the teaching class in general as the principal object of study.

There are some who think that the principle of competition should not be introduced into education at all, and that there are better ways of teaching industry even to children. This may be an extreme view; but I am sure that competition is a dangerous principle, and one the working of which ought to be most jealously watched. It becomes more dangerous the older the pupil is, and therefore it is most dangerous in Universities. It becomes more dangerous the more energetically and skilfully it is applied. At Cambridge it is wonderful to see the power with which it works, and the unlimited dominion which is given to it. And therefore here it produces most visibly its natural effects,—discontent in study, feverish and abortive industry, mechanical and spiritless teaching, general bewilderment both of teacher and taught as to the object at which they are aiming. The all-worshipped Tripos produces, in fact, what may be called a universal suspension of the work of education. Cambridge is like a country invaded by the Sphinx. To answer the monster's conundrums has become the one absorbing occupation. All other pursuits are suspended, everything less urgent seems unimportant and fantastic; the learner ridicules the love of knowledge, and the teacher with more or less misgiving gradually acquiesces; there is something more necessary, more indispensable, something that cannot so well wait,—

> ἡ ποικιλωδὸς Σφίγξ τὰ πρὸς ποσὶ σκοπεῖν
> μεθέντας ἡμᾶς τἀφανῆ προσήγετο.

I hold, then, that the influence of competition at Cambridge has increased, is increasing, and ought to be diminished; that the teaching class should set their faces against it, and study to use every means by which it may be moderated. If, therefore, it appears that one main reason why learning does not flourish is that education, depending mainly on the examination system, does not require learning, I consider that education itself suffers from this system. I would deliver education from its dependence, and, without renouncing the undeniable advantages of strict and well-conducted examinations, I would use them as little as possible for the motive or incentive to study. I would appeal directly to the student's love of knowledge; I would endeavour in all ways to kindle it, but especially by improving the quality of the teaching; and, even if the result were some diminution of industry, I should find full consolation in the improvement of tone.

But those who maintain that the interests of learning and education in a University are conflicting have still another argument. They say that the German system, which favours learning, leaves the student entirely without personal care or moral discipline; that it simply provides him with food for the understanding, but takes no pains to preserve him from vice or bad habits. The English system, they say, provides moral and religious instruction, and attaches greater importance to this than to the imparting of mere knowledge. It is thus driven to make certain arrangements which, as it happens, are not favourable to learning. No doubt the *college* system makes the great difference between an English and foreign University. Instead of leaving our students to live as they please in the town, we have established large boarding-houses called colleges, in which the students live under a certain discipline, and with a certain family life. It is very plausibly maintained that here the English system is superior to the German, and that for this superiority we may be content to sacrifice something in learning. It is certainly true that the college system keeps down the character of the teaching class. I have already pointed out that, the lecturers being chosen from the fellows, and the fellows as a general rule from the students of the particular college, it may easily happen that a man may rise to be a lecturer, without any par- ticular merit, through happening to be the best man at a small college. I have also remarked that, as each college undertakes to give its students a complete training, the lecturers are required to lecture on too many subjects, and so prevented from that concentration which is a condition of profound learning. But are these evils inseparable from the college system? Is it not possible to give the students family life and discipline in a boarding-house without at the same time undertaking their whole education? And, again, is it necessary that having lived in a particular boarding-house should confer a claim to the greatest reward of merit that is known to the University, a fellowship?

But what are the definite changes for which I plead? I plead for much more than an alteration in machinery; still there are two or three changes[1] which I regard as essential. These are as follows:—

1. Let the fellowships at every college be thrown open to the whole University. In other words, let the greatest rewards of learning, and the position of teachers, be given to the ablest men and best teachers. This requires, I believe, no change in the statutes of any college. It requires simply a change of practice. Now why do the colleges make a general practice of giving their fellowships to their own men? Without denying

[1] I confine myself here to such changes as the colleges may make for themselves. It seems to me possible in the way here indicated to bring the University back to a healthy state without any new legislation. If Parliament were called in, another way of attaining the same end would more naturally be adopted, some such way as that sketched out in the evidence given by Professor Jowett and Mr. Fowler before Mr. Ewart's Committee.

that they may be partly influenced by the consideration that they know their own men best, and have had better opportunities of testing their worth, we may safely affirm that their principal motive is different. Their object undeniably is to attract students. A college is considered attractive where the fellowships are good and the competition is not excessive; in other words, where a little merit gets a great reward. It is surely unnecessary to use arguments in order to show that it is not for the interests of the public that there should exist this protection for mediocrity. The colleges might come to consider it not less opposed to their own interests, if they would cease to pride themselves upon the number of wranglerships, Porson prizes, &c. carried off by their undergraduates, and begin to place their pride in the number of learned and distinguished men they could assemble in their Combination-Room.

2. Let the instruction given in the University be made altogether independent of the college system. That is to say, let the lectures at every college be open to the whole University; let it no longer be considered necessary for each college to furnish a complete course of instruction; and let each lecturer be directly interested in increasing the numbers of his class. In other words, remove the protection which is now given to secondrate lecturing by the college system. The existing abuse is obvious. It is not possible that the staff of a small college should, as a rule, furnish lectures equal to those given, for example, in Trinity. Even a small college man must allow the rule, though he may remember distinguished exceptions. Yet Trinity refuses to let the men of other colleges attend its good

lectures, and the small college refuses to excuse its own students from attending its own inferior lectures. The system of private tuition is applied as a rough remedy, but it is a remedy which is scarcely better than the disease. If, on the other hand, all the lecture-rooms were open, and each lecturer received a capitation fee for each attendant in his lecture-room, there would spring up a competition among lecturers which would at once inspire life into a dying organization, and the private tutor would almost disappear. Nor is it to be supposed that the effect of such a change would be to crowd the lecture-rooms of Trinity and St. John's, and to empty those of the small colleges. The small colleges are not so completely inferior, and their inferiority would be removed by the throwing open of their fellowships. Their character would perhaps be changed. Instead of being copies of each other, they might find it advisable to give themselves a more individual character, and to devote themselves to special studies. One might make itself a school of law, another of theology, another of natural science. But the proper character of the college, as exerting control and enforcing discipline, would remain what it is. The tutor would, just as much as now, require attendance at a given number of lectures, only they would not necessarily be lectures within the college.

The college organization might also be very serviceable in providing for the wants of the poll-men. There are at Cambridge a vast number of students who want either abilities or inclination for serious study, or both, or whose education has through special circumstances been neglected. There are also a certain number of

considerable intelligence and cultivation who come to
the University rather for the sake of the society than
with the intention of going through any regular course
of study. These two classes of men are very different;
but they are alike in this, that it is not for them that
the University exists, and that they are there by a kind
of sufferance. It has even been questioned whether
such sufferance should be extended to the former class,
and it is certain that their preponderance in lecture-
rooms is a perpetual discouragement to lecturers; and
their preponderance in society, if it adds a certain
vivacity to university life, lowers the intellectual tone
and makes it more difficult to maintain discipline. In
this Essay I have left them entirely out of consideration,
and have throughout regarded the undergraduate as
advanced intellectually a stage before the sixth-form
schoolboy, though I well know that he is often several
stages behind. I have done so because it seems to me
clear that this intellectual element, whether or no it be
tolerated at Cambridge, ought never to be allowed to
interfere with the proper work of the place, and must
be entirely neglected when we are considering how the
studies of the University should be arranged. But we
may make it welcome to any surplus power and any
accidental conveniences we may find at our disposal.
Now, as every college must have a staff of officers who
are much occupied in the mere management of the institution, and are thus unable to concentrate themselves, as
I wish to see university teachers doing, upon a special
department of learning, but who are learned men and
not without leisure time, it would seem that we have
here the surplus power required. Besides affording to

genuine students discipline, which they do not much
need, and the society of mature and enlightened men,
which they need above all things, the colleges may
undertake to supply an inferior kind of instruction in
separate classes, conducted by a different set of teachers,
to those various descriptions of the intellectually indigent
that make up a large proportion of the poll.

3. But these changes would not by themselves give
the teaching a high quality, though they would make it
effective for its purpose. So long as the tripos domi-
nates, the teachers will always be trainers, though they
may be good trainers. This evil is chiefly felt at Cambridge, and the way to remove, or at least diminish,
it, without losing the advantages of the examination
system, is pointed out by Oxford. Let the names in
each class of every tripos be arranged alphabetically.
This simple change would, I think, at once clear away
all that vulgarity of competition of which I have spoken.
The abler men would feel just so much restraint in the
necessity of securing their first as would keep them
sober in their studies; but within these limits they
would be free. They would have leisure to look around
them and before them, without fancying an examiner
in every bush. They would begin to use their minds
naturally, instead of warping and straining them to suit
an artificial model. They would sometimes indulge,
instead of habitually stifling, intellectual curiosity, and
they would not accustom themselves to dismiss every
thing new or original in thought as being certain not
to be *set*. By the same change the teacher also would
be set free. He would no longer feel it almost a duty
to be commonplace. He would no longer be afraid

of making the pupil think, lest thought should damage his chance in the examination. The *frigida curarum fomenta* would be left behind, and the intercourse of teacher and pupil would become intellectual, elevating, fruitful to both.

It is to be hoped, at the same time, that the triposes may become smaller. Competition will be less stimulated by the chance of being high in a list of twenty or thirty men than in a list of ninety or a hundred. And this result may be obtained by means which will at the same time benefit the University by encouraging variety of study. By fostering as much as possible the smaller triposes, and by constantly recommending students to take up some branch of moral or natural science, we should at last obtain a number of triposes all held in nearly equal respect, and all of moderate size. Besides the allaying of the competitive fever, which would follow, I think this change would operate beneficially upon the tone of undergraduate society. The intellectual part of the conversation of undergraduates must be mainly furnished, however morbidly unwilling they may be to *talk shop*, by their studies; and if these studies were made more various, there would be more intellectual unlikeness, more ideas to be communicated, and conversation would become richer.

It may be urged that a new difficulty will be created by introducing the alphabetical order into the triposes, at the same time that the fellowships are thrown open to the University. In this system, it may be said, how are the fellowships to be awarded? It will not then be possible, as it is now, to determine the comparative merit of two candidates by simple reference to the calendar. It will be necessary to introduce fellowship examinations held by the colleges, which will produce just as much competition as the present tripos, and which will not be regarded with so much respect or deference. The university examination, it is said, is entirely above all suspicion of corruption, and is also most searching. A college examination would of necessity be less searching and less free from suspicion. You would abolish a perfectly satisfactory method of awarding fellowships and introduce a very unsatisfactory one. I grant that the tripos does, on the whole, very satisfactorily test the merit of the students in special departments. Mischievous as I believe it to be in its indirect influence through attempting too much, I do not deny that its decisions on the whole and roughly are correct. It would be very unreasonable for the colleges to set them aside and supersede them by private decisions of their own, which would neither receive nor deserve half so much respect. But to admit this is not to admit that fellowships ought to be awarded by a simple reference to the calendar. The calendar can only prove that a candidate is good and sound in some special branch of study. Every one will admit that a fellow should be such a person, but it is quite another thing to affirm that such a person has a right to be a fellow. A fellow of a college is a member of a learned society, of a society that exists for the purpose of promoting science and scholarship, and that is occupied in education. Now, it may easily happen that a high wrangler or a high first-class man has very little pretensions to be a member of such a society. The wrangler may chance to be totally

P

without what we have learnt lately to call "cultivation." He may, in fact, be for all the ordinary purposes of life an entirely uneducated and ignorant man. He must, indeed, possess a considerable power of consecutive thought and considerable industry. But there is no necessity whatever that he should be in any sense of the word intellectual, or that he should take any pleasure even in his own special pursuit. It is not to be imagined that he is always a man with a natural taste for science. He is often merely a shrewd man of business, who has seen his way through mathematical study to a pension of two or three hundred a year. The same shrewdness which procured him the pension is likely to reveal to him the inutility of pursuing his studies after it is won. If the high wrangler may easily be uncultivated, the high classic may just as easily be a dilettante. A little natural taste for literature, a good memory, and a good school suffice to place many in the first class of the classical tripos, though their reasoning power is very slightly trained, their range of information very narrow, and though they have not even formed, what the mathematical man has formed, the habit of industry.

In short, the merit of the tripos as a standard for fellowships is merely negative. It is a serviceable means of preventing thoroughly bad elections. But for this purpose it is not necessary that the man should be placed. It might be an understanding in the colleges that no one could sit for a fellowship who had not taken a first in some tripos. If this rule were adopted, no gross corruption would be possible. The only question is, How would you compare two men who had both taken a first? Now, for this purpose the placing is assuredly of no great use. The two men often went out in different years or different triposes; in which cases they cannot be compared at all. Even when their names appeared in the same list, the comparison between them is perfectly nugatory. For it is only their acquirements in one department that are compared, whereas the fellowship should be a reward of general intellectual merit. On this system a tenth wrangler, grossly ignorant of all ancient and modern literature, may be preferred to a twentieth wrangler who reads Goethe. It seems to me that the difficulty would be best solved by requiring all the candidates, assumed to be first-class men, to write an English essay upon one of several subjects put before them. In this way you might discover whether the classical man had any power of thought and the mathematician any power of language. The mere classic would be detected by his reasoning, and the mere mathematician by his spelling; and in this way you would readily distinguish the truly intellectual man from the highly-trained schoolboy.

The reader will see that my object is not merely to alter the machinery of the University, though I think some alterations in the machinery most important, but to recommend quite a different conception of what a university education should be. He will see my drift clearly by considering education under three heads: the motive to study, the instruction, the examination or test. Of these three parts, Cambridge regards the last, that is the test, as all-important, and it finds that it is possible to combine with a very accurate system of examination an exceedingly powerful motive, viz.

competition. In this plan the second part, that is the instruction, becomes dependent on examination and competition. Nothing is taught with any care, but what is likely to be set in the examination, and nothing is learnt except with a view to success in it. In place of this I recommend a plan which has the instruction as its focus. I would have the instruction made at all costs the best possible, and every means taken, first to procure the ablest teachers, and next to enable them to cultivate their powers to the utmost. For the motive I would trust mainly to the stimulating power of good instruction. I allow that this motive would be less powerful than competition over the average man, but I maintain that it would be a purer and wholesomer motive; and that it would exercise a ripening instead of a retarding influence upon the character. It would produce moderate industry continued through life and producing great results, whereas the present system produces overwork, followed by listlessness and achieving nothing. Moreover it would be reinforced by a rational and manly ambition—an ambition for the great prizes of life, honour or fortune or station, an ambition for success according as each man conceives success; whereas the present system drops a curtain over the coming life, consigns the student blindfold to his private tutor, and expects him to take for granted that these same marks, the currency of the University, if a man can hoard up a sufficient fund of them, are legal tender for everything that human beings covet.

I will conclude by briefly enumerating the advantages of what I may call the teaching system over the examining system.

First, it is incomparably better for the teachers. The present system does not consider the interest of the teacher at all. It is wonderful how much interest is taken in the student until he takes his degree, and how little afterwards. It is of course quite right that control and supervision should cease, but it seems to me most important that, in assigning the duties of the younger lecturers, pains should be taken to give them as much opportunity and as much inducement as possible to prosecute their studies further. I have no doubt that this is often done as far as the system permits: it is not the men that are in fault; it is the examination system, which makes learning in the teacher superfluous, and the college system, which puts the good and bad lecturer upon the same footing. The result is, that there is a perpetual difficulty in prevailing upon the abler men to stay at Cambridge; and various methods have been proposed for bribing them to remain and devote themselves to teaching. You could bribe them if you offered them a career. Many men who are driven to the bar would be contented with a moderate income that they might increase by their own exertions, leisure to follow their tastes, a position of real influence, and an opportunity of rising to distinction.

The influence of the teaching system upon the reading-man I have already discussed. His studies would be made more manly and free: he would pass rapidly out of the schoolboy stage, instead of being artificially detained in it. But there is a further advantage of which I have not spoken. It is often said, in arguing against the professorial system, that, after all, the student only gets from a professor what he might get as well from a book. This is true of a professor who merely delivers formal harangues and then disappears. But it is one of the greatest advantages of the system of learned lecturers which I have advocated, that it gives the reading-man the society, and to some extent friendship, of a man who is an authority on his subject. It is deceptive to compare him to a book. In the first place he is a great number of books; next, he is a book that can be questioned; and a book that can put questions; and a book that can recommend other books; and, last not least, he is a book in English. As a rule, good books are in German, and it may happen that the student does not read German.

Next, the teaching system would be most beneficial to that class of students who, without being in the strict sense reading-men, are intelligent, and can take an interest in literature, science, and scholarship. Upon this class the general cultivation of a country depends, as its eminence in the commonwealth of learning depends upon the reading-men. The present system, with its monotonous drill, its sedulous elaboration of minute details, is not calculated for them. What they want, and what is really best for them, is general views; and these the reading-men also cannot dispense with. A good course of lectures would offer such general views, and the class I speak of, the dilettanti of the lecture-room, would be infinitely the better for them.

Lastly, the teaching system would be beneficial to the whole country. Those who propose to sacrifice learning for what they consider the good of the students, do not seem to me distinctly to conceive the magnitude of the sacrifice they propose. They propose to sacrifice the intellectual rank and character of the country, which is left to chance when the Universities renounce learning. Private thinkers and amateur writers may by accident rise to support our credit, just as, if we should disband our army, volunteers might succeed in defending the coasts. But how much we all lose, nay, how much we have already lost, by our strange system, may be judged by any one who will consider what has been done by university professors in the countries where the professorial system is adopted. If we take the single department of philosophy, is it not evident that, if the English system had been followed in the Scotch Universities, there would have been no Scotch school of philosophy? And has not the German school sprung entirely from the Universities? Were not Kant, Fichte, Schelling, and Hegel, without exception, university professors? That barrenness in ideas, that contempt for principles, that Philistinism which we hardly deny to be an English characteristic now, was not always so. In the seventeenth century, the author of "Argenis" considered the principal fault of English people to be their reckless hardihood in speculation, their love of everything new and untried. In the eighteenth century, Montesquieu called us the philosophic nation; and at the same date, Holberg, the Dane—to mention one more among many instances—describes England as the land of heroes and philosophers. It is not then the English character which is averse to thought; we are not naturally the plain practical people that we sometimes boast, and sometimes blush, to be. If in the present century we have fallen somewhat behind, and instead of overrunning the Continent with our ideas, as in the days of Locke,

Newton, and Bentley, have suffered in our own island the invasion of French and German philosophies, it is assuredly from no inherent weakness. We must seek for other causes, and among them we shall find this, that in the warfare of thought we have hoped to resist regular troops with volunteers.

## VIII.

## ENGLISH IN SCHOOLS.

In the great controversy which rages between the advocates of a scientific education and the advocates of a classical education, both sides appear to me to make good half their case. The men of science are irresistible when they allege the superiority of things over words, of a knowledge of actual facts over a knowledge of opinions, and of what has been said about facts. The men of scholarship are unanswerable when they point out that the knowledge of things is mainly derived through the knowledge of words. Each party has an excellent watchword. We cannot do without facts in education, and we cannot do without words. If there is any result which may be said to have been fairly attained in the educational controversy, it is this,—that science must come in and that language must not go out.

I say this at starting in order that you may know my standing-point. I am frankly with the classicists to this extent, that I consider language to be one of the most essential and important parts of the educational course. But I find myself widely differing from them as to the manner in which language should be taught. The method which they would make universal, and continue through the whole educational period, seems to me suitable only to the later stages of education, and to a certain class of boys. What I would make the universal basis of instruction in language they omit altogether.

This is the subject, upon which I ask your attention this evening. Education has been for a long time an interesting question; since the Reform Bill it is acknowledged as the question of the day. With the advance of democracy not only does the question become more pressing, but it changes its character. Education must henceforth not only extend its area, but it must become a much more intense influence, because it has to cultivate not only a new class, but a rude class. Hitherto but a small part of what is properly education has been given in schools and colleges. That politeness which Mr. Carlyle finds in its perfection in our aristocracy was not imparted to them at Eton or Oxford. It is the tradition of their families and homes. All that a gentleman asks of a schoolmaster for his son is book-learning; the higher moral education, almost all that is included under the word "cultivation," he furnishes himself, by his own example, by the society, by the books in the midst of which his children are reared. But the problem before us now is to educate the whole nation. We have to educate a class who have none of these domestic traditions, no inherited refinement, no common stock of literature forming an intellectual atmosphere around every child. If we teach this class what we have hitherto taught the other class, the result will not be the same. For them the schoolmaster must do much more, because the parents and the home have done much less. To them he must become a kind of priest or missionary of culture. He must no longer content himself with imparting naked facts, or rules, or book-learning, as though he taught those who are surrounded with other ennobling and refining influences. On the contrary, he must consider that just so much enlightenment, breadth of view, liberality, and magnanimity as he can contrive to impart to his pupils, just so much and no more will they carry with them into the world. If then the present classical system is inadequate already as the instrument of education to a class, much more will it be found inadequate to the civilizing of a nation.

In what shape, then, is language to enter into education? This is the question, and the answer of the classicists is, "In the shape of Latin and Greek." We are all familiar with the arguments by which they support this. They speak of the unrivalled merit of the classical literatures, of the vast influence which those literatures have had upon modern thought; again, they speak of the perfection of the classical languages, of the invaluable mental training which is involved in learning them; they tell us also that as instruments of education they are all the better for being dead languages, and for being unlike our own, because they demand on that account more effort, and are more stimulating to curiosity. In short, they recommend the learning of Latin and Greek on two principal grounds: first for the process itself, and next for the results; for the benefits derived in the learning, and for those furnished by the learning.

Now I admit the force of both arguments, but of both with a limitation. The learning of Greek and Latin is an admirable mental exercise, but only to minds in a certain state and after a certain preparation; the Greek and Latin literatures are a most valuable acquisition, but it is only those who study Greek and Latin very deeply and very long that can be said to make this acquisition. In short, if in classical education there is a valuable process and a valuable acquisition, a large proportion of those who receive a classical education begin too soon to reap the benefit of the process, and leave off too soon to make the acquisition.

I will now try to establish these two points. First I will endeavour to show that Latin is properly an advanced subject, that it should not be placed early in education, and that it presupposes a certain preparation of the mind.

Grammar is certainly not a very easy science. If we intended to proceed from what is easiest to what is more difficult, we should certainly not begin with grammar. We should prefer to begin either with some natural science, dealing with visible things of a particular kind, and classifying them, or with some science like geometry or arithmetic, which, though abstract, yet deal with one or two abstractions such as magnitude or number at a time. The abstractions of grammar are numerous and difficult; it deals with things which are not visible, and things which are symbolical; it deals with a double system of symbols, words and letters; it deals with mental processes, and requires that which is most unnatural to children—introspection.

Nevertheless, there are two very strong reasons why grammar, in spite of its difficulty, should be taught early. The first is, that grammar systematizes a knowledge which the child already possesses. Every boy begins his education with one great intellectual acquisition—he can talk. The power of talking implies a quantity of knowledge, an activity of the powers of generalization and abstraction, which we do not always sufficiently appreciate. Words are the boy's strong point. There is no other class of facts of which he knows anything considerable. If you were to undertake to teach him botany, you would find perhaps at the outset that he knew the names of half a dozen flowers; all facts beyond these you would have to communicate at the same time that you communicated the laws of them. But when the boy begins to learn grammar, he already knows several hundred words; and he not only knows them, but he can arrange them with considerable accuracy into sentences. The science may be a difficult one, but he already possesses an implicit knowledge of it; its laws may in form be new to him, but their substance he is familiar with already; he recognizes their truth as soon as they are stated; his memory furnishes him with illustrations of them; he is able to devise new illustrations, and his whole life, every speech he hears uttered, every speech he utters, every story-book he looks into, increases the mass of facts which these laws explain.

The other great reason is, that words are pleasurable and delightful things in themselves. They are also the means or instruments of almost all our intellectual pleasures. Whether or no you teach a boy grammar he will certainly be occupied the greater part of his day with words. His memory will be full of rhymes and songs, good or bad; his imagination will be crammed with tales and stories. He will himself talk and write; he will be influenced by the talk and writing of others. Therefore, though the laws of words be difficult, yet in teaching them early you follow the bent and irresistible bias of the boy's mind. If you can introduce clearness and order into his thoughts on this subject, you introduce clearness into a good half of his thoughts. It is better to make a road in the direction in which people actually travel, even though the engineering be difficult, than to make it on smooth ground where nobody comes.

There are, therefore, overwhelming reasons for teaching grammar, and for teaching it early. But—and it is this to which I would call your attention—neither of those reasons apply to the Latin grammar. It is good, I have said, to teach the laws of words, because the boy already knows a multitude of words, and has a practical knowledge of the use of them. True, but the words he knows are English, not Latin ones; and it is English, not Latin speech, with which he has a practical acquaintance. By substituting Latin for English, you deprive him entirely of his advantage; you cheat him of all that he has gained. He had mastered in infancy one difficult acquisition, speech, and in this a store of implicit knowledge: what the boy already knows, let him learn to know consciously, give him names for the different kinds of words that he is able already to distinguish practically, and for the different linguistic operations he already performs with ease. On the basis of speech in this way grammar would naturally be placed as the first story of the tower of human knowledge. But at this point the schoolmaster steps in, and stays the building by confounding the language.

Again, I have said that it is a good thing to teach the laws of words, because the boy is, and must be, constantly occupied with words. But it is English, not Latin words, with which he is occupied. The Latin grammar does not help him to express himself clearly, or understand a speech or a lecture or a play better; the books which feed his imagination are not Cæsar's Commentaries or Livy's History, but Ivanhoe, or Robinson Crusoe; within his experience the object seldom stands in the accusative case, and the instrument never in the ablative; the poems of Scott and Tennyson are not written in hexameters and pentameters. The Latin grammar, therefore, whatever use it may have, does not answer this particular purpose of introducing order into the boy's habitual thoughts, and classifying facts with which he is continually occupied.

Thus, while I see strong reasons for teaching grammar early, I see no good reasons for teaching Latin grammar early. And I see this strong reason against it, that grammar is a very difficult and intricate science, and that Latin grammar is particularly difficult. It may seem strange to you that I should speak of Latin grammar as difficult, though boys of every degree of intellect have been put through it, and a great many, not particularly clever, have been supposed to master it without much trouble. But the truth is, they have not really mastered it. By using the memory a good deal, and the reason a little, they have acquired the practical knowledge of it which is necessary to read and write Latin. But as a science they have not learnt it; in fact, as a science it is not taught; to attempt to teach it to children would be too hopeless. What is taught for grammar is not principles, but arbitrary rules, conveyed often in doggerel verses. Here, indeed, is the great proof of the unfitness of Latin grammar for young boys, that it is necessary to deprive the subject of its scientific character before you can teach it. In the contest between the children and the grammar the children have the better. They have more influence upon it than it has upon them; instead of the children becoming grammatical, the grammar becomes childish.

My conclusion, then, is that when the classicists recommend Latin and Greek as being an admirable discipline for the mind, they are right indeed, but only if they speak of a mind considerably advanced. For a boy of nine or ten—and many boys begin Latin a good deal earlier—I do not think it a good study. It is too difficult and too remote from the affairs of life, and gratifies no curiosity that is ordinarily felt at that age. But the case would be very different at the age of thirteen or fourteen. Let us suppose that by that time the boy has been familiarized with the great principles of grammar in his own language, that he has read with care in class several English classical books, that he has tried his hand at English composition, that he has been taught to understand rhythm and metre, that he has committed to memory much English poetry, and has been taught to recite it with just emphasis. I believe that after this preparation he would take up the Latin grammar with different feelings. One half of its difficulty would be removed. He would be familiar with the general laws of the construction of sentences; what is common to the syntax of all languages he would have mastered in his own. If we suppose him to have learnt some French, he would have had an introduction to the laws of inflection. He would pass, by regular gradation, through a slightly inflected to an abundantly inflected language, and instead of being suddenly overwhelmed, as he now is, by a host of inflexions, he would cope with them and overcome them in detail. He would also take up the subject with stronger interest and curiosity. The analysis of his own language would have constantly shown him Latin in the background; French would bring it still nearer; and he would take up the Latin grammar at the moment when his mind was full of questions to which it would furnish the answer. And if among the English books read in class was the translation of Plutarch, he might already at fourteen have a familiarity with the ancient world and an interest in it which is altogether wanting now to many finished scholars.

I pass to my second point of disagreement with the classicists. It is in the estimate they form of the value of the classical literatures themselves to those who can read them in the original. I agree with them heartily when they speak of the humanizing and educating power of great works of genius. All cultivation lies in this. There is nothing else in education which could not better be spared. That the common spirits among men should pass under the influence of the greater and rarer spirits, this is the chief thing for us to aim at. All mere knowledges seem to me of less value. Mr. Carlyle somewhere proposes the question—"Which would we English people sooner give up, our Indian empire or our Shakespeare?" A similar question may be proposed in education, and I should be disposed to answer it as Mr. Carlyle does. For works of genius I would give up the multiplication table. But between this position and the position that we ought to teach all boys to read Cicero and Plato in the original there is a great gulf. I shall not enter here into the interminable and unpractical question of the comparative excellence of the ancients and the moderns. My objection to the plan proposed is simply that it cannot possibly be executed. You cannot teach all boys to read Cicero and Plato in the originals. You may teach *some* boys. Those whose tastes and circumstances mark them out for a life of study can and ought to be made intimate with the great classical writers. I hope there will always be a large class undergoing this higher kind of education. But the other class, which will always be still larger, of those who leave school at fourteen or sixteen, *cannot*—nothing is more certain—master Latin and Greek enough to read the greater classical writers with pleasure in the originals. Obviously they do not. Look around you at the men of business who received a classical education up to the age of sixteen. Are their minds full of the 'Idea' of Plato? Do they judge of a new play by a Greek standard? Do they bring their Aristotle to bear on the politics of the day?

Now I would ask the classicists, on their system what becomes of these boys? Their system is literary. They say, and I heartily agree with them, that if you would cultivate the mind, you must imbue it with good literature. If, then, the mind of the classically-educated boy who leaves school at sixteen is not imbued with good literature, on their own showing it is not educated. The more you exalt literature, the more you must condemn the classical system. Of what advantage is it, if the boys do not, after all, gain the treasure, to have spent several years in straining after it? What avail all the merits and beauties of the classics to those who never attain to appreciate them? If they never arrive, what was the use of their setting out? That a country is prosperous and pleasant is a reason for going to it, but it is not a reason for going half-way to it. If you cannot get all the way to America, you had better surely go somewhere else. If you are a parent, and think that your son is not fit to go to Cambridge, you send him into the City or into the army. You do not send him part of the way to Cambridge; you do not send him to Royston or Bishop Stortford.

Probably the classicists would represent this comparison as inexact. They would say that appreciation of the classics is not a thing of which you must have all or none; that the men of business I speak of gain something from the great writers of antiquity, though not all that might be gained, and that they gain the power of reading them, though not, perhaps, with ease. I believe, however, that this is not generally the fact. I believe that of those who leave at sixteen very few have received any perceptible influence from the classics considered as literature, and that even the power of reading them is soon lost, the exercise of it being attended with no pleasure or satisfaction.

You will have perceived by this time what position I wish to give to Latin in education. I regard it as the beginning of the higher, the professional, or learned education. But as I do not think it a good subject to learn early, I see no reason for separating those boys who are intended for the professions from the others, nor for sacrificing in any degree either class to the other. I would have a common education for all boys up to about the age of fourteen. At this age I would have Latin begun. Those, therefore, who leave at fourteen would learn no Latin. Those who leave at sixteen would learn

Latin for two years; and this I think would be well, not because of the beauties of the classics, but because of the mental exercise, which at this age I think invaluable, and because of the light which is thrown from Latin upon modern languages and literature.

But now, of what is this common education to consist which I would give to all boys up to the age of fourteen? A large part of it, I think, should be scientific; but it is not of this that I would speak now. I do not quarrel with the principles of the classicists, but with their means. I would reach their goal, but by a different way. I think they are right in the importance they attach to words, but I would substitute English words for Latin ones. I think they are right in introducing boys to great works of genius, but I would substitute modern genius for ancient. In a word, I advocate a comprehensive and elaborate English education.

I do not think it can be necessary to give reasons why boys should be taught their own language thoroughly. Everywhere but in England, I imagine, the native language makes a prominent part of the educational course. And I do not suppose there is any rational man who would not admit it to be a most desirable thing that the great mass of our population should have a real intelligent interest in English literature, a knowledge of the great English writers of past ages, a discrimination of the best English writers of the present. I am not generally a very sanguine reformer; yet I confess I see no reason in the nature of things for that gross ignorance with which we are surrounded. It is surely not a necessity that persons in decent circumstances, in decent society, persons who have passed several years at school, should go through life without any intellectual tastes, without any sense of literary excellence, falling victims with barbarian simplicity to every tinsel allurement of style, entirely outside the influence of living genius, and scarcely aware, even as an historical fact, that they are the countrymen of Bacon, Shakespeare, and Milton. I confess that this seems to me as remediable as it is lamentable. The schoolmaster might set this right. Every boy that enters the school is a *talking* creature. He is a performer, in his small degree, upon the same instrument as Milton and Shakespeare. Only do not sacrifice this advantage. Do not try by artificial and laborious processes to give him a new knowledge before you have developed that which he has already. Train and perfect the gift of speech, unfold all that is in it, and you train at the same time the power of thought and the power of intellectual sympathy, you enable your pupil to think the thoughts and to delight in the words of great philosophers and poets.

No one, I say, denies the desirableness of teaching English. The position of the classicists is, that English is taught indirectly in teaching Latin and Greek, and that it is exceedingly difficult or impossible to teach English directly.

Now the first assertion I must answer, for want of space, in a single sentence. I admit that in the thorough learning of Latin and Greek a good deal of English is indirectly learnt. But the boys we are speaking of, those who leave school at fourteen or sixteen, do not learn Latin and Greek thoroughly, and I believe that very little, if any, knowledge of English is conveyed in the learning of a little Latin and Greek. I pass to the alleged difficulty or impossibility of teaching English directly.

It is easy to understand the embarrassment of a teacher who endeavours to apply to English the methods he has been accustomed to use in teaching Latin. The two languages do not stand in the same relation to the pupil's mind. A native language cannot be taught in the same way as a foreign language. In a foreign language, if the pupil does not know a rule, he breaks it; but in his native language he observes it from habit, whether he knows it or not. In a foreign language the pupil, if he does not understand a word, looks it out; but in his own language he rarely perceives his own ignorance, and attaches some idea, right or wrong or half-right, to almost every word he meets with. In a foreign language the pupil has a definite problem to solve; he has to find out the meaning of the foreign words before him, and to represent them in their English equivalents: in his native language he perceives the meaning at a glance, and he has no other language in which to represent it. All this proves plainly that it is impossible to teach English in the way in which you teach Latin, but it does not prove that you cannot teach English in some other way.

An attempt is sometimes made to meet the difficulty by falling back upon our oldest writers. Chaucer is to an English boy not unlike a Latin classic; he is sufficiently foreign to need the same kind of explanation, so that lessons in Chaucer may be given very similar to the lessons ordinarily given in Virgil. Now I sympathise strongly with the attempt now making to revive the knowledge of our early literature; and if we see, as I hope we soon shall, a regular series of English classics introduced into our principal schools, I should desire to see Chaucer and Piers Plowman read occasionally in the highest class. But I think it would be altogether perverse to give these writers precedence over those of the later and greater centuries. Let us introduce our native language as such, and not in the disguise of a foreign language. Let us give it a method of its own, as well as a place of its own, and find new bottles for the new wine.

If we dismiss from our minds altogether the misleading analogy of Latin, and consider simply the end we have in view, and the direct way towards it, we shall find, I believe, that the proper course of an English education is nearly as follows :—

The boys being assumed able to read, the first thing is to teach them to read well. By reading well, I do not mean merely correctly, but distinctly and expressively. I mean, in short, that they should be taught elocution. To this I attach great importance. It is more than one hundred years since Bishop Berkeley propounded the question, whether half the learning and talent of England were not lost because elocution was not taught in schools and colleges. The same question might be repeated now, so slow are we English people in taking a hint. But it is not for its practical use that I wish to see elocution introduced into education ; not so much to prevent English people from swallowing their words as they do now, to the astonishment and dismay of foreigners who are trying to learn our language, nor yet in order that those whose profession or business in after-life demands public speaking may be taught to speak with effect. It is mainly because I think that by this means more than any other may be evoked in the minds of boys a taste for poetry and eloquence. This taste is really very universal ; generally where it appears wanting it is only dormant, and it is dormant because no means have ever been taken to cultivate the sense of rhythm, and to make the delightfulness of speech understood. Along with elocution would go naturally English prosody; boys should be made familiar with the principal metres used by our poets: and all this they should be taught as much as possible by practice. They should be called upon to commit to memory a great deal of poetry, and then to recite it with due attention to the laws of metre and emphasis.

I put this at the beginning, because it requires little brain-work or reasoning, and because it may be made interesting to the youngest boys. The next step is the analysis of the language. The first part of this of course will be grammar. I would teach it carefully, and with perpetual examples from English authors, but I would not make mere grammar a very prominent part of the course. In the learning of a foreign language we know that when the grammar is mastered there remains a higher and a more difficult acquirement, upon which, however, depends all fineness and niceness of scholarship,—the exact determination of the meanings of words, and the distinguishing of synonyms. Now in the study of one's native language this may fairly be put much earlier, because the syntax, having been already practically taught in the nursery, requires much less attention.

I think that an exact knowledge of the meanings of English words is not very common even among highly educated people, which is natural enough, since their attention has been so much diverted to Latin and Greek ones. But the ignorance in this department of the class I have most in view, those who leave school at fourteen

or sixteen, is deplorable. It is far more than a mere want
of precision in the notions attached to words. It is far
more also than a mere ignorance of uncommon and philosophical words. There is a large class of words in the
language, originally perhaps philosophical, but which have
passed so completely into the common parlance of well-
educated people that they cannot now be called philosophical, but which remain to the class I speak of perfectly
obscure. The consequence is that such people, in reading
not merely abstruse books, but books in the smallest degree
speculative or generalizing, constantly mistake the meaning
of what they read. It is not that they understand their
author imperfectly; they totally misunderstand him, and
suppose him to say something which he does not say. It
is no wonder that such persons have no turn for reading;
in fact, it is scarcely to be wished that they should. But
all this is plainly owing to the fact that they have never
been taught English. It has always been supposed that
they knew their own language: but the language of
Bacon and Locke cannot be taught in the nursery. Our
language is full of terms invented by philosophers ancient
and modern, which from the philosophers have passed
into the mouths of educated men, and into books, but
which have not passed into the nursery, and are seldom
heard in family conversation. Those who pass through
a long and thorough education infallibly pick up these
words, but those whose education terminates sooner
do not, and for want of understanding them they are
shut out from all the more instructive part of English
literature.

I would therefore devote much time and care to the
explanation of words. I would take the words as they

occurred in the reading of English authors, and require a rigid account of them. Not only would the boy in this way gain an understanding of words hitherto unintelligible to him, but he would gain the utmost benefit from the effort to explain such words as he understood. The exertion of clothing a thought in a completely new set of words increases both clearness of thought and mastery over words. It is the test of a solid thought, that it will bear a change of clothing. Hollow and delusive thoughts are known by their always wearing the same formula, as spectres always appear in the same dress. Under this head of the explanation of words comes the distinguishing of synonyma. Almost all niceness of literary taste depends upon this. It is therefore by this exercise more than any other that your pupils will be brought gradually to appreciate those writers whom we call elegant. And this is the more important, because without some such training these writers will always be a sealed book. Whether or no Shakespeare be read in schools, he will continue to be in some degree appreciated by every one who has human feelings or imagination; every one who has an ear will admire Milton's music; but Addison and the poetry of Goldsmith will have little charm for those who have not been led to reflect on the finer proprieties of language.

Next after the explanation of words comes what I hope I may call, without being misunderstood, rhetoric. I do not mean here by rhetoric the art of persuasion, but all those arts and contrivances by which a limited number of words are made to express a practically unlimited number of conceivable things. Of these the principal is metaphor; and I think it important that the pupil's attention should be fixed on this subject long enough to make him perceive clearly what a large proportion of language is metaphorical, and also to make him distinctly aware of the presence of metaphor when he meets with it in reading, and conscious of it when he uses it himself. For this purpose, I would require him to give a precise account of the metaphors which may occur in the author who is being read, and to express the same thoughts in direct and unmetaphorical language.

There is one more most important subject which may conveniently be coupled with English—I mean logic. It may occur to you that this is too abstruse a subject for young boys, and also that, if taught at all, it should be taught independently. But the outline and leading principles of logic are not too abstruse for young boys, provided they are not presented to them in too technical a form. As every boy comes to your school a talking creature, so he comes to it a *reasoning* creature. The teacher has only, as I said before, to turn implicit knowledge into explicit. It will not be hard for him to show the pupil that when he makes general inferences he uses induction, and that when he draws particular conclusions he uses the syllogism. I would go no further than this— to bring out distinctly the notion of induction and deduction, and to make the pupil familiar with the syllogistic formula. But why connect this with English? For this reason: I am presuming throughout that a series of English classical writers is being read in class, and the problem is to draw as much instruction as possible from them. I have suggested, first, that the reading itself shall be accompanied with an explanation of the laws of elocution; next, that the syntax of each sentence shall be investigated; next, that the words shall be carefully explained, and their shades of meaning brought out; next, that the rhetorical contrivances, particularly the metaphors, shall be pointed out. But the analysis will evidently be incomplete unless we examine the writer's reasoning. For this purpose we require logic. I would have the pupils constantly exercised in stating the grounds upon which the writer's assertions were grounded, and drawing out his arguments into syllogisms.

The selection of the series of writers to be read in the classes is an important question. I should like to see it differing in different schools, but constant in some main features. You would naturally begin with what is most attractive to young boys, such as Macaulay's Lays, Kingsley's Heroes, Scott's poems and Tales of a Grandfather. You would put at the end of the course the older poets and the philosophical writers. But I should like to see introduced everywhere, about the middle of the course, Plutarch's Lives, in the translation, Pope's Iliad, and Worsley's Odyssey. I will undertake to say that the reading of these three books would more than counterbalance all that the boys might lose in the knowledge of antiquity by giving up the classics.

I have not forgotten that books of such size as those I have mentioned could not be read through and analysed in class. I am well aware that this could be done with only a very small part of each. The same is true of the Latin books which are now read, and the result in the case of these Latin books no doubt is, that either grammar or literature is sacrificed. The books read cannot influence the imagination and taste of the pupils unless they are read through; on the other hand, if they are read through, the grammatical analysis must be slurred for want of time, and they cease to discipline the reasoning powers. But with English books there is a way out of this difficulty. A small part of the book being read in class, the pupil might be required to read the rest at home, and might be put through some not too close examination in it. In this way a certain gentle constraint would be exerted over the boy's private reading. He would first find that he had not time to read trash; he would be driven against his will to good literature, and in due course he would find to his astonishment that good literature was much the more delightful reading.

This is the scheme of English education which I picture to myself, and I could detain you very long in enumerating its advantages. But I have already detained you long enough, and therefore I will only insist for a moment in conclusion upon one broad recommendation. Under this system any boy who goes to school at ten and leaves it at fourteen will have passed four years in reading the best sort of literature, books always instructive, elevating, and in many cases also delightful. In his own home, perhaps, he sees no books at all, or feeds only on monstrous romances, or becomes prematurely wise and rancorous and cynical by perpetual reading of newspapers. I am pleading for a class which have no intellectual atmosphere around them; in the conversation to which they listen there is no light or air for the soul's growth; it is a uniform gloomy element of joyless labour, bewildering detail, broken with scarcely a gleam of purpose or principle. Such a boy goes to school, and at fourteen he is taken away, having read a book and a half of Cæsar's Commentaries, two or three epistles of Ovid, and a book of Xenophon. In his mind, at the end of this time, what images have been deposited? There are some chaotic conceptions of Cæsar exhorting his troops, and of Grecian soldiers marching indefinitely through Asia at the rate of so many parasangs a day. What happened when these soldiers reached their destination it is likely enough he has never found out, because that is recorded in another part of the book. Towards cultivating his imagination and taste, towards enlarging his contemplations, this is all that has been done, whatever may have been done for his reason and memory. This is all that has been done in the only years of his life that are redeemed from money-making, the only years in which the missionaries of civility and cultivation can reach him. He goes back to the mill with no conception gained of a larger life, of a freer and clearer atmosphere, sharpened, if you will, a little, but cultivated not at all.

Even this statement is hardly strong enough. It is bad that his education should not have put him in the way of becoming a thoughtful and cultivated man. But that it should leave him in total ignorance of the literature of his own country is more and worse than this; it means that he is left not merely uncultivated, but absolutely uncivilized. He can have no link whatever with the past, he can have no citizenship, no country. Classical studies may make a man intellectual, but the study of the native literature has a moral effect as well. It is the true ground and foundation of patriotism. Now that the Americans, the Germans, the Italians, are almost drunk with the sense of their national greatness, it would surely be well if our own population could be brought to think of England otherwise than as a country where wages are low, manners very cold, the struggle for life intolerably severe. In the past we might find food for self-respect; surely we might find something interesting to tell our boys about their ancestors. We too are a great historic nation; we too have "titles manifold." This country is not some newly-discovered island in the Northern seas; even this London is no mere dreary collection of shops. It is literally true that in this city, in which I am now speaking to you, Hamlet was first brought out. The Long Parliament sat within two miles of you; Milton is buried in Cripplegate Church. These are simple facts, but it is the province of education to make them sink into the mind, and influence the character. The name of Milton sounds like any other name to those who have not pondered over his verses. I call that man uncivilized who is not connected with the past through the state in which he lives, and sympathy with the great men that have lived in it. And that the English people in general, and not merely a small class of them, should be civilized in this sense, does not seem to me a Utopian dream. Ordinary English boys seem to me quite capable of appreciating great thoughts. They seem to me quite capable of taking delight in the achievements and writings of their ancestors. No doubt they are liable to be led astray; they will not take most naturally to the best books; a little gentle constraint, as I have said, has to be used; their books must be prescribed for them at first, until the effort of coping with a great writer, the labour of following a high flight, has begun to be felt as invigorating and refreshing. But the chief thing they want is the opportunity and the guidance. The good books do not fall in their way, and they have no one to tell them what is good. What then might they not do, what growth in liberality and magnanimity might we not expect from them, if for four years of boyhood at least such books were forced into their hands, and such guidance were given to them?

Yet, certainly, if we only looked around us, it might seem a most Utopian dream. If we judge of what can be done by what has hitherto been done, we should pronounce it impossible that the lower half of our population could ever receive either cultivation or civilization; we should conclude that things must remain always as they have so long continued, and that a small number of cultivated men will always live in England in the midst of a vast half-barbarous population. We should think ourselves happy that this half-barbarous multitude belongs to the better class of barbarians, that it is hard-working, tolerably honest and good-natured, and that its worst faults are narrowness and dulness. What higher hopes could we form if we looked at the lower section of the middle class, and marked the small traces left upon the ordinary Englishman by several years of education? He has all the good qualities that nature gave him; he is industrious, conscientious, benevolent, persevering. But what remains to him of his education? What marks him out as civilized? Has he any high or liberal pleasures? Has he any intellectual dignity, any breadth of view? Does he ever generalize, ever philosophize? Has he any worthy end in life, any ideal? Or does he creep and labour, and "discuss the sewage question," and provide for his family?

From the past of our country, from the masterpieces of

our literature, would come most naturally the influence that might give back to the Englishman his self-respect. All the pride and strength of an aristocracy comes from the sense of ancestry, and every member of a historic nation may have something of this sense and something of the pride that springs from it. He has but to make himself familiar with the past. There is something in what Mr. Carlyle says, that the true Bible of every nation is its own history. And these same English people, whose deficiencies we have been lamenting, are at the same time—the coincidence is worth noting—singularly ignorant and incurious about English history. The National Portrait Gallery has lately been closed.[1] It has put before the eyes of London the whole eighteenth century of England. What an interesting, what a fascinating spectacle, provided for us by the life-long labours of a Hogarth, a Gainsborough, a Reynolds, and putting before us in one brilliant and grandiose pictorial epic all the gallantry and intelligence of our ancestors and the beauty of our great-grandmothers! They say it was a failure; it did not attract the public; and of those who visited it I wonder how many enjoyed what they saw. There you might see Pope's wrinkled mouth, and the delicate face of Addison. You might see the old traitor Lovat, and the Kitcat Club sipping their *thé*, and the poring eyes of Sam Johnson, and Goldsmith writing in his study, and the black brows of Thurlow. But all this people did not care to see. They did not even care to see the Duchess of Marlborough in her youth, nor the Gunnings, nor that village-maiden who went hanging on

[1] 1867.

the arm of her landscape painter to visit Burleigh House by Stamford Town. No! this did not hit the popular taste.

Yet for all this forgetfulness of the past, even though it lead to an equal carelessness of the future; for all this dull pre-occupation with the sordid present, I do not see why our countrymen should be despised. Is it their fault, or is it the fault of their education? We might despise them if in the hurry of business and money-making they had forgotten the lessons of their youth. But what lessons have they forgotten? What lessons have they ever had? What right have we to expect that they should look with interest upon the portraits of Addison, or Pope, or Johnson, or Burke, or Franklin, or Pitt? They left school at fourteen or sixteen, and their occupations in life have been such as to prevent them from forming new intellectual tastes since. They have had leisure enough, or they were bound to make leisure enough, for continuing the studies begun at school, provided they found their minds the better for doing so; but they have not had leisure enough to enter upon totally new studies. And a totally new study was the study of literature to them, after all the years spent over the Latin grammar and the Latin classics. Their education stopped short of this. It taught them, perhaps, something—if you will, something valuable—but one thing it did not do. It did not give them the key to literature, it did not open to them the world of books, it did not put them in possession of that inheritance which has been provided for every Englishman by the labours of philosophers, poets, and wits of three centuries. This inheritance belongs, I say, to every Englishman, but whether every Englishman shall enjoy it lies with the schoolmaster.

I do not blame the Englishman, then: I blame his education. And who is responsible for his education? Is it the parents or the schoolmaster? I fancy one reason why so little is done in the way of improvement is because there is so much shifting of responsibility. And in particular it seems to me that the schoolmaster does not assume the authority in the question to which he has a right. He regards himself as employed to teach some definite thing, and as having no concern with the question whether it be the best thing to teach. In the meanwhile the parent throws the question back upon the schoolmaster. He sends his son to school, trusting that there he will be taught the proper things. And thus the question what should be taught is not considered with a sense of responsibility by any one.

Whether or no it be his duty to consider it, certainly the schoolmaster is in the most favourable condition for doing so. Education is his business, and therefore he has opportunities of watching the effect of different sorts of instruction such as no one else can have. But it seems to me that he generally confines himself to studying methods and processes of teaching, and neglects the more important question what should be taught. He is, indeed, almost driven to take this for granted, not only by the force of tradition, but by that multitude of prizes and scholarships offered for proficiency in definite subjects, under the weight of which education in England is almost stifled. Still I will propose the question—Would not the schoolmaster take a higher view of his functions, and support the dignity of his profession better, if he took this matter also into his hands? He may, if he pleases, sell knowledge, and undertake to teach whatever parents require, without inquiring whether by doing so he is doing good or harm to the pupil. But is it not better that he should undertake to *educate* his pupil, to develop his powers and cultivate them to the utmost? and if he does so, must he not assume the right of judging, not only in what way subjects should be taught, but also what subjects should be taught?

## IX.

## THE CHURCH AS A TEACHER OF MORALITY.

Upon the question whether the Christian community is to be regarded by its teachers as one and homogeneous, or as divided between a small number of true believers, the children of light, and a large number of merely nominal believers, the disguised children of darkness, depends more than is commonly perceived the whole character of Christian teaching. Those teachers who take the latter view will practically abandon all moral questions; those who take the former will, unless some counteracting influence intervenes, occupy themselves as much with morality as with religion.

That the High Church party, who have generally shrunk much more than the Evangelicals from drawing the perilous line of demarcation, have nevertheless not occupied themselves much more with moral questions, is due to such a counteracting influence. They have been (until quite recently) for the most part conservatives, attached by temper and tradition to the existing order of things both political and social. They have been disposed to regard all moral questions as settled already; and when they have possessed activity of mind, they have exerted it not so much in speculative investigation of what ought to be held as in antiquarian inquiries into what has been held. But suppose a large and liberal Christian feeling to inspire men unshackled by a spirit of deference to authority, and it seems to me evident that it can only issue in a most searching revision and criticism of all the institutions, usages, and customs of society; in short, in a new political and a new ethical doctrine.

That no such result flows from Christian feeling, even when it is warm, in the case of the teacher who divides his congregation, is intelligible enough. Moral teaching seems to him thrown away upon the great majority of his flock; for they have not yet, as he thinks, received the inward spirit without which all external morality is worthless. On the other hand, though it would be useful to the small minority, yet he cannot think it absolutely essential to them; for they, he holds, are safe already, and he cannot spare them more than a hasty and occasional thought, occupied as he is in the urgent and infinite labour of saving those who seem to him to be perishing before his eyes. Besides, all the reforming zeal which any high-minded man might feel in observing the condition of society, and which might be expected to become a furnace seven times heated in the Christian minister, is cooled in him by his habit of taking the evil for granted. He is not surprised at anything in a world which, he is accustomed to repeat, "lieth in wickedness." In fact, much as he inveighs against the ungodly world, his secret vexation is that he cannot clearly make it out to be as bad as his theology declares it to be.

The consequence of this fact, that the pulpits of England are in the hands either of men who are slaves

to tradition or of men who divide their congregation,
is that lamentable one which drives many patriotic men
who are not hostile to religion into active hostility to all
religious bodies,—namely, that the people of England
are not taught morality at all. The task is entrusted
to the clergy of teaching the community what is right
and what is wrong, and it cannot be said that in any
practical sense of the word they perform it.

To say this is not to say that they do nothing, or
that what they do is not in itself as valuable as what
they leave undone. Christianity founds morality upon
theology, and besides theological doctrines it offers other
influences,—the human example of Christ, the lives of
prophets, apostles, and saints,—in order to accomplish
that which it regards as the essential and difficult preparation for morality; namely, the general disposing of
the will towards right and orderly action. It is in laying this theological basis and in bringing to bear those
preparatory influences that Christian teachers occupy
themselves almost exclusively. I do not find fault with
what they do, but it seems to me none the less lamentable that they should leave the direct teaching of morality
almost entirely undone.

By the teaching of morality I do not mean the teaching that we ought to be moral, but the teaching what is
moral and what is not. The former kind of teaching
enters into most sermons, though I am afraid not quite
all. The latter is, of course, not entirely absent; but,
when we are speaking of the average of sermons, it is
impossible to concede more. Obvious vices are stig-
matized, but the less obvious parts of morality, which of
course need most explanation, receive very little, and the

great extent and the constantly shifting and progressive character of moral duty is not recognized. Any one who inquires for the moral result of so much zealous preaching will discover, I think, just this,—a moral sense really awakened, but instructed only on one point; namely, the duty of relieving distress.

A school of Christian teachers has sprung up of late years which neither divides the congregation nor defers to tradition. The Broad Church party, like the High Church party, or still more like the Catholic Church, aspires to guide, not a small selection out of the community, but the community itself. It has none of the old pietistic shyness, none of that shrinking from the affairs of the world and society which is so visible in all sectarian Christianity, and which sometimes assumes the form of an intense nervous antipathy to human beings. It admires the mediæval Church and Cromwell; it sympathises with all the attempts which Christianity has made to influence secular government, and to impose its law upon whole communities. But it is unlike the modern Catholic Church, or the old High Church party of England, in not being conservative. By being intensely conservative at a time when society moves with a speed like that of the planet itself through space, the ecclesiastical systems that aspire to government become more hateful to the world than the inoffensive pietistic societies which pretend to nothing of the kind. But the Broad Church party is thoroughly liberal. It hates obstruction, finality, and every sort of unnatural constraint. It hates in an especial manner what may be called ecclesiasticism; so that the clergy of this school are in a manner at war with their own order, deplore constantly the weakness

and mistakes of "divines," and in all disputes appeal to
the judgment of the laity. It repudiates the principle of
authority in the investigation of truth; and if it abides
by some ancient beliefs, and would retain them as the
basis of modern order, does so on the ground that
they are true, and that they are the best and strongest
foundation upon which modern order can be based.

Before this party, then, there evidently lies a task to
which the older parties were not equal. No conservative prejudices, no theological despair, need hinder
them from giving the people a Christian morality suited
to the age.

Nor is there any reason why the people should not
receive them as their instructors. That the people should
have little confidence in existing religious bodies is natural.
A conservative Church linked to the governing aristocracy could not hope to gain the full confidence of any
class but the aristocracy; the classes that were intolerant
of the aristocracy were naturally dissatisfied with the
Church. On the other hand, the Churches of the converted, which so ostentatiously proclaim themselves the
Churches of an extreme minority, must expect to be
regarded by the majority they excommunicate with the
same feelings with which the Irish Church is regarded by
the Irish population. Broad Churchmen, without party
ties, without theological exclusions, may reasonably hope
to win the confidence of every class. Nor does there
seem to be any other agency by which the people can be
satisfactorily instructed in morality. The proposal is
sometimes made to take morality away from the clergyman and hand it over to the schoolmaster. I should
like very well to see some direct teaching of morality

introduced into schools. But the art of living well cannot be despatched in a few school lessons. It is evidently an art which demands the study of a life. Adults as well as children require instruction in it, and in any properly ordered State such instruction would be most solicitously and amply provided. The need for it is so great that other agencies have been tempted to do something towards furnishing the supply which the clergy have neglected to furnish. Journalism has evidently among its other functions assumed this of moral guidance. Most Englishmen probably get their morality from their paper as exclusively as they get their religion, when they get it at all, from their favourite preacher. And the best journals no doubt discharge this function exceedingly well. But a clergy earnestly occupied with the task would be in many respects a better agency than journalism. The ministry of journalism, so to speak, is a sectarian and voluntary ministry. The journalist is to a great extent bound to the opinions of the particular section of the public for which he writes. He is more absolutely dependent on his flock than any nonconformist preacher. To this are added the evils of irresponsibility, perpetual acrid controversy with rival journalists, and want of influence over the large class of people who never read.

If, then, the Broad Church clergy (who are scattered through all sects, though I suppose the largest number of them to belong to the Established Church) are willing to undertake this great and necessary work of the moral education of the people, let us consider what will be the conditions of performing it efficiently. First, a large and deep intellectual cultivation. They will have carefully to avoid the example set by the schools that have preceded them in the Church. If, like High Churchmen, they intended to teach a conservative doctrine to a stationary people, they might well dispense with this. They might dispense with it if, like the Methodists and Evangelicals of the last century, they had the mission of teaching the simplest lessons of Christianity to a neglected and barbarized population. But their doctrine allies itself with progress, and travels in company with education. It intends to rule and organize a complicated society. Its priests, therefore, must be qualified to guide men in thinking rather than to save them from the trouble of thought, and to teach, not the rudiments, but the more advanced lessons of morality. It is evident, therefore, that they must be learned, but not with the conservative erudition, the knowledge of authorities and precedents, which has characterized the older schools of divinity. Their learning must be the instrument and material of original thought, not the substitute for it; it must be a knowledge of modern affairs rather than ancient, of the present rather than the past.

Indispensable as this qualification is, it is difficult to see how a sufficient number of clergymen possessing it can be procured. The clergy in England have scarcely any special training. Their theological knowledge is, on the average, hardly greater than that of the laity, and to raise the standard seems at present to be impossible. They are to be regarded simply as a section of the better educated class of Englishmen. Education itself must be reformed before the kind of cultivation just described can be introduced among the clergy. Just what is most needed, the progressive spirit, the insight into the present age and the actually existing society, this is what our system of education most completely fails to supply. For it most sedulously avoids the present and occupies itself with nothing that is progressive, nothing that is not fixed and frozen up in antiquity.

Partly from timidity, partly from the real difficulty of explaining what is nearest to our own time, what men are still quarrelling about, what men have not seen the end of; partly also from a notion of laying a very deep and sure foundation, education in England commonly leaves a man very ignorant of the actual state of the world. He has been taught ancient history, theoretically because it is the true key to modern history; but his education terminates before he has any opportunity of applying the key, and his historical researches close when he is still a century or two short of the present time. He is taught the classical languages because all modern literatures have sprung from the literatures of Greece and Rome, and the consequence of this method is, that he commonly remains all his life in ignorance of modern literatures. The Latin language is considered so important as explaining to him his own, that his own language remains a riddle to him to the end of his days. If he dives into philosophy, he cannot of course be introduced too soon to Plato and Aristotle, and they effectually prevent him in too many cases from acquainting himself with the great living philosophies which move the actual world, with the Baconian logic of discovery, and all that has flowed from it, with the ethics of Kant and the Utilitarians, the inductive psychology that was founded by Locke, and the social philosophy that began with Adam Smith.

The dulness and languor that is complained of in our modern sermons is not due to any cause that operates upon the clergy alone. The Church clergy represent pretty well the average of the educated classes. If, when they undertake to discuss religious and moral questions, they are dull, it is because the education they have received—that is, the ordinary English education—has not roused their minds, has not filled them with strong ideas. Nor, indeed, could it do so. If there be such a thing as progress in human affairs, if modern society be more developed and complex than ancient, the study of the remote past can never impart a knowledge of the present, nor can the crude and rudimentary wisdom of antiquity qualify men to guide the moderns on their intricate way. It is, however, a special disadvantage under which the clergy labour, that they have not the inducements and facilities that some other classes have for supplying, in after-life, the defects of their early training. The lawyer, for example, is introduced by his profession to a mass of new and most important knowledge, and at the same time spurred on by ambition and by the certainty that success will bear some proportion to real desert to make himself master of it. The consequence is that he receives a second education far more thorough and profound than that of his youth. But the clerical profession is not so situated. In the Church it is demoralized by a system of promotion which has little reference to merit. In dissenting bodies perhaps merit is theoretically more considered, but the kind of merit which is most rewarded is not high, a rhetoric which corresponds fairly to the Socratic definition of rhetoric, a knack of flattery; and the judges who distribute the rewards are ill qualified to do so, mixed congregations unskilled in distinguishing sound doctrine from unsound, and easily hoodwinked by a cheap and vulgar fluency. The clerical profession, therefore, is not favourable to progressive intellectual cultivation; and the result is that, whereas other classes of men readily fling off the prejudices and the inertness produced by an antiquated education and educate themselves anew, "in dem Strom der Welt," the clergy not unfrequently finish their education at college, and continue drowsily quoting Horace all their lives.

Education, however, is rapidly reforming itself. It is adapting itself to the new age which we may hope is beginning, in which the powers and patriotism of the whole nation will be enlisted in the nation's service. So long as the conservative view of society prevails, an education founded on the remote past will prevail. Thinking about the actual state of society leads to seeing its faults, and that leads to change and reform. Therefore, under a conservative *régime* education instinctively avoids the actual state of society, and it does so by the contrivance of antiquarianism. Antiquarianism in education answers to conservatism in politics. On the other hand, we cannot throw ourselves into a progressive political course without adopting a progressive education. There is no middle course in education between the antiquarianism that secures the mind from the intrusion of disturbing thoughts and the modernism which deals with them unreservedly and exhaustively. We must turn our backs or our faces upon the questions of the day. There is nothing but disquiet and danger to be reaped from looking at them sideways. This is already felt in the educational world, and a breath of new life is passing through schools and colleges. In the general re-invigoration the clergy will naturally share. But they should spread their sails at once to meet the breeze. The supply of men capable of the great work of moral instruction above described will constantly increase, but it will increase the more rapidly the more distinctly the want is recognized. Broad Churchmen must not be content with a negative teaching, with merely repudiating what is obsolete. They are called upon heartily to adopt the conception of a progressive ethic, to forget the outworn petition of the Collect, "that we being freed from the fear of our enemies may pass our time in rest and quietness," to accept movement as the law both of Churches and States, and to assume the position of guides in the movement.

As I have said, the special training of the clergy in England is very slight. Such as it is, however, might it not be modified in this direction? Like the rest of our education, it is corrupted by antiquarianism and formalism. The Church stands undoubtedly upon a basis which was laid in antiquity. If it is desirable that every layman should know his Bible, it is still more desirable that every clergyman should do so. It is also desirable that there should always be in the Church a certain number of theologians minutely acquainted with Biblical criticism. But it seems to me that the special training of the average clergyman should not be philological. It is a fact perversely overlooked in England that philology is a science of which a little knowledge is particularly useless. We hear much of the importance of being able to read ancient books in the originals. But we do not hear of the immense difficulty of acquiring this power, nor of the absolute certainty that nine-tenths of those who attempt to acquire it will fail. If the study of Greek (and sometimes of Hebrew) is required of the clergy in order that they may be able to form an independent judgment of the true meaning of Biblical texts, then nothing is more certain than that the whole time spent in the study is in the majority of cases thrown away. It is not a little knowledge of Greek, but an accurate and extensive knowledge of it, that will qualify a man to form an opinion of his own upon a doubtful or difficult passage. The average clergyman should, no doubt, be superior to the average layman in knowledge of the Bible, but his superiority should consist in a greater knowledge of the best commentaries, not in any pretension,—which must necessarily be groundless,—of knowing the originals.

To gain, however, this little knowledge, which is so perfectly useless, a great deal of time is devoted. If this time were better spent, the standard of clerical efficiency might be considerably raised. A considerable knowledge, for example, of modern history, and particularly of the influence of the Church upon society in all ages, might be demanded of candidates for ordination. And there is another study which would have the effect of raising the clerical order indefinitely in public estimation. They are the almoners of the people; to their hands a great part of the vast machinery of philanthropy is entrusted. Now philanthropy, unless directed by foresight and knowledge, is very far from being twice blessed; if it blesses him that gives, it frequently has a contrary effect upon him that takes. Moreover, almsgiving without sufficient system leads to waste; some distresses it perpetuates, others it overlooks, and others it relieves two or three times over, while every failure of philanthropy damps and discourages the Christian feeling in which it originated. Yet it is matter of common complaint that the clergy are seldom men of business. May it not be urged, not as a thing merely desirable, but as imperative and as essential to the credit of the clerical profession, that the clergy should master the whole political economy of philanthropy?

If the clergy should rise to a proper conception of the magnitude of the work entrusted to them, and should become through the improvement both of general education and of their own special training not wholly unequal to the performance of it, they will find it a comparatively easy matter to sharpen, as much as may be required, the mere tools they work with. Their principal tool is speech, and unless they study the art of speech carefully and methodically, they must expect to fail in their enterprise. But they will fail, however much they study it, if they do not rigidly subordinate speech to thought and matter—reversing the Mephistophelian precept; and, on the other hand, when the matter of speech has been acquired in abundance, skill in speech will come with moderate study, though not with none. We may then reasonably expect a new pulpit rhetoric to spring up adapted to the cultivated ears of the first English generation that will have been to school. That new rhetoric will differ from the style now in vogue, as it seems to me, in two principal points.

First, it will recognize that the most effective images and illustrations are those which are drawn from the actual experience of the audience addressed, and that the most effective language is the most vernacular that is not vulgar,—that is, the most familiar, and in its choice of words the most colloquial. A reform in sermons will take place similar to that which at the beginning of the century took place in poetry. At that time poetry had accustomed itself to deal in images that answered to nothing in contemporary experience, and that were only faint and vague reflections of those which earlier poets had drawn from the actual life of their own age. At the same time poets had adopted as part of poetic refinement a practice of denoting things by names which were not their current names in the language of the time. We may call the first fault conventionalism, and the second euphuism. Now both faults are still as apparent in sermons as they once were in poetry. As the poets described imaginary shepherds and shepherdesses living in scenery partly Sicilian, partly Italian, and partly English, a state of things answering to nothing in their readers' experience, so are we still introduced in sermons to an artificial and conventional world. We are sometimes warned against the vice of idolatry, which has been extinct in England since the time of the Saxon Heptarchy. We hear declamations against Babylon, a city which lost all independent power to do mischief about 2,400 years ago. Of course these phrases are not used literally; in the same way the shepherds of the old pastoral often stood symbolically for lovers, or poets; but such symbolism serves not to illustrate, but positively to darken thought. It is explaining what is unknown by what is incomparably more unknown. The power of the Pope in the modern world may resemble that of

Babylon in antiquity; but the audience know something already of the former, and will not learn more by hearing him compared to the latter, of which they know nothing. Not less vicious than the conventionalism of the modern pulpit is its euphuism. As the pastoral poets called a shepherd a swain and a woman a fair, so a clergyman will often call interest usury; a farmer he describes as a husbandman; and he retains the old verbal inflection in "eth" which two hundred years ago began to displease the taste of Milton. But more ruinous to rhetorical effect than all such faults of commission is his studied avoidance of all those words and phrases which he ought particularly to affect, those namely which answer to the commonest facts and reflect the homeliest and freshest experience, and which, though they want the sanction of immemorial use, and therefore call for more tact in selection and application, have a force peculiarly their own, being fully charged with the electricity of new and vivid associations.

Conventionalism and euphuism are the inevitable vices of all speaking that is perfunctory. The speaker intent upon his subject, and ardently hopeful of attaining the end he proposes to himself, slips them off as unhesitatingly as the cricketer rids himself of all superfluous incumbrances of dress. The new race of preachers that I have been imagining, having undertaken a task in which they may hope for success, but only through the utmost exertions—the task of the moral education of the nation—will soon find the artificial decorums of the pulpit intolerable to them. They will soon rub away from their style the rust of antiquarianism. Pressed on the one hand by the necessity of being grave, and on the other by the still more imperious necessity of being intelligible and forcible, they will be driven to a certain classical distinctness and severity of outline, and the leading preachers of such a school may be expected to give new masterpieces to English literature. These leading preachers will no doubt be few, but it seems not visionary to expect that a large number, braced by the distinctness of their object and elevated by the greatness of it, may acquire the power of interesting an audience profoundly, and may make the church once more a place not merely of devotion, but also, as Protestant churches should be, of solid, continuous, and methodical instruction.

It is not indeed to be supposed that such a style would be the most popular of styles. It would be rarely pathetic, because it would be above all things honest. Depending for effect entirely upon the importance of the thing said, it might be in danger of falling into a didactic dryness. It would shrink from a lavish or spasmodic use of language as from a sin. It would give much less pleasure, and so be much less popular, than a style less severely restricted. A preacher who adapts himself without reserve or self-respect to the taste of his audience, and who tricks out his style with the flowers of Oriental poetry, such a preacher, to his own cost, will always defy competition, for he imparts pleasure in the greatest quantity and to the greatest number. Even in arts, whose main object it is to give pleasure, the best artists are seldom the most popular. Tennyson and Browning are our best poets, but they are not the most widely read. The best is never the best liked; but, on the other hand, it is equally true that the best is always liked. Tennyson and Browning, though not read the most, are read much, and such a school of preachers as I have described would always command attention, though not enthusiastic applause. And the influence they would exert would be out of all proportion to the applause they would receive. For their words being well weighed and seriously meant would be important; the response they would elicit would be not empty praise, but bitter opposition, angry denial, and all the higher, rarer, and more gratifying forms of popular applause. In scriptural language, such preaching would be "as the hammer that breaketh the rock in pieces."

There would however be, as now, a third class of preachers who, from sheer want of intellectual power, would always be dull. Assuredly no reform will ever expel dulness from the pulpit any more than from the bar. But a dull preacher is not necessarily either a bad or an ineffective teacher. The advice he gives may be good, however feebly given; and it may be followed, however coldly received. Of all those who complain of the dulness of sermons, a very small proportion ever seriously doubt that what they contain is true; a very small proportion do not, in some general way, intend to be guided by them. As I have already said, the only practical lesson which can be clearly collected from the sermons now preached,—namely, the duty of relieving distress,—has been very thoroughly learnt by the nation, and is very generally practised. If other moral rules equally reasonable were preached with equal unanimity, however feebly, they would meet with equal acceptance.

I intended to speak first of the manner of moral teaching, and then of the matter. At one point, however, manner and matter may be said to merge in each other, and I come naturally to this point in making the transition.

Teaching in all subjects proceeds as much by example as precept; in morals, the importance of example is even greater than in other subjects, and it is characteristic of Christianity that it makes a greater use of example than any other system. Christianity starts from the unbounded admiration of a Person, and it seems to me that all true moral progress is made through admiration; in other words, that before you can rise to a higher moral standard you must become aware, by actual experience, of the existence of that higher standard. Now while all Christian schools have agreed in putting forward Christ as the supreme Example, no Christian school has ever treated Him as the only one. The early and mediæval Church surrounded the central figure with a host of inferior objects of admiration. Protestants have put aside this ancient calendar, but they have not repudiated the principle of it. They hold the admiration offered to have been excessive in degree or superstitious in kind, and the objects of it to have been, in many instances, ill chosen. But the principle of setting up objects of imitation other than Christ is admitted by them as much as by Catholics. The lives of Moses, David, Ezra, St. Paul, furnish the material of a large proportion of Protestant sermons. Nor does any school theoretically maintain that such objects of imitation are to be found only in the Bible. No preacher is blamed for referring in the pulpit to modern examples of virtue;

but it is supposed to be advisable, in the main, to keep within the limits of scriptural history.

This notion seems to me to have the same origin as the notion, which almost brings Christianity into contempt, that all sermons should be of an extreme simplicity. It arose in the missionary preaching of the Methodists of the last century. Addressing an almost barbaric population, they naturally simplified their teaching to the utmost limit; and for the same reason they confined themselves to the one book which they knew thoroughly themselves, and had any chance of making their disciples know. But a practice which in such circumstances was inevitable is very ill adapted to a preaching addressed to the educated classes, and therefore to preaching generally in the age to which we look forward of universal education. To an intelligent audience, the best examples of virtue are not, as a general rule, those of the Bible, but examples taken from modern times, and from a society like our own. The men of the Bible lived, in the first place, in circumstances unfamiliar to us; it follows that it must cost us an effort to realize their actions and characters. Nay, more than this follows. It follows that we may often make mistakes in estimating their characters, and conceive them not merely imperfectly, but wrongly. Must not this frequently happen to a preacher of only ordinary intelligence and information? Do not persons acquainted with antiquity often smile at the innocent modernism with which the acts of Jacob or Deborah are discussed in the pulpit? Do not travellers tell us of the contempt with which, after becoming acquainted with Oriental manners, they recollected clerical interpretations of Old Testament history? Now, there is no reason why the clergy should expose themselves to the risk of making such mistakes. Incomparably the larger portion of Scripture history is entirely unnecessary for the establishment of any theological doctrine. When it is discussed in the pulpit, nothing is drawn from it but example; and this might be drawn equally well, and without running any risk, from modern history.

The most impressive and practically useful of biographies, *ceteris paribus*, are those of fellow-countrymen of the most recent date. Their characters are legible to us without effort, their conduct imitable without much modification, and everything about them is interesting to us. The places where they lived we have seen or may see. We may stand where they stood and touch what they touched. Their *relics* are among us, ready for a worship which need not be pushed to extravagance. To disregard all these moral influences, to suffer the great and good to pass away from among us without any memorial that really keeps them in memory,—unremembered by three-fourths of the population and unknown in the next generation to all but a few students,—and in the meanwhile to concentrate our admiration upon the Hebrew judges and kings of an epoch separated from us, as we may say, by three civilizations—what does this involve? It involves an enormous gap or break in the gradations of our moral feelings, which should extend in regular series from what is near to what is remote. From our family affections and admirations we ought not to pass abruptly to the largest and most comprehensive admirations. Cosmopolitanism, said Coleridge, is not possible but by antecedence of patriotism. And patriotism is only another name for the worship of relics. We should begin by admiring all the virtue which is near us in time and space. We should contemplate all the greatness which appears in our neighbourhood, until, as in natural course it will, the very land which has been the stage of it acquires a sacredness. From this we should pass regularly backward through time, adding our great fellow-countrymen of a past age to those of the present; then we should pass to other countries and times, rising to those names which are highest of all, but remote, through those which are less high but near to us. We should form, as it were, a national calendar, consecrate our ancestors—keep their images near to us—and so reap the inestimable advantage of living always *coram Lepidis*.

I suggest, then, that the clergy should draw largely upon English history and biography for illustrations of their moral teaching. Carlyle has said that every nation's true Bible is its history. If the Hebrew history be a cosmopolitan Bible, or rather the first part of one, I think there should be national Bibles also, and I can imagine no more proper and nobler task for a clergy than the perpetual shaping and elaborating of such a national monument. Such a task they would practically undertake if they habitually resorted to English history for examples. However many mistakes might be made in the estimate of character, however many false idols set up, however much exaggerated declamation delivered, however often the truth of history might be warped to gain a moral, the continual application of a large number of minds to the work of sifting our history for the purpose of preserving in memory whatever in it was memorable, would, I believe, result in nothing less than this. The clergy themselves would have a task to perform which would demand some reading and thought; they would have to make their Bible, instead of merely citing it by rote. The people would listen to matter intrinsically interesting to them, and hardly capable of being made dull by any feebleness in the preacher; and in the end there would spring up an idealized history, which would become familiar to every imagination and give a new sureness and continuousness to the progress of the national mind, and a new elevation to individual character.

Let us now proceed to consider more closely the matter of moral teaching. This divides itself naturally into what men should not do, and what they should do.

On the first of these two heads I shall not linger long. I have only to remark that the moral censorship of the clergy can only be influential when it is founded upon a real study of human life. Their criticisms must above all things be particular. General declamations against immorality are easy, but of scarcely any use, especially when couched in Oriental language. The special cause of immorality, against which preaching may be effective, is that indistinctness of conception which prevents people from seeing under what general head particular actions are to be classed. All agree to censure dishonesty, but people will differ on the dishonesty of particular actions; and what can be done by preaching is to prevent men from persuading themselves that wrong actions are not wrong, or from entirely overlooking the criminality of them. For this purpose the preacher must especially inquire what are the criminal acts to which people are most tempted, what are the particular vices of particular classes of men, or professions, or trades. The fault to be found with the present school of preachers is, not that they neglect altogether to do this, but that they do not do it with sufficient study and thoroughness. Our censors content themselves too much with generalities. When great public scandals arise—as lately, for example, in the commercial world—the censorship of the press is vigorous and useful; but where is the censorship of the pulpit? The journalists either had or procured the necessary special knowledge; but the clergy generally knew too little of the subject to be able to deal with it. Alarmists sometimes come forward with strong assertions of the utter demoralization of large classes of the community, or of the gradually advancing demoralization of the whole. Mr. Herbert Spencer writes an essay on the "Morals of Trade," in which he maintains, with a quantity of detailed evidence, the universal dishonesty of the trading classes. If all this is true, should the clergy leave it to be discovered by amateur moralists and preachers? Is it not their business to find it out and proclaim it?

But much more may be done by positive precept than in the way of negative criticism. The inadequacy of sermons to restrain vice is proverbial. A strong temptation undoes in a moment the work of many sermons. On the other hand, when virtue is regarded not negatively but as a system of positive actions, exhortations have not the same inutility. The majority of men have a certain desire, when they are not influenced by strong temptation, to do their duty, and will listen, I think, with remarkable docility, to any one who will intelligently explain to them what it is, and give them advice as to the best way of doing it. That the Christian Church has much influence in diminishing crime it is possible to deny, and would be difficult to prove; but its positive results—the charitable institutions with which it has covered the country—are visible to all.

This one great and undeniable achievement of the Church seems to me instructive, as showing what sort of enterprise the Church may engage in with real hopes of success. The Church will be listened to when it prescribes definite deeds the good results of which are easily seen. In such a case, so far from preaching to deaf ears, it wins an obedience which is excessive and unreasonable. Men give and give in defiance of reason and political economy. Are there no other duties equally plain which the Church might inculcate with equal effect?

My own profession constantly brings before me instances of an immorality—so I think it should be called —which proceeds simply from want of instruction in morals, which has most disastrous consequences, and which, I believe, the Church could cure. I mean the habit which fathers have of delegating altogether to others the education of their children. Not from any indifference to the welfare of their children, not from any deliberate contempt for moral obligation, but simply from never having had this particular duty pointed out to them, they become guilty of a neglect the immediate consequences of which are sometimes startling, and the less direct and obvious consequences beyond calculation. I have met with young men who have been suffered to grow up in an incredible intellectual barbarism, the father working conscientiously for them all the time, but delegating altogether the particular work of education. I do not suppose such extreme cases are common; the majority of parents are not so unfortunate in their choice of delegates; they find teachers for their sons who are tolerably competent to teach, and they persuade themselves, no doubt, that it is really best not to interfere with those who have made a special study of the art of education. The principle of division of labour is adopted. The father has not time to do all that is necessary to be done for his children; part he will do himself, but part must be entrusted to others. He hands over to others the child's education, his mind, his soul. He reserves to himself the finance department. It is not easy to estimate the mischief produced by this division of labour. I know scarcely any cause from which the community suffers so much. In the first place, consider the effect produced upon the parent himself. It is open to him to give so much time and thought to educating his children, or the same amount of both to making the money to pay for their education; and he elects the latter. In other words, he chooses an occupation which is in many cases the most sordid and illiberal drudgery, and in very few cases can be highly improving, instead of the most improving occupation in which he can be engaged. Surely there is no task which life brings with it, at least to the average man, calculated to raise him so much as the task of educating his children. It is by far the greatest and most delicate problem which he ever has to solve. It demands all his powers of thought and contrivance, and by making so constant a demand upon them forms and disciplines them: at the same time it disciplines the affections. In short, a man cannot educate his children without at the same time in a much greater degree educating himself. What trade or profession does as much for the man who follows it? Not perhaps the most intellectual of all; and assuredly a good many of the occupations by which men make money are for all other purposes a mere waste of time. What then are we to think of the division of labour by which a father devolves upon others all that is valuable and dignified in fatherhood, and retains only its burdens and anxieties? What an impoverishment of character must be the effect of such an abdication of the paternal dignity! It must lead inevitably to those low views of the actual prevalence of which we are always complaining, that money-worship, that morbid industry, that insensibility to the highest interests and enjoyments.

But what is the effect upon the children themselves? I am not of course maintaining that the father should take the place of the schoolmaster, but that he should actively co-operate with the schoolmaster and supplement his work. Now his neglect of this duty to a great extent paralyses the schoolmaster. We have recently been told on good authority that the high average culture of the Scotch is due mainly to parental influence in education. It is to find an equivalent for this in England that we are always hopelessly labouring. That division of labour by which the parent loses so much is, even for its special purpose, a mistake. The teaching of special subjects may be delegated, but there is much in education which cannot be delegated, very much which can only be done at home, and a good deal which can be done only by the father. But if the child's intellectual loss is great, his moral loss is perhaps still greater. When the father elects to perform his parental duties entirely in the counting-house, he practically surrenders his claim to filial affection. Instead of sympathy, personal care, and intimate friendship, such a father only gives his son money, a gift which will not inspire any enthusiastic gratitude. Distant respect is all that he can look for, and in the want of filial feelings the son loses more than the father loses by not inspiring them.

Here, then, is an example, as it seems to me, of an abuse which the Church might remove. It is an abuse which springs from no inveterate vice of human nature, but from a moral rudeness, an ignorance which a little instruction might cure. Without much eloquence, preachers might make men ashamed of a negligence like this. And if a better way of thinking on such a point were introduced, the effects would be incalculable. The standard of national cultivation might be permanently raised and a kind of self-denial introduced which Englishmen seldom practise, the self-denial not of giving money but of refraining from earning it.

My profession, as I have said, brings this matter particularly before my notice. The teacher can do little for the pupil for whom his parents have done nothing, and to show parents their duty is evidently in the province of the teachers of morality. It is therefore at this particular point that it becomes most clearly visible to me how little teaching of morality there really is in England, and in how unenlightened a condition is the moral sense of a great proportion of the nation. I dare say other illustrations of the same fact will occur to many of my readers. Other instances might no doubt be cited of plain moral duties which are very generally neglected out of sheer ignorance and want of instruction. A great many maxims which literary men call platitudes are to a large majority of people so unfamiliar as to deserve rather to be called paradoxes. It does not follow because they are worn out for literary purposes that they ought not continually to be repeated in the pulpit,—repeated, if possible, with a perpetual variety of language and illustration; but, if this is not possible, with the dullest monotony rather than not at all. But they will not be found dull if they are expressed with only a little conviction, with only a little simplicity of language. What a few simple platitudes made up the whole of Thackeray's philosophy!

If it be inquired why such a plain duty as that to which I have called attention is so little inculcated, the answer seems to be that it does not rise very obviously out of any text of Scripture. As, however, no one probably will dispute that it is a duty, and one of the most important duties, this example may serve to show how far preachers are misled by their inveterate habit of resting morality upon the Bible. If the "canon of inspiration be closed," as they say, if we have no means of determining whether an action be right or wrong but by referring to certain Greek and Hebrew formulæ, then indeed they are justified, then indeed is the teaching of morality an insane pretension. But it is not so.

"Die Geisterwelt ist nicht verschlossen :
Dein Sinn ist zu, dein Herz ist todt."

Since I have introduced the question of education, and since we have learnt of late years—what we might have learnt from ancient philosophers long ago—the great importance and the great difficulty of the art of education, let me go on to suggest that it is an art which it behoves the clergy especially to study. Education will not probably, for the future, be strictly in their hands so much as it has been. But if, as I hold, parents are bound to take a great share personally in the education of their children, and if at the same time education is a most difficult art, it follows that the clergy must teach the parents this art. There exists no other machinery by which they can learn it, and this machinery is both adapted to the work and placed everywhere within reach. The diffusion of really solid information upon an art which men and women of all ranks, competent or incompetent, have to practise, and are, for the most part, really anxious to practise well, the art of educating children,—this is an inestimable benefit which it is within the power of the Church to confer upon the nation.

Enough for the present of direct instruction in morality. The sum of my argument hitherto has been that the sermon ought not to be purely theological, nor purely hortatory, but ought to contain direct moral teaching. Such moral teaching, I hold, should be explicit and detailed, not confining itself to principles and leaving rules to be inferred, but rather stating the rules in such a manner as to make the principles appear through them. But there is another subject besides theology from which morality ought not to be severed, and cannot be severed without losing most of its vitality. This is political and social science. It is common to sneer at political religion, and to maintain that the clergy should have nothing to do with politics. Yet it is evident enough that in relinquishing politics the clergy practically renounce their influence over men, and become mere spiritual directors to women and children, and that the effect of this is to lower the clerical character, and to give to the proceedings of the clergy, when the interests of their own order force them into politics, all the helplessness, cowardice, and recklessness of inexperience. That the clergy should not engage themselves in party conflicts is true; it may even be true that they should refrain as much as possible from political action of any kind. But if so, this is not because politics are out of their province, but in order that they may exercise a more elevated kind of political influence. If they are not to engage in political strife as combatants, it is in order that they may be better qualified to act as umpires; it is that they may be more efficient as expounders of political principle that they are to avoid political action. Taken in any more absolute sense, the maxim that the clergy are not to meddle with politics degrades the clerical function in the most pitiful manner, and condemns it to a feebleness and insignificance which must make all men of strong character disdain to take it upon themselves. Morals cannot be severed from politics any more than the individual can be isolated from society. If the individual is profoundly modified by the character and condition of the corporate body, if morbid moral states affect whole classes at once, and the moral health of the whole makes itself seen in the separate parts, how is it possible for the teacher to confine himself to the individual and neglect the State? Besides, an important part of the moral duty of the individual is his duty to the

State: and how can the teacher in any effective way give instruction in this without entering into political questions? Once more: this particular part of moral duty is one which especially requires to be carefully explained, because it is an advanced and abstruse part of the subject. Natural affection may make a man a good husband or father, but nature by itself will not make a man a good citizen in a community like ours. This virtue can only be the fruit of much reflection; and who is to excite and direct this reflection if the clergy do not? If in other parts of morality one often has occasion to remark the rudeness of the national mind, it is perhaps especially manifest here just because there is so much political activity. Almost every one must have his political opinions, must take his side; but as there is no diffused political education, no generally understood political principles, each question is decided by itself really at the dictate of a faction, nominally by the arguments furnished by the heads of the faction, and politics degenerate into the senseless bickering of opposite prejudices and the interminable controversies of parties not open to conviction.

If people considered the Bible as a whole, and not merely in its separate texts, they would surely see that no book presents morals in such an inextricable union with politics. Did those Hebrew prophets, who are the prototypes of our modern preachers, refrain from meddling with politics? Are not their utterances instinct with the sense of the national life, the national vocation, and the continuity of the national history? These prophets, in fact, were not so much what we should call moralists as politicians of a doctrinaire school, addressing rather classes than individuals, and dealing with public affairs rather than private. I do not certainly urge that they should be closely imitated; but modern preachers seem to think they are following the Bible when they omit all mention of politics, and treat English history with complete indifference. Because the prophets speak of Jerusalem—their own city—they too speak of Jerusalem—a foreign city, and, by way of imitating men in whom patriotism was a burning passion, are silent about their own country and the events of their own age.

It may be answered that if the Old Testament is national the New is universal, and that the latter should be followed rather than the former. Assuredly, when I urge that patriotism should be inculcated, national history closely connected with morality, and civil duties carefully explained, I do not mean that this is the ultimate lesson of morality. There is a higher doctrine still,—of which the New Testament is the text-book,—a universal morality, which it is still more important to teach. But as the race rose to the universal morality through the national, so, it seems to me, must the individual. And I find it a capital mistake, in the present school of preachers, that they omit this middle class of duties altogether. The morality of the Old Testament and of Plutarch has still its place, and is indispensable. It ought to be taught both as a step to the higher morality and to prevent it from becoming a hindrance to it. English prejudices, insular selfishness, and contempt for foreigners, are no doubt as much opposed as possible to Christianity. But they are to be cured, not by leading people to forget that they are Englishmen, not by severing morality from all those associations of locality and circumstance by means of which it most naturally attaches itself to the mind. The abuse of patriotism is not to be cured by destroying patriotism itself; but patriotism is to be strengthened by being purified, by being deprived of its exclusiveness and ultimateness. The Christian unity of mankind is to be taught as a final lesson, which will be easiest learnt, or rather will only be learnt, by those who have already realized the unity of the State.

Politics, then, should be a part, and a principal part, of the studies of the clergy. To discover and popularize the lessons that may be drawn from our history, to idealize the nation and familiarize it in its unity to the minds of its members, is a most vital part of the moral teaching of the community. The phrase, political religion, may have very different meanings; there are two senses in which it signifies a hateful thing, but there is a third sense in which it is an admirable and necessary thing. It is a hateful thing when it means religion made the tool of a political party or governing class, as when the Church consecrated the absolutism of the Stuarts, or, on a smaller scale, when the parson preaches submission to the squire. It is a hateful thing when it means the Church interfering with public affairs merely with a view of strengthening its own position, of preserving its own influence or privileges or endowments. But when a Church is independent of political parties and sure of the respect of the people, when it can speak with impartiality and with authority, then political religion means only the purifying of politics by connecting them with duty, honour, and piety; it means only the discouragement of faction, the assertion of general principles, the keeping before the eyes of the people a political ideal. And as in the former senses political religion is only another name for corrupt religion, in the latter sense it is another name for worthy and noble politics.

Besides the general duty of proclaiming political first principles, there seems to be a more special political function belonging to the clergy. Taken indifferently from all classes, and addressing assemblies composed indifferently of all classes, they are the natural mediators in the perpetual warfare between class and class. This warfare is the fundamental political fact, and the leading political problem is to moderate it. Nothing can be more plainly written in the New Testament than the mission of the Church to reconcile all such differences, to pull down all barriers, and to establish unity among men. No institution would seem better adapted to forward this perpetual process of reconciliation than the institution of a clergy. An order of men taken from all the warring classes, and removed, as it were, from the arena of conflict, expected to have intercourse with the poor and admitted to intercourse with the rich, enabled to hear both sides of the controversy, highly educated, so as to form an intelligent opinion, not dependent (that is, where the Church is well ordered) on the favour of either side, and provided with frequent opportunities of addressing both sides together,—such an order should do much to remove the principal cause of discord between classes—which is ignorance of each other's interests and feelings,—and they should be able to pronounce with more authority than any other men the verdict of justice.

If morality cannot be properly taught without entering into political questions, neither can it be separated from what is called social science. Those minor arrangements of society by which the welfare of sections of the community are affected and the course of their lives determined, have incalculable moral consequences. This is so plain that no one doubts that such questions fall within the province of the clergy. When the periodical famine begins at the East end of London, the papers are full of the letters of clergymen, and they become the leaders of a philanthropic campaign. The only question is, whether the clergy do not confine themselves too much to effects, and neglect causes too much. Is their province limited to the pointing out of social evils and the application of remedies? Should not rather cure give place to prevention? Is not the removal of the causes of social disease more important than the alleviation of its effects? If this be so, it would seem that a field of study lies open before the clergy which they have as yet very imperfectly occupied. Take as an example the condition of the agricultural poor. This is universally admitted to be one of the most difficult social problems. What renders it specially difficult is the fact that the active intelligence of the country is chiefly collected in the towns, and therefore withdrawn from the study of the subject. Now the Church furnishes an organization by which the presence of at least one man of cultivation is secured even in the most secluded districts. This problem, therefore, is one which specially falls to the Church: from the Church, surely we may say, the country has a right to demand the solution of it. Yet among the country clergy,—who are most zealous in the care of their parishes,—how few generalize upon the facts before them, how few penetrate to the causes of the evil! We hear of few Kingsleys and few Girdlestones.

Let me now try and gather into one view all these considerations. The clergy are charged with the task of pplying to the wants of men, both individuals and societies, the remedy provided by certain religious and moral principles and a certain organization established eighteen hundred years ago. They need, therefore, to study two things,—Christianity, and that modern society to which Christianity is to be applied. Society is constantly shifting, it is extremely complex, and philosophy during the last hundred years has thrown much light upon the laws which govern its changes. If therefore a system of morality is to be built on the basis of Christian theology, as it must be if Christianity is the universal religion, it will not be sufficient for the clergy to read the New Testament and imbue themselves with its maxims. They must read with equal diligence in the book of the modern time. Their business is not merely to repeat a message; they are charged with an embassy which demands the employment of their own independent judgment and discretion. They must add a philosophy to their religion, they must originate, combine, adapt. They must be not merely passive channels of ancient wisdom, passive administrators of ancient rules, but thinkers, interpreters of the age, the living legislators of a living society. Their function is high, not merely by the sacredness of the interests committed to them, but also by the high powers, the wide cultivation, and the vigorous originality which they are required to exercise.

When a view like this is presented, it is commonly met by two objections; the one, that such work is above the powers that any large body of men can be expected to possess; the other, that it would be degradation for the clergy to occupy themselves with work so secular. When both these objections issue from the same mouths they may be thought to refute each other, but they are tenable separately. The first objection, then, says that the average educated Englishman—and the average clergyman will never rise above this standard—does not understand political economy or the principles of political and social science, nor has he fresh views of moral philosophy, nor is he versed in English history, still less in modern history generally. How can you expect a large class of men to be qualified to lecture on all these subjects when we do not find that any large class of men has any considerable acquaintance with any one of them? But, in the first place, this is somewhat unjust to the average educated man. Most men of intelligence, after a few years of intercourse with the world, form independent views upon these subjects. Their views are not always very clear or comprehensive; but then it is to be remembered that to form them has not been a business, but rather a recreation. They are the fruit of accidental and occasional reflection upon the facts of life. Might not then the average clergyman—assumed equal in intelligence to the average layman—be expected to form more intelligent views on these subjects if he once understood it to be part of his duty to study them? Not perhaps at once, not at the time of taking orders; but after twenty years of continuous and methodical study, why should not a man of ordinary intelligence be able to say something worth attention, at any rate on some one of them?

"But then the clergyman has no time for study! He is expected to do so many things; his congregation intrude so constantly upon his leisure; so much activity and publicity are forced upon him." But in the first place the studies of which I have been speaking are not of the kind which specially require seclusion from the world. I have been advocating the study of actual life and society; such a study absolutely requires a good deal of contact with society and experience of life. Still it must be admitted that a certain amount of solitude is the indispensable condition of all study; the facts collected in the world must be arranged and generalized in private. A perpetual round of petty engagements is fatal to progress even in practical studies. We suffer from this malady in all departments of culture at once at the present time. Not only in the Church, but among the teaching class at the Universities and in schools, as idleness was the besetting sin of the last age, industry is the besetting sin of the present; or, more correctly, the idleness has been succeeded by a merely external and superficial industry. Our conversion seems to have begun not at the heart but at the extremities. The hands and feet have thrown off their listlessness and move to and fro indefatigably; the tongue, throat, and lungs tax themselves prodigiously; but the change will be more in form than in substance till it penetrates to the brain and will. In all the professions a man's first duty now is to renounce the ambition of becoming distinguished for activity; the temptation chiefly to be avoided is that of undertaking more work than he can do in first-rate style. The quality of work must be improved, and for that end, if necessary, the quantity reduced. A higher and calmer sort of activity must be arrived at—economy in energy, expenditure without waste, zeal without haste. The moral teachers of the community should set the example of an industry thus tempered, of a proper distribution of life between solitude and society, between contemplation and action. They are the last persons in the world who should allow their work to be spoiled by the unreasonable expectations of others. How can they direct the actions of others if they have not independence enough to direct their own? The question for all people, but particularly for them, is not how they are expected to do their work, but how their work may best be done; and the higher the kind of work, the more necessary it is that the worker should claim and use the privilege of doing it in his own way. If he is to submit to any other opinion in such a matter, at least let it be an authority above him, not an ignorant clamour from beneath.

The other objection represents the clergy as degraded or drawn away from their true function by becoming teachers of morality. Their province, it is said, is the higher one of religion and theology; however important morality may be, the clergy have work more important still which they cannot neglect for it. Those who urge this objection generally either assert or imply that morality is practically taught in the teaching of religion, and that it is sufficient if a little practical advice is thrown in at the end of a theological discourse as it is at the end of some of St. Paul's Epistles. I trust

I have shown that this is not really sufficient, that the teaching of morality is no such simple matter, but requires deep and various study, original thought, and copious explanation and illustration. I trust I have shown that the want of moral teaching is a great evil, whether it be unavoidable or not. But I do not wish theology to be thrown into the background in order to make room for morality. I am not one of those who think that theology can be dispensed with. Not so much morality as life itself seems to me to require the support of a hope that goes beyond calculation, and a faith transcending knowledge. And if a faith in goodness and a divination of happiness lie at the bottom of our life, then I willingly concede the foremost place in the ministrations of the clergyman to the inspiring and cherishing of such sentiments of trust and ardent anticipation, which are the elastic spring that sets virtue in motion. Nothing is sounder, as I think—at any rate, nothing is more Christian—than the method which puts the motives to virtue and the temperaments or affections of virtue before the deeds in which they result. But whatever may be said against morality without religion, is there not also something to be said against a religion that is without morality? The religions of antiquity were more or less of such a kind, and the religion which superseded them did so mainly because it was not of such a kind. This religion placed human life under a stern law; it did not consecrate the usages it found existing, but subjected them to a searching criticism, referred them to an ideal standard. If the first Christians had been so busy with their theology as to find no leisure for a protest against the "infamis arena," their religion might have remained (and would it not have deserved to remain?) undistinguished from the pagan worships that surrounded it. A religion that has exhausted its moral force, that has become unexacting and conventional in its discipline, has the feebleness of religion divided from morality, of Paganism itself. Has Christianity exhausted all its destructive and reconstructive powers? Has it no new prohibitions, no new commands? If so, let the clergy confine themselves to theology. If society is finally set on its right basis, if the proper way of living is as clear as daylight to every one, and there remains nothing to struggle against but the weakness of individuals, the human tendency to "step aside," then let the clergy confine themselves to theology. But most of them believe the millennium to be still future. If so, why are they Conservatives?

One thing remains to be said. I have had, of course, the average clergyman in view throughout this essay; to men of uncommon ability I have no pretension to offer advice. In considering what work ordinary men should do, we have to take account not merely of the importance of the work, but also of their ability to do it. One of the greatest practical difficulties is the necessary incompetence of the average clergyman to that part of his work which is most important. It is not impossible, as I have argued, to find a great abundance of men who, well educated and with facilities and motives for continuous study given them, would be able to discuss questions of duty, whether private or public, questions of social arrangement, details of philanthropic plans, with sufficient ability. It is not hopeless that it should be possible to attain a high tone in the Church, so that a large number of men might be inspired with a genuine ardour of religious feeling. What is difficult is to imagine how a large number of men can be found competent to treat of the deepest and most delicate subjects that can occupy the human mind, "the springs of life, the depths of awe," without degrading them. Is it possible for any one who remembers the proverbial dumbness of Englishmen on all topics of deep feeling, to listen to the unrestrained effusion of pulpit rhetoric without the strongest suspicion of hypocrisy? Such hypocrisy can scarcely be avoided by those who have to treat of matters too high for their powers. The congregation demand the expression of more ardent feeling than the preacher has, the discussion of deeper questions than he understands. The supply rises to the level of the demand, but by means often of insincerity and superficiality.

Since, then, the great difficulty is in the want of a sufficient supply of ability, there is the most urgent necessity for increasing this supply by all possible means. I have already remarked that an improvement in general education is among these possible means, and that something also may be expected from an improvement of special clerical training. Perhaps also the ability which is already at command might be better distributed. We might have two kinds of sermons preached by two different classes of men. The common parochial sermon might be of a simple and practical kind, and confined in the main to questions which are within the range of an ordinary preacher. Then, besides, you might have in the larger churches of towns lectures delivered by the ablest men, and dealing with the deepest subjects.

But, above all things, if there be any cause already

at work which depresses the average of ability in the teaching class, let us remove it if possible; let us, in any case, avoid increasing the intensity of its operation. One such cause there is, a practice which, though it belongs peculiarly to religious bodies, yet is to be found in secular institutions as well, lowering the standard of ability among orders of men who, for various purposes requiring high ability, are constituted by election. This is the practice of narrowing the area of choice, of diminishing by disqualifications the number of eligible candidates. What lowers ability in the American Congress? The rule which requires a man to belong to the particular State for which he is returned. In the same way, Mr. Hare argues that half the elective wisdom of England is lost by the rule which confines a man's vote to a special locality. To come to a case more closely resembling the Church: the standard of teaching ability at Universities is lowered when Fellows are elected only from the members of particular colleges, or only from the particular University. Now, this *closeness* prevails most intensely in religious bodies. It is practised on grounds which are perfectly tenable, which are most plausible; nevertheless it depresses everywhere the efficiency of religious teaching. Not from any selfish or corrupt motive, but from zeal for what is believed to be truth, each religious denomination refuses to be taught by any one whose belief does not exactly coincide with its own. It is certain that such a rule will be most exclusive of the highest order of teaching power. Genius refuses to be thus fettered. And in a lower rank power will constantly be postponed to correctness or supposed correctness. Extensive belief will be preferred to intensive. A great number of half-convictions will be preferred to a smaller number of entire, intense, and infectious convictions.

Now that we have become familiar with great national schemes of education for the young, if we turn our attention to the provision which exists for adult education, the suspicion may strike us that it also requires to be made national. Adult education, so far as concerns religion and morals, is given in churches and chapels, and it is depressed, just as schools have been depressed, by want of unity. As each neighbourhood furnished itself as it was inclined, or as it best could, with schools, so has each sect furnished itself with its own religious teaching. If the sect is large, or belongs to a cultivated class, or both, it is able to procure good teaching; but if its adherents belong principally to the less educated classes, or if it is small, then of necessity its teaching will be of bad quality.

Thus from my own starting-point I arrive at the same conclusion at which the other contributors to this volume have arrived from theirs,—namely, that in religion we want comprehension and union. Others may show that division means narrowness, illiberality, and ignorance, and that union brings enlightenment, moderation, and tolerance. My object is to repeat the old familiar maxim, that division is weakness and union strength. Differences of opinion we cannot avoid, but we can avoid divisions in organization and action. On one object all religious bodies are agreed,—namely, in wishing to give people good advice for the conduct of their lives. What I urge is, that if they divide they will give worse advice and with fainter effect than if they combine. Attempts to narrow the basis of the Church of England, and to multiply the conditions of teachership in it, whether directly or by the indirect method of severing its connection with the State, are intelligible when they are made by a certain class of men, and even justifiable when made by another class. Men who do not care whether the people are taught religion and morality or not, but are irritated with the Church for some party reason, may intelligibly take this way of disabling it. Those who wish to demolish all existing systems with a view of erecting another on their ruins, may be justified, by the morality of revolution, in adopting this most promising contrivance for doing so. But Christians, and even religious indifferentists that are not also revolutionists, must be blind indeed to take such a course. It is the direct way to discredit Christianity, and, in a Christian country, to discredit Christianity is to discredit morality.

# X.

## THE TEACHING OF POLITICS.

### AN INAUGURAL LECTURE DELIVERED AT CAMBRIDGE.

It is natural to me on this occasion to call to mind the Lectures on Modern History of Sir James Stephen, to which I listened in this place seventeen years ago. I recollect the Professor and his audience, the merit of his lectures, and the degree of attention with which they were heard. The recollection is discouraging. I do not hope to give better lectures than Sir James Stephen. I remember that he was master of his subject, skilful in the exposition of it, and not sparing of pains. Yet, of his audience, most were there by compulsion; few of them were what we called "reading men;" I myself only went because I was ill and had been recommended not to study too hard. It was—and I think the Professor felt it—a painful waste of power. There was teaching of the highest and rarest kind, and no demand for it, or only such artificial demand as can be created by a protective system.

I do not suppose that matters are quite the same now; I have heard that Professor Kingsley was able

to command an audience worthy of his earnestness and
eloquence. But the causes which were at work in Sir
James Stephen's time to depress the study of modern
history have not quite ceased to operate, though they
may operate less powerfully; and, therefore, it is in no
sanguine spirit that I commence my labours.

After this day, my words will only reach those who have
already elected to study modern history; but it is possible
that I have before me now many who have never fairly
considered the claims of this subject upon their attention.
For this reason, and also because, in my opinion, the
theory of education, apart from practical educational
details, is too little discussed in Cambridge, I will propose
the question of the value of modern history in education.

The reason why this subject is not taken up by most
undergraduates in this University is not, I may take it
for granted, to be found in any conviction of their own
that other subjects in themselves deserve the preference.
The question is settled for them, partly by the competi-
tions and prizes of the place, which give an artificial
value to classics and mathematics, partly by the advice
of their elders and teachers. These two influences taken
together are nearly overwhelming, but that of the two
which deserves to have the least weight has, I fear, the
most. I must always regard it as a misfortune that
prizes and fellowships, which have been admitted into
education under the notion of incentives to industry or
aids to deserving poverty, should be practically used so
as to produce other and more questionable effects, and
should be converted into a protection of particular studies
and a prohibition of others. The other influence—advice
of elders and teachers.—I certainly am not interested to

discredit. The undergraduate who deviates from the ordinary course of study in this place may indeed deserve praise if he prefers his own intellectual progress to material rewards; but his conduct is much more questionable if he merely prefers his own opinion to that of wiser people. I can remember well the doubts that disturbed me when I was an undergraduate, as they must have disturbed many others, in considering the course of studies prescribed by usage in the University. What should a student do who doubts whether this course of studies is really the best for him? Is he to sacrifice his own judgment to that of the men who have prescribed this course, or is he to try the hazardous experiment of chalking out a course for himself? I do not intend here to offer any hasty solution of this delicate question. But it seems to me that both teachers in advising particular studies, and students in receiving such advice, should carefully separate in their minds their educational value from their pecuniary value. Let not a subject which is useful towards winning a fellowship, be confounded with a subject that is useful in developing the mind. The two things may chance to be different; nay, we have only to consider the process by which fellowships are awarded to perceive that they can only by accident be the same. Let the student by all means elect for himself which path he will follow. If he cannot secure at once distinction in the University and a good education, let him make his choice between these objects, or let him study, if he will, to reconcile them; but in any case let him not mistake the one for the other.

I must venture to suggest to the student another reason for not sacrificing his own judgment too readily. To the unanimous opinion of good authorities it would certainly be presumptuous in him not to yield, but when those authorities differ he must, whether he will or not, make himself arbiter between them; and it is mere laziness, not modesty, to abandon himself to the guidance of those advisers who happen to be in a majority in his immediate neighbourhood. A few years ago no student here had any strong reason to think he could go far wrong in devoting himself to classics or mathematics. But the case is very different now. Let a man thumb his Thucydides to pieces, and fill his Poetæ Scenici from the first page to the last with annotations; all this zeal and enthusiasm will not save him, when he goes out into the world, from being treated, and that by men whose ability he cannot deny, as a mere ignoramus—as a man who has acquired no knowledge, though he may have gained some cultivation. The mathematician hardly fares better. He had always to endure some contempt from the scholar, as uncultivated; then philosophy fell upon him, represented by Sir William Hamilton, and attempted to prove that his studies were ruinous to the intellect; and now physical science includes him in the sweeping condemnation it passes upon all who do not make observations and try experiments.

Let me not exaggerate the difference of opinion that prevails. There is no school that does not hold both classical and mathematical studies in respect as far as they go. The student who has a pronounced taste for either is still safe in indulging his taste. Every student may feel convinced that, if he brings a sufficiently liberal spirit to either study, he will acquire at least something valuable, if not the most valuable thing. But beyond this, whether he will or not, he must decide for himself. Between those who attach a great value to the study of words and those who cast contempt on words in comparison with things; between those who value the abstract sciences and those who rate the sciences of experiment far higher; between those who would study man and those who would study nature; between those who would study the ancient world—whether in language, literature, or history—and those who would study the modern; the student must inevitably choose for himself. He does not escape the necessity by devolving the choice upon advisers, for those advisers themselves have to be chosen.

So long as education is in its transition state in this country, there must be some confusion and some perplexity in the minds of students. This is unavoidable; but if he frankly accepts the situation, the student may discover that it offers compensations. While so many studies are competing with each other, the student's mental range will be widened; the comparison of sciences will become familiar to him; the world of knowledge will be revealed to him as a whole, and each part of it will be better known when it is known as a part. This University, if it abandons its old simple routine of Classics and Mathematics, may perhaps seem to become for a time a scene of confusion—science struggling with science, and tripos elbowing tripos. The change has already advanced some way, and I cannot plead the cause of Modern History to-day with any effect without advancing it further. The old boast of Cambridge, a certain modest thoroughness, exactness within a narrow range, will perhaps suffer when we try, as we are beginning to do, to teach and to learn everything; but even during the transition there will be no small compensation in enlargement of ideas, and when the transition is complete it may be found possible to recover the old exactness within a wider range. Lastly, the new obligation which falls upon the student of deciding for himself between several courses of study calls him to make an effort which may certainly be very beneficial to him. The old uniformity which was so tranquillizing to the mind, when if a man would know it seemed as if he must apply himself to one of two sets of things—to Greeks and Romans on the one hand, or to magnitudes and numbers on the other—and no third department of knowledge anywhere existed, this uniformity deprived the student of one of the most wholesome mental exercises, the exercise of appraising or valuing knowledge. To know the value of a science, the relation it bears to life, the utility of it—I use the word utility in no sordid sense—is quite a different thing from knowing the science itself. It is not only a different but a very separable thing, and from this separation come two great evils—pedantry in the learned, and contempt for knowledge in the ignorant. If by the new variety of our studies, and the new difficulty of choosing between several courses, students should be led to a habit of intelligently comparing the different departments of knowledge, a great gain would accrue from a temporary embarrassment.

I turn now to the question of the place of History in education. Why should History be studied? Mathematics may teach us precision in our thoughts, consecutiveness in our reasonings, and help us to raise general views into propositions accurately qualified and quantified.

Classics may train in us the gift of speech, and at the same time elevate our minds with the thoughts of great men and accustom us to exalted pleasures. Physical science may make us at home in nature, may educate the eye to observe, and reveal to us the excellent order of the universe we live in. Philosophy may make us acquainted with ourselves, may teach us to wonder in the difficult contemplation of that "dark fluxion, all unfixable by thought," the personal subject, and to watch its varied activities of apprehending, doubting, believing, knowing, desiring, loving, praising, blaming. Such are the manifest claims of these great subjects. Does History recommend itself by less obvious uses? Are its claims upon our attention less urgent? Are they obscure, difficult to state or make good?

On the contrary, in discussing them I should feel embarrassed by the very easiness of my task, by the too glaring obviousness of the thesis I have to maintain, if I did not remember that after all the claims of History are practically very little admitted, not only in this University, but in English education generally. Let me say, then, that History is the school of statesmanship. If I were not addressing the students of Cambridge, I might take lower ground. I should choose rather to say, that as in a free country every citizen must be at least remotely interested in public affairs, it is desirable both for the public good and for the self-respect of each individual that great events and large interests should make part of the studies which are to prepare the future citizen for his duties, in order that he may follow with some intelligence the march of contemporary history, and may at least take an interest in the great concerns of his generation, even though he may not be called to take any considerable part in them, or to exert any great influence upon them. This more modest view is well worthy of consideration even here. The mass of those that are educated here will work in after-life in some very limited sphere. They will be compelled to concentrate themselves upon some humble task, to tread diligently some obscure routine. In these circumstances, their views are likely to become narrow, their thoughts paltry and sordid, if their education received here have not given them eyes to see whatever is largest and most elevating in life. Who has not met with some hard-working country curate, living remote from all intellectual society, and clinging with fondness to the remembrance of some college study which seems still to connect him with the world in which thinkers live? Who has not wished that he had some stouter rope to cling to than such reminiscences as college studies generally furnish—that he could remember something better, something more fruitful and suggestive, than scraps of Virgil or rules of gender and prosody? The most secluded man is living in the midst of momentous social changes, whether he can interpret them or not; the most humble task upon which any man is engaged makes part, even though he forgets it, of a total of human work by which a new age is evolved out of the old; the smallest individual life belongs to a national life which is great, to a universal life of the race which is illimitably great. There are studies which show a man the whole of which he is a part, and which throw light upon the great process of which his own life is a moment; the course along which the human race travels can be partially traced, and still more satisfactorily can the evolution of particular nations during limited periods be followed. Studies like this leave something more behind them than a refinement imparted to the mind, or even than faculties trained for future use; they furnish a theory of human affairs, a theory which is applicable to the phenomena with which life has to deal, and which serves the purpose of a chart or a compass. The man that has even a glimpse of such a theory, if the theory be itself a hopeful one, cannot but feel tranquillized and reassured; his life, from being a a wandering or a drifting, becomes a journey or a voyage to a definite port; the changes that go on around him cease to appear capricious, and he is more often able to refer them to laws: hence his hopes become more measurable, and his plans more reasonable, and it may. be that where his own efforts fail he is supported by faith in a law of Good, of which he has traced the workings. Such a study—teaching each man his place in the republic of man,[1] the post at which he is stationed, the function with which he is invested, the work that is required of him—such a study is History when comprehensively pursued.

History, then, I might well urge, is the school of public feeling and patriotism. Without at least a little knowledge of history no man can take a rational interest in politics, and no man can form a rational judgment about them without a good deal. There is no one here, however humble his prospects, who does not hope to do as much as this. There are, it is true, men who, without any knowledge of history, are hot politicians, but it would be better for them not to meddle with politics at all: there are men who, knowing something of history, are indiffer-

---

[1] "Humana quâ parte locutus es in re."—Persius.

entists in politics; it is because they do not know history enough. But what I choose rather to say here, is not that history is the school of public feeling, but that it is the school of statesmanship. If it is an important study to every citizen, it is the one important study to the legislator and ruler. There are many things, doubtless, which it is desirable for the politician to know. It is so much the better if he acquires the cultivation that characterized the older race of our statesmen, the literary and classical taste of Fox and Canning. In the same way a lawyer or a clergyman will be the better for being a man of letters and scholarship. But as the indispensable thing for a lawyer is a knowledge of law, and for a clergyman the indispensable thing is a knowledge of divinity; so I will venture to say that the indispensable thing for a politician is a knowledge of political economy and of history. And, though perhaps we seldom think of it, our University is, and must be, a great seminary of politicians. Here are assembled to prepare themselves for life the young men from whom the legislators and statesmen of the next age must be taken. In this place they will begin to form the views and opinions which will determine their political career. During the years they spend here, and through influences that operate here—perhaps not in the lecture-room, but at any rate in the meetings of friends, or in the Union—their preparation for political life is made. It may seem a somewhat exaggerated view of my function, but I cannot help regarding myself as called to join with the Professor of Political Economy in presiding over this preparation. What will at any rate be learnt *at* the University it should be possible, I hold, to learn *from* the University, and I shall consider it to be in great part my own fault if this does not prove to be the case.

If Professor Smyth delivered his inaugural lecture in this hall, it is very possible that among his hearers sat the young Lord Palmerston. It is possible that at this moment some one sits there who will occupy the position of Lord Palmerston in the last years of this century. In Professor Symond's lecture-room I dare say there may sometimes have been seen, wearing a Pembroke gown,[1] an undergraduate named William Pitt. It would be hard, certainly, to trace in the career either of Lord Palmerston or Pitt the influence of any of my predecessors. The influence of Cambridge upon Pitt is discernible rather in the command of finished language which his classical studies gave him, and the strong precision of thought which he got from mathematics, than in any wide historical views. But history was not then the practical study that it is now, and the kindred subject of political economy was not then taught in this University. The acquirement which more even than his eloquence or his mathematical knowledge raised Pitt above the other politicians of his time was one which, though it was not made here, might, had the University been in a more efficient state, have been made here, and could most certainly be made here now; it was his knowledge of Adam Smith.

But when I say that a knowledge of history is indispensable to the statesman, there will rise up in the minds of many a doubt which it is desirable to lay. Political economy is indispensable; yes! but is history so neces-

[1] I am told that this is a mistake, and that in Pitt's time the undergraduates' gown was the same for all the Colleges.

sary? After all, how easy for a profound historian to be a very shallow politician! The light which is shed upon contemporary affairs by the experience of remote ages and quite different states of society is surely faint enough. How utterly inapplicable seem inferences drawn from ancient Rome or Athens to the disputed political questions of the present day! Even less connection is there between mediæval barbarism and the complicated civilization we live in the midst of. Cannot high authorities be quoted to prove the uselessness of history in politics? No statesman ever towered above his contemporaries, not only in power, but in statesmanlike qualities, more decidedly than Sir Robert Walpole, who was a contemner of every kind of learning. On the other hand, Carteret, full of historical knowledge, makes but a poor figure. The most influential politician of the last age, Cobden, was never tired of sneering at the pedants who busied themselves with the affairs of other ages. Can we avoid suspecting him to have been in the right when we remark the evident superiority as a statesman of a man so unlearned and so moderately gifted as Cobden, to such a prodigy both of ability and historical acquirement as Macaulay? Outmatched in eloquence, in acuteness, in cultivation, and most of all in knowledge of history, how did Cobden succeed in winning the race at last? Was it not evidently by occupying himself exclusively with the questions of the time and the place, by encumbering himself with no useless knowledge, by not obscuring plain matters with ambitious illustrations, curious parallels, and obsolete authorities?

There is a very simple answer to all this. It is an argument that presupposes that history refers only to what is long past. Now it is not unnatural to give this meaning to the word history. We often in common parlance use the word so. We say that a thing belongs to history when it is past and gone. The title of history is given to books which contain narratives of occurrences that are past, and in most instances long past; it would not be given to a simple account of existing institutions or communities. We must remember, however, that the language of common life is one thing, and scientific language another. I do not intend on this occasion to give an exact definition of history as I understand it. The attempt to do so would lead me too far. But, however we determine the province of history, it must be understood that I use the word, and shall throughout use it, without any thought of time past or present. There are multitudes of past occurrences which do not belong, in my view, to history, and there are multitudes of phenomena belonging to the present time which do. Phenomena are classed together in science according to resemblances in kind, not according to date. If history were taken to have for its subject-matter all that has happened in the world, it would not be a single science, but the inductive basis of all sciences whatever. Evidently it must be taken scientifically to deal only with occurrences and phenomena of a certain kind, and this being so it is evident that *vice versâ* phenomena of that particular kind must be reckoned as historical, to whatever period they belong. Now, whatever phenomena we exclude, it is evident that we must include political institutions within the limits of historical phenomena. Every one, therefore, who studies political institutions, whether in the past or in the present, studies history.

It is therefore a misconception to think that a politician disregards history because he disregards the remote past. It is misleading to call Macaulay a student of history and Cobden a contemner of history. Both men evidently were occupied with phenomena of the same kind; they laboured at perfectly similar problems. The power and weakness of states, their advance and decline, their chances of success in war, their political and social institutions, the stability or transience of their order, the state of civilization, the influences promoting it and the influences retarding it, the character and qualifications of public men—these and similar questions occupied both. However you describe the studies of the one, you must give the same name to the studies of the other. It cannot be just to rank them among the students of different sciences because the one examined the power of Louis XIV. and the other that of the Emperor Nicholas, the one studied the struggle of political freedom with despotism, and the other the struggle of commercial freedom with monopoly, or because the one was rather too much disposed to measure a country by its eminence in literature, and the other by its activity in manufactures and trade.

But after this explanation you will perhaps be disposed to think me guilty of a truism; for it now appears that when I said that the study of history is indispensable to the politician, all I meant was that a politician must needs study politics. But is it a truism to say this? Is it a truism to say that a politician must study politics? I fear not. I fear that there is just as much unwillingness in this profession as in the other professions in England to acknowledge any general principles or build on any scientific basis. As in England your lawyer seldom knows jurisprudence, your clergyman is seldom a theologian, your medical man seldom a physiologist, so is it with the politician. He may know a great deal, but what he knows is not in the proper sense politics. He has much knowledge that is useful for a politician, but little of the knowledge that is indispensable and fundamental. He stores his memory with information about persons—how So-and-so voted on this question or on that. He becomes acute in party tactics, ready in popular arts, skilful in scaling the ladder of power. He watches perhaps the tides of opinion, knows what measure it is safe to propose or support, and what measure is inopportune, however salutary in itself. But for a politician who is serious in his profession, and who has higher ends than mere success or power for himself, all these things are secondary. What is primary is a solid knowledge of political and social well-being in its nature and its causes, and more particularly a strong apprehension of the place of government in human affairs, of its capacities and the limits of its capacities. Finesse, adroitness, eloquence, it may be desirable to have; but after all they are useful principally for those who have nothing better. A grain of real knowledge, of genuine uncontrollable conviction, will outweigh a bushel of adroitness, and to produce persuasion there is one golden principle of rhetoric not put down in the books,—to understand what you are talking about. Now any one who knows how much study it takes in the present complication of human affairs to arrive at solid political convictions, and how much taste for study there is in the ordinary Englishman, whether he belong to the class of politicians or not, will arrive at the conclusion that our politicians must be insufficiently educated, from the mere fact that political science is so little taught in schools and colleges. An Englishman often extends in after-life his knowledge of the subjects to which he has been introduced at school or college, but does not very often travel into quite new regions of knowledge; and perhaps a political career, once begun, is too absorbing to leave much leisure or tranquillity for abstract investigation. In these days, when we are all more alive than our fathers were to the difficulty of the science of government, I may venture, perhaps, to make the assertion that we shall never have a supply of competent politicians until political science—that is, roughly, political economy and history together—are made a prominent part of the higher education.

But what are we to think of that difference of opinion among statesmen on the subject of history? For Walpole and Carteret, Cobden and Macaulay, though they do not really differ about the importance of history, do certainly differ about the proper way of studying it. What, then, is the exact point of difference between them, and to which of the two parties ought we to attach ourselves? Now, remembering the perpetual sneers of Cobden's school against classical studies, we may be inclined to answer the question by saying that they measure the importance of historical phenomena by their nearness to ourselves, while the opposite school measure them by their intrinsic greatness; so that the one school cares for nothing that is not modern, while the other, considering that some of the most memorable things happened in remote times, gives a great prominence in historical studies to antiquity. If this were really the difference, I for one should have little hesitation in siding against the modernists. Dr. Arnold maintained that we allow ourselves to be misled by the word ancient, and that much of what we call ancient history is, for all practical purposes, more modern than most of that which is commonly called modern history. I agree with him heartily. I think that we shall derive more useful lessons to guide us in politics from Thucydides than from Froissart; and even times much more modern than those chronicled by Froissart seem to me barren of instruction compared to some periods of the ancient world. I feel more at home at Rome in the times of Cicero, than at Paris in the disturbances of the Fronde. If, then, the school of Cobden maintain that historical phenomena deserve study in proportion to their nearness to the present time, I have no agreement with them. Men and things and occurrences are not memorable in proportion to their chronological relation to ourselves; some which are very near to our own times we cannot too soon forget, and some few we ought always to remember, however far we drift away from them upon the stream of time.

But you will observe that Dr. Arnold's own argument tacitly assumes that there is a historical period more important than even the most memorable periods of ancient history. For why does he attach so much importance to the classical periods? Because of their likeness to our own time; because of the light they throw upon our own time. It is implied in this that contemporary history is, in Dr. Arnold's opinion, more important than either ancient or modern; and in fact superior to it by all the superiority of the end to the means. Now, if after making this observation we reconsider the language of the Cobden school, we shall see that it is of contemporary history, and not merely of modern history, that they are thinking; and that they are not advocates of modern times against ancient, but of the present against the past. In his famous sneer at Thucydides, Cobden did not compare him with Froissart, or even with Clarendon, but with the *Times* newspaper. And in spite of all his contempt for Athens and the Ilissus, I think it very likely that he might have agreed with Arnold that Pericles and Demosthenes are better worth remembering and studying than Cœur de Lion or the Black Prince, and even than the Stuarts or Louis XIV. But then he would have added were he among us now, and Arnold we have seen tacitly agrees, that time spent upon either period, upon the fifth century before Christ or the seventeenth century after Christ, would be equally wasted if it did not lead to a clearer comprehension of the age of Queen Victoria, the Emperor Napoleon III., the Czar Alexander II., and President Grant. Here, again, there is agreement. This is not the point of difference between the two schools, for no school denies, or can deny, that the especial business of the politician is to understand, not some other age, but the age he himself lives in. It is necessary, therefore, to ask once more, What is the point of difference?

Evidently the difference is here, that the school of Cobden are for attacking the problem directly, while the other school approach it by a circuitous route. Cobden scarcely sees any difference between the proposition that the present time ought to be understood and the proposition that the knowledge of it ought to be imparted

in schools and colleges. He would have the student
buckle to at once, occupy himself without the least delay
in collecting and classifying and analysing the facts of
the time. In his view other ages are of quite secondary
importance, intrinsically indeed of no importance whatever, but not altogether to be despised on account of the
illustrations that may occasionally be drawn from them.
The opposite school, the school in possession, have
precisely the same end in view, but approach it in quite
a different way. To them the present time is like a
fortified city, which must be attacked by opening trenches,
working underground, and gradually stealing nearer and
nearer. They think it necessary, before introducing the
student to the phenomena which he is ultimately to
consider, to set before him analogous phenomena drawn
from other ages. He is to store up a mass of facts which
he will afterwards find useful as illustrations. While
he is acquiring them it is of course impossible for him to
appreciate their illustrative value, because he has not
yet been acquainted with the phenomena which they
illustrate, but when this is done it is supposed that they
will at once recur to his memory—that all the dead
knowledge will suddenly become alive, the dry facts
give up their kernel of philosophical truth. And such
vast importance is attached to this preparatory process
that absolutely the whole time at command is spent
upon it, and the day never comes in our course of
education when the phenomena themselves, which it
is the object of the whole process to explain and teach,
are even in the most summary way stated to the student.

Here, then, are the two views. It is not necessary
to accept either without qualification. Cobden, I think,

greatly underrated the instruction to be derived from the past, and he had probably no idea of that philosophy of universal history which, if a number of great thinkers appearing in succession, from Vico and Herder to Comte and Buckle, are sufficient indications of the set of thought, will sooner or later be worked out. But, on the other hand, I earnestly urge that in preferring the direct method to the indirect in the teaching of political science or contemporary history he is right. I will give my reasons.

First let me point out that, though an indirect method may sometimes have its advantages, the presumption must always be against it. For it multiplies the number of things to be learnt, it increases the tax upon memory and time. The history of an age is composed of a vast mass of minute facts, which again are substantiated by other minute facts which we call evidence. To learn the history of an age is to commit to memory this whole mass and to weigh all the evidence. If, then, there is some age of which it is urgently important that the student should master the history—and such an age always is the age that is present—it is surely a serious matter to double or quadruple for him this already formidable task, by requiring him, as a mere preliminary exercitation, to master the history of two or three other periods. It may not indeed be a great burden upon a man whose life is passed among books; to him the additional labour thus imposed may be merely delightful; but for the man whom an active life awaits—we are thinking principally of the politician—as soon as his education is over it is such a burden that the very object of imposing it is defeated. If we will look facts in the face, we shall confess that the student commonly breaks off his historical course in the middle. He learns, more or less perfectly, those periods of remote history, whether ancient or modern, which are so rich in illustrations of our own time; but when the comparison between the present and the past comes to be made, when the analogies are to be traced, and the results of the whole complicated process to be obtained, the student is tired, or has not energy to enter upon the new task, or the business of life has come upon him and left him no more leisure.

This danger, however, may be unavoidable; and if so, it must, of course, be faced. If the knowledge of the political world around us cannot be come at by the direct route, we must, of course, make a circuit, in spite of the risk that some of our pupils will grow weary before they reach the goal. But is it so? Is there any insuperable difficulty in the direct route? I do not believe it, and I think that we have here an example of the prevailing vice of English education, which is just this indirectness. Indirectness in education is a great evil. It is an evil, not merely because it wastes time and energy, but still more because it conceals from the student the end of his studies. The student's interest in his studies will always be very much in proportion to the progress he perceives himself to be making, while it is impossible for him to perceive his progress at all unless he has his goal in sight. It is, therefore, most desirable that studies should have an object not merely good, but visibly and plainly good. Compare in your minds the student who studies politics in the living time and him who studies them in the mirror of remote history. Think which of

the two will bring the greater ardour or earnestness to
the pursuit. There is indeed for drowsy imaginations a
certain charm about the remote past which the present
wants. It is so romantic, people say; that is to say, the
characters are all in stage-costume, and speak in quaint
language; the rhetoric and literary art of succeeding
generations have given an artificial dignity to the persons
and incidents, and all the more prominent personages
appear (as they never appeared to their contemporaries)
with the halo round their heads of posthumous renown.
No doubt, in that peaceful world of the past you escape
all that is most uncomfortable in the present—the bustle,
the petty detail, the slovenliness, the vulgarity, the hot
discomfort, the bewildering hubbub, the humiliating spites
and misconstructions, the ceaseless brawl of objurgation
and recrimination, the painfulness of good men hating
each other, the perplexingness of wise men flatly con-
tradicting each other, the perpetual sight of failure, or
of success soon regretted, of good things turning out to
have a bad side, of new sores breaking out as fast as old
ones are healed, the laboriousness and the littleness of all
improvement, and in general the commonness and dulness
and uneasiness of life. We escape from all this in the past,
but after all we escape from it only by an illusion; and in
truth he who desires pleasing and fascinating pictures for
his imagination should have recourse to poetry, which
expressly undertakes to furnish them, and not to history,
where, if they are admitted, it is most commonly through
the weakness of the historian. After all, it is another
kind of interest that the present time has, in spite of all
its discomfort; it is the interest of reality, the interest
that our own private affairs have for us, an interest at

least scarcely less keen and personal, and more ennobling, because connecting us with grander issues. Nay, to one who is to be a politician—and it is this case that I am principally considering—contemporary history not only resembles a personal affair, but actually is a personal affair. Can any one question the eagerness with which such a student would apply himself to this subject when introduced to him by his teachers; remembering that for him—in addition to its speculative interest which it shares with the rest of history, in addition to the interest which it must have for all people, because it concerns persons and things of which, as being contemporary, they must needs know a good deal and have thought a good deal beforehand—it would have the close and special interest of being the subject of all subjects which it would be most useful and most advantageous to him in after-life to understand?

That the history of the past is useful the student takes upon trust; that contemporary history is useful must needs be palpably evident to him. It is useful, like past history, for the lessons it gives, the principles it illustrates; but, unlike past history, it is also indispensable to the politician for its own sake. He who studies contemporary history, therefore, at the same time masters the principles and becomes familiar with the age, while he who studies the past learns only the principles and remains a stranger to the age. The latter, therefore, at the end of the process has still a necessary stage to traverse which the former has left behind him. They may have acquired an equal amount of historical information, have stored up an equal number of facts; but the one is still unprepared for want of knowledge which is indispensable, while the other has all the knowledge which is necessary to start with. And this advantage being felt from the beginning, cannot fail to give the student of contemporary history an ardour and an interest in his work which the student of the past must want. For he not only makes progress, but feels and knows that he makes progress. What he learns is not merely stored up for future use, but tells immediately upon his views and judgments of things around him. It sheds at once upon the political world, the world of states, nationalities, parliaments, armies, parties, and interests, an illumination like that which natural science sheds upon the world of physical and vital forces, of light and heat, the plant and the animal. Studied in the past, history is rather entertaining than stimulating, except to those who have a natural inclination for it, or who come to it specially prepared. Studied in the present, I doubt not that it would be among the most stimulating and fascinating of studies. Like natural science, it is a study which a man may always carry about with him, and prosecute in almost all circumstances. "Pernoctat nobiscum, peregrinatur, rusticatur." If the botanist and geologist cannot walk across the fields or along the high road without being reminded of their favourite studies, neither can the man who studies his age ever be in want of stimulants to reflection. To him, too, the fields and the roads read lessons, though of a different kind—lessons about the division of property, about the progress of industry. Meanwhile the town is his almost exclusively. He has the clue to the whole human movement; he is at home in the world of purpose and utility; all human activities he watches with a curious eye, and sees laws where others may see only a dull and bewildered confusion. He finds sermons in streets, and good in newspapers.

To turn history away from the past to the present is in fact to give it the interest of an experimental study. Our knowledge of both is necessarily imperfect. Of the past much is unrecorded, and many records have perished. The present has not yet been recorded perfectly, and the records have not been collected or made accessible. But in the present there is more room than in the past for the original and independent inquiries of the student. In ancient history, what can any student here do beyond reading intelligently his Grote and his Mommsen? To make new combinations is not to any important degree within his power. And in the past generally, though there remains much to be done for laborious investigators exploring archives and for great thinkers generalizing the newly acquired facts, there is wanting a field in which the ordinary student, who has neither exceptional opportunities nor exceptional gifts, may without presumption make his own observations and venture upon original speculations. Yet no study which does not afford such a field can be in the highest degree stimulating or improving. Now contemporary history affords such a field. Ἀσήρατός ἐστ' ἔτι λειμών. Any one may join the reapers in that harvest. The phenomena are not hidden away in libraries, but are before our eyes. To every one of us a certain proportion of them, a larger one perhaps than we sometimes think, are within the range of personal observation. Another large section lies scattered about the journals and magazines of Europe. Neither collected nor compared nor classified they lie, and there is no one

who might not do for himself some work in sorting
them—work which, though, like the collections of the
private botanist or geologist, it may do nothing ultimately
to advance the science, may yet do much towards improving the student's mind, and making his studies
delightful to him.

Again, the past is a less stimulating contemplation than
the present, because it is a thing complete and finished.
It consists of controversies for good or for evil closed,
questions answered whether rightly or wrongly, problems
together with their solutions. But the present consists
of problems which still await their solution, questions
which the time is still struggling to answer, controversies
in which we are called on to take a side. Now the mind
is roused and stimulated by questions, not by answers.
In education the essential thing is to offer problems of
some kind to the student, and the solution must not be
given along with them. The student's own solution is
what it is important to get—some genuine exertion of
his own faculty; and this it is barely possible to get
when a solution is already before him. Every one can
take an interest in divining what will happen next, for
that is still unknown, and the issue will confirm or con-
found the prophecy; but it seems idle to stand guessing
what might have happened next when the next page of
the history tells you what did actually happen. We read
in one sentence of the distress of the Roman peasantry,
and of the agrarian law by which Tiberius Gracchus
tried to relieve them; and few readers pause to consider
what were the possible solutions out of which Gracchus
made his choice. Surely it is much more stimulating
to the intellect to consider, as we have been doing for

some months, the distress of the Irish peasantry, and to conjecture the provisions of that agrarian law by which Mr. Gladstone yesterday evening proposed to relieve it.

In short, past history is a dogmatist, furnishing for every doubt ready-made and hackneyed determinations. Present history is a Socrates, knowing nothing, but guiding others to knowledge by suggestive interrogations.

All this is said in no spirit of disparagement of the past. Though I have several times mentioned the name of Cobden, it is not because I have any sympathy with that contempt for the old learning which is generally, and for all I know justly, attributed to him. Let us reverence the past, say I; let us cherish the records of it; let us often revert to it. What I urge is not that it is less instructive than is commonly supposed; what I wish to see is not a neglect of past history, whether contemptuous or respectful. Would rather that we realized the past less drowsily, that something better prevailed among us than what I may call the Waverley view of other times! The past is in my eyes the best commentary on the present. What is it, then, that I urge? This, that the text should be put before the commentary, and the present before the past. Illustrations are valuable, but only when there is something to be illustrated; the analogies of past and present are full of interest, but not to one who is ignorant of the present. It is for this reason that the taste for history is commonly observed to come late. Not till people have seen the world a little, and have had some experience of affairs, are they able to realize, except in the theatrical spurious-poetical fashion, the order of phenomena with which historians are concerned. But this knowledge of the world, this experience of affairs, might be given earlier if the student were brought at once face to face with the living present, encouraged to follow the drama which is now being enacted on the stage which is all the world; accustomed, not in his hours of recreation, but as part of his education, to thread the maze of the world's affairs, to take the measure of public men before the world is unanimous about them, study tendencies before they have reached their limit, predict the growth of power not yet mature, or calculate the stages of its decline; accustomed, in fact, to work out for himself at his desk the very problems which are awaiting the solution of Time.

History the school of statesmanship! This was what I began with. It is a maxim which to many practical men sounds, I know, somewhat hollow. To give it another sound, to vindicate it as a sober maxim in this University, is a task to which I feel very unequal; nevertheless it is what I understand myself to be called upon to attempt. If I succeed in any measure, I hope to do so by the method I have now indicated, by giving due precedence in the teaching of History to the present over the past.

THE END.

www.ingramcontent.com/pod-product-compliance
Lightning Source LLC
Chambersburg PA
CBHW022018240426
43667CB00042B/934